COMPLETE MANDARIN CHINESE

THE BASICS

By Janet Lai

Published in the United States by Living Language, A Random House Company

www.livinglanguage.com

Editor: Zviezdana Verzich
Production Editor: Lisbeth Dyer
Production Manager: Thomas Marshall
Interior Design: Sophie Ye Chin

First Edition

ISBN-10: 1-4000-2273-8

ISBN-13: 978-1-4000-2273-1

Library of Congress Cataloging-in-Publication Data available upon request.

This book is available at special discounts for bulk purchases for sales promotions or premiums. Special editions, including personalized covers, excerpts of existing books, and corporate imprints, can be created in large quantities for special needs. For more information, write to Special Markets/Premium Sales, 1745 Broadway, MD 6-2, New York, New York 10019 or e-mail specialmarkets@randomhouse.com.

PRINTED IN THE UNITED STATES OF AMERICA

10 9 8 7 6 5 4 3 2 1

CONTENTS

INTRODUCTION

Living Language® Complete Mandarin Chinese: The Basics makes it easy to learn Mandarin Chinese. In this course, the basic elements of the language have been carefully selected and condensed into forty short lessons. If you can study about thirty minutes a day, you can master this course and learn to speak Chinese in a few weeks.

You'll learn Chinese the way you learned English, starting with simple words and progressing to complex phrases. Just listen and repeat after the native instructors on the recordings. To help you immerse yourself in the language, you'll hear only Chinese spoken. Hear it, say it, absorb it through use and repetition.

The *Living Language® Complete Mandarin Chinese* coursebook provides English translations and brief explanations in each lesson. The first five lessons cover pronunciation, laying the foundation for learning the vocabulary, phrases, and grammar, which are presented in the later chapters. If you already know a little Chinese, you can use the book as a phrase book and reference. In addition to forty lessons, there is a summary of Chinese grammar and a section on writing letters and e-mails.

This course also contains three 60-minute CDs, where all forty lessons are recorded with pauses for repetition, and a *Wallet Phrase Card for Travelers,* which contains the most essential Chinese words and sentences you can use on the go.

Also included in the course package is the *Living Language® Mandarin Chinese Learner's Dictionary.* It contains more than 10,000 entries, with many of the definitions illustrated by phrases and idiomatic expressions. You can increase your vocabulary and range of expressions just by browsing through the dictionary.

Practice your Chinese as much as possible. Even if you can't manage a trip abroad, watching Chinese movies, reading Chinese magazines, eating at Chinese restaurants, and talking with Chinese-speaking friends are enjoyable ways to help you reinforce what you have learned with *Living Language® Complete Mandarin Chinese: The Basics.*

Now let's begin. The instructions below will tell you what to do. *Zhù nǐ chénggōng!* Good luck!

COURSE MATERIALS

1. Three 60-minute CDs.

2. *Living Language®* *Complete Mandarin Chinese* coursebook. This book is designed for use with the recorded lessons, but it may also be used alone as a reference. It contains the following sections:

Basic Chinese in 40 Lessons

Summary of Chinese Grammar

Letter and E-Mail Writing

3. *Living Language®* *Mandarin Chinese Learner's Dictionary.* The Chinese/English–English/Chinese dictionary contains more than 10,000 entries. Phrases and idiomatic expressions illustrate many of the definitions.

4. *Wallet Phrase Card for Travelers* with dozens of the most essential Mandarin Chinese words and phrases.

INSTRUCTIONS

Look at page 1. The words in **boldface** are the ones you will hear on the recording.

Now read Lesson 1 all the way through. Note the points to listen for when you play the recording. The first word you will hear is **bāng**.

Start the recording, listen carefully, and say the words aloud in the pauses provided. Go through the lesson once and don't worry if you can't pronounce everything correctly the first time around. Try it again and keep repeating the lesson until you are comfortable with it. The more often you listen and repeat, the longer you will remember the material.

Now go on to the next lesson. If you take a break between lessons, it's always good to review the previous lesson before starting a new one.

In the manual, there are two kinds of quizzes. With matching quizzes, you must select the English translation of the Chinese sentence. The other type requires you to fill in the blanks with the correct Chinese word chosen from the three given directly below the sentence. If you make any mistakes, reread the section.

Even after you have finished the 40 lessons and achieved a perfect score on the Final Quiz, keep practicing Chinese by listening to the recordings and speaking with Chinese-speaking friends. For further study, try Living Language® *Ultimate Chinese Beginner–Intermediate* and Living Language® *Business Companion: Chinese*.

LESSON 1

A. CHINESE SOUNDS AND THE *PĪNYĪN* ROMANIZATION SYSTEM

The Chinese language does not have an alphabet. Instead, each word is represented by a unique character or combination of characters, which may be composed of just one stroke or line or as many as several dozen strokes or lines. To represent Chinese sounds for those who do not read the Chinese script various systems of Romanization have been devised. In the Living Language® *Complete Chinese: The Basics* course pack we use *Pīnyīn,* the standard system used in China and the one most commonly used in the United States.

However, students should be aware that the sound values of some *Pīnyīn* letters are different from the sound values of their equivalents in English, such as the sound values of the letters *j, q, x, zh, ch* and *sh.* All *Pīnyīn* symbols and Chinese sounds are discussed with examples in lessons 1 to 5.

B. INITIAL SOUNDS

Each syllable in Chinese has an initial consonant sound and a final vowel sound. There are twenty-three initial sounds (consonants) and thirty-six final sounds (vowels or combinations of vowels and consonants). Below is the list of *Pīnyīn* initials, with their approximate English equivalents. It is the best that you listen to the words on the recordings to learn how to pronounce these sounds correctly.

1. *b* is like *b* in *beer*

bāng	to help
bù	not

bàn	half
bìng	sick
báisè	white
biàn	to change

2. *p* is like *p* in *poor*

pán	plate
pēn	to spray
pá	to crawl
pīngpāng	Ping-Pong ball
pén	basin
pǔtōng	common, ordinary

3. *m* is like *m* in *more*

mái	to bury
mén	door
māma	mother
mǐ	rice
mài	to sell
míngbai	to understand

4. *f* is like *f* in *fake*

fèi	lung
fá	to punish
fēnbiàn	to distinguish
fěn	powder
fāxiàn	to discover
fēng	wind

5. *d* is like *d* in *dare*

dǎ	to beat
dānchē	bicycle
dà	big
dǎn	gallbladder
dài	to bring
diàn	electricity

6. *t* is like *t* in *take*

tiào	to jump
tuō	to tow
tǔ	to spit out
tūn	to swallow
tuī	to push
tiān	sky, day

7. *n* is like *n* in *now*

niǎo	bird
nóngfū	peasant
nǐ	you
nǎo	brain
niú	cow
nán	difficult

8. *l* is like *l* in *learn*

lái	to come
lèi	tired, exhausted
làzhú	candle
lěng	cold
là	hot and spicy
líhūn	to divorce

9. *g* is like *g* in *get*

guā	squash
gōngpíng	fair
guǎfu	widow
gàosu	to tell
gòu	enough
gāo	tall

10. *k* is like *c* in *cow*

kāfēi	coffee
kǔ	bitter
kāi	to open
kuān	wide
kǒu	mouth
kuài	fast

11. *h* is like *h* in *help*

hé	and
huā	flower
hǎo	good
huángsè	yellow
hǎi	sea
huílái	to come back

12. *j* is like *g* in *gene*

juān	to donate
jiǔ	liquor
jūnduì	army
jiǎo	foot
jiù	old (opposite of new)
jiǎngjīn	prize

13. *q* is like *ch* in *cheese*

qián	money
qù	to go
qiān	to sign
qiú	ball
qíguài	strange
qǐng	please

14. *x* is like *sh* in *shoe*

xuě	snow
xìng	last name
xuéxiào	school
xīn	new
xióng	bear
xièxie	thank you

15. *z* is like *ds* in *yards*

zuò	to sit
zúqiú	soccer
zuǒ	left
zīběn	capital
zǒu	to walk
zìjǐ	oneself

16. *c* is like *ts* in *its*

cíqì	china
cuòwù	mistake
cóng	from
cūn	village
cígōng	to resign
cù	vinegar

17. *s* is like *s* in *sibling*

sān	three
suì	years old
sì	four
suìdào	tunnel
suān	sour
sùdù	speed

18. *h* is like *dg* in *judge*

zhuō	to catch
zhuī	to chase
zhū	pig
zhú	bamboo
zhǔn	to permit
zhuōzi	table

19. *ch* is like *ch* in *church*

chē	car
chángcháng	frequently
chán	cicada
cháng	long
chī	to eat
chá	tea

20. *sh* is like *sh* in *shhhh*

shìjiè	world
shídào	esophagus
shì	to try
shōujù	receipt
shǒu	hand
shū	book

21. *r* is like *r* in *rubbish*

rén	person
ruǎn	soft
rù	to go/come
rè	hot
ròu	meat
rì	sun

22. *w* is like *w* in *weed*

wū	house
wūguī	tortoise
wěi	tail
wǒ	I, me
wèi	stomach
wén	mosquito

23. *y* is like *y* in *you*

yuè	moon, month
yú	fish
yòu	again
yǒuqíng	friendship
yòng	to use
yǒngyuǎn	forever

LESSON 2

A. CHINESE AS A MONOSYLLABIC LANGUAGE

A large number of words in Chinese consists of only one syllable, e.g., the word for "person" in Chinese is *rén*. Some compound words have more than one syllable (and are written with more than one character in Chinese writing), e.g., *chéngshì* "city," which consists of *chéng* and *shì*.

B.   FINAL SOUNDS

There are thirty-six final sounds and sound combinations.

1. *a* is like *a* in *ma*

fāshēng	to happen
mǎ	horse
nà	that
shā	sand
bàba	father
tā	he, she

2. *ai* is like *y* in *my*

zài	again
mǎi	to buy
hái	still
wàiguó	foreign country
tài	too, excessive
tái	to lift up

3. *ao* is like *ou* in *pout*

gāo	tall
nǎo	brain
zǎo	early
hǎo	good
zhǎo	to look for
yào	medicine

4. *an* is like *an* in *elan*

tānxīn	greedy
bù	not
bàn	half
rǎn	to dye
dānchē	bicycle
fàn	cooked rice

5. *ang* is like *ong* in *throng*

ràng	to let
tāng	soup
máng	busy
bàngqiú	baseball
láng	wolf
fāngbiàn	convenient

6. *o* is like *o* in *or*

bó	thin
bòhe	mint
fó	Buddha
pòchǎn	bankrupt
mó	devil
bōcài	spinach

7. *ou* is like *oa* in *float*

chǒu	ugly
lóu	building
tōu	to steal
ròu	meat
yǒu	to have
zǒu	to walk

8. *ong* is like *ong* in *long*

tòng	pain
lóng	dragon
dōngtiān	winter
hóngsè	red
kōng	empty
gōnggòng	public

9. *e* is like *er* in *nerve*

hē	to drink
gēzi	pigeon

10. *ei* is like *ay* in *day*

bēizi	cup
fēi	to fly
shéi	who
měi	pretty
péi	to accompany
féi	fat

11. *en* is like *un* in *under*

mén	door
hěn	very
rén	person
fēn	minute
pén	basin
bèn	stupid

12. *eng* is like *ung* in *mung (bean)*

dēng	light
mèng	dream
péngyou	friend
téng	pain
zēngjiā	to increase
fēng	wind

13. *i* (after *z, c, s, zh, ch, sh*) is like *er* in *thunder*

cízhēn	compass
chī	to eat
sǐ	to die
shì	matter
zhīfáng	body fat
zīběn	capital

14. *i* is like *ee* in *see*

tī	to kick
dī	low
xǐ	to wash
jī	chicken
bǐ	pen
qí	flag, to ride

15. *ia* is like *yah*

jiǎ	fake
xiā	shrimp
qiàqiǎo	by coincidence
xiā	blind
jiā	home
jiàqian	price

16. *iao* is like *eow* in *meow*

jiāo	to submit
diào	to hang
miào	temple
tiào	to jump
xiǎo	small
liáotiānr	to chat

17. *ian* is like *yan*

biānfú	bat
diàn	electricity
liánhuā	lotus
jiān	shoulder
qiǎn	shallow
biàn	to change

18. *iang* is like *yang*

qiāng	gun
jiāng	ginger
xiāng	fragrant
liǎng	two

19. *ie* is like *ye* in *yes*

bié	don't
jiē	street
qiē	to cut
tiē	to stick
xiě	to write
piē	to have a quick look

20. *iu* is like *yo* in *yo-yo*

xiùzi	sleeve
qiú	ball
jiǔ	nine, wine
liù	six

21. *iong* is like *young*

xiōng	chest

22. *in* is like *in* in *sin*

xīn	heart
qīnqi	relatives
míngē	folk song
línjù	neighbor
jīn	gold
bìnyíguǎn	funeral home

23. *ing* is like *ing* in *sing*

bīng	ice
qǐng	please
yīngwén	English
jìng	quiet
dīng	nail
míngbái	to understand

24. *u* is like *u* in *flu*

zú	foot
bù	step
wūyā	crow

tūrán	suddenly
sùdù	speed
shū	to lose (opposite of "to win")

25. *ua* is like *ua* in *suave*

huā	flower
shuā	brush
zhuā	to grab

26. *uai* is like *wi* in *wide*

shuài	handsome
kuài	fast

27. *uan* is like *wan*

zhuānjiā	expert
chuán	ship
huán	to return

28. *uang* is like *wong* with a strong *u* at the beginning

shuāng	pair
huángsè	yellow
chuāng	window
zhuàngchē	car crash

29. *uo* is like *wo* in *won't*

guójiā	country
cuò	wrong
huǒ	fire
duō	many

luòtuo	camel
kuòyīnjī	loudspeaker

30. *ui* is like *weigh*

tuī	to push
zuǐ	mouth
shuǐ	water
ruìlì	sharp
huì	know how to
guǐ	ghost

31. *un* is like *won* but with a shorter *o* sound

lúnyǐ	wheel
hūnlǐ	marriage ceremony
kùnnán	difficult
gǔn	to roll
dūn	to squat
cùn	inch

32. *ü* is like *ee* in *see*, but with lips rounded into a pout
   (cf. German *hübsch* or French *tu*)

yú	fish
xūyào	to need
qù	to go
júhuā	chrysanthemum
nǚ	female

NOTE:

The vowel *ü*, unlike the vowel *u*, can combine with consonants *j*, *q*, *x*, and *y*. So when *ü* combines with *j*, *q*, *x*, and *y*,

the two dots above the letter "u" can be omitted. Since both
ü and *u* can combine with *l* and *n,* the two dots above *ü*
cannot be omitted in this case.

33. *üan* is like *ü* followed by *en* like in *pen*

yuǎn	far
xuānbù	to announce
quánlì	power
juān	to donate

34. *üe* is like *ü* followed by *e* like in *debt*

juédìng	to decide
xué	to study
yuè	month
quēdiǎn	disadvantage

35. *ün* is like *ü* followed by *n*

qúndǎo	archipelago
yùndòng	sports
jūnduì	army
xùnliàn	to train

36. *er* is like *are*

ěrduo	ear

LESSON 3

A. MORE ON THE *PĪNYĪN* SYSTEM

1. Use of apostrophe

When a syallable starting with *a*, *o* or *e* comes after another syallable in a word, the apostrophe is added to separate the two syllables:

píng'ān (*píng + ān*, not *pín + gān*)   safe
pèi'ǒu (*pèi + ǒu*, not *pè + iǒu*)   spouse
Cháng'é (*cháng + é*, not *chán + gé*)   Lady in the
                                           Moon/Lunar Fairy

2. Spaces between syllables

When a word consists of more than one syllable, the syllables are put together without any spaces in between.

diànshì   television

There is a space between different words in a sentence, just like in English.

Nǐ hǎo ma?   How are you?

3. Capitalizing letters

Proper nouns are capitalized in *Pīnyīn*.

Běijīng   Beijing
Měiguó   America

B.   TONES

Chinese is a tonal language. This means that there are
words which consist of all the same sounds, but still differ
in sound by virtue of the difference in the tones their vowels carry. There are four tones in Chinese: first, second,
third and fourth.

First tone:	**mā**	mother
Second tone:	**má**	linen
Third tone:	**mǎ**	horse
Fourth tone:	**mà**	to scold

Some words, referred to as "toneless," are pronounced with
a neutral tone. There are no tone markers above the vowels
in such words. The Chinese particles **ma** and **ne** are words
pronounced with a neutral tone.

Nǐ hǎo *ma?*	How are you?
Wǒ hěn hǎo. Nǐ *ne?*	I am fine. How about you?

C.   TONE MARKERS

Tone markers are placed above the vowel of each syllable
in *Pīnyīn*. Take the vowel *a* as an example:

First tone:	**ā**	prefix attaching to first names
Second tone:	**á**	an interjection expressing doubt or a question
Third tone:	**ǎ**	an interjection expressing surprise
Fourth tone:	**à**	oh (interjection)

In the case of diphthongs (or compound vowels), the tone is
marked over a vowel that is closer to the left end of the following vowel priority list: *a, o, e, i, u.*

ai

First tone:	āi	dust
Second tone:	ái	cancer
Third tone:	ǎi	short
Fourth tone:	ài	love

When *i* and *u* combine together to form a diphthong, the tone marker is always placed over the second vowel. For example, the tone marker is placed over *u* in *iu* and over *i* in *ui*.

ui

First tone:	tuī	to push
Second tone:	tuí	declining
Third tone:	tuǐ	leg
Fourth tone:	tuì	to withdraw

iu

First tone:	liū	to skate
Second tone:	liú	to flow
Third tone:	liǔ	willow
Fourth tone:	liù	six

LESSON 4

A. TONE CHANGES

1. Third tone followed by a third tone

When two syllables with third tones join, the first syllable with a third tone is usually pronounced as a half third tone, which sounds like a second tone. In writing, both tones are still written as third tones. For example:

Nǐ hǎo ma?   How are you?

2. **bù** (not)

Bù undergoes two types of tone changes.
When it is used alone, at the end of a word, or when it precedes the first, second or third tone syllable, it remains unchanged and is pronounced **bù**.

Bù! Wǒ bù chī.   *No!* I don't eat it.
Wǒ *bù* zhīdào.   I *don't* know.

When **bù** precedes a syllable with the fourth tone, it is written and pronounced as **bú**.

Wǒ *bú* huì qū.   I *won't* go.

When it is found between two words that are repeated, it is written and pronounced with the neutral tone **bu**.

Hǎo *bu* hǎo?   Okay? (*lit.,* Good or *not* good?)

3. **yì** (one)

Yī has three different types of tone changes.
When it is used alone, at the end of a word, or as an ordinal number, it is written and pronounced with a first tone.

yī, èr, sān   one, two, three
xīngqī*yī*   Monday
dì*yī*   the first
yī-qī-qī-liù nián   year 1776

When it precedes a syllable with a fourth tone, **yī** is pronounced as **yí**.

*yì*húir	a while
*yí*wàn	ten thousand

When it precedes a syllable with the first, second, or third tone, **yī** is pronounced as **yì**.

*yì*qiān	one thousand
*yì*zhí	straight, all along

If it comes between two duplicate syllables, **yī** is pronounced as **yi**.

shì *yi* shì	try a little bit
zuò *yi* zuò	do a little bit

LESSON 5

A.   MORE PRACTICE WITH SIMILAR INITIALS

1. **z** and **zh**

zū	to rent
zhū	pig
zǎo	early
zhǎo	to look for

2. **c** and **ch**

cū	rough
chū	out
cūn	village
chūn	spring

3. **s** and **sh**

sān	three
shān	hill
sǎo	to sweep
shǎo	few, a small amount

4. **zh, ch, sh** and **j, q, x**

qī	seven
chī	to eat
jī	chicken
zhī	to know
xī	west
shī	poem
sǎo	to sweep
shǎo	few, a small amount

B.   MORE PRACTICE WITH SIMILAR FINALS

1. **i** and **e**

shí	stone
shé	tongue
zhì	to cure
zhè	this

2. **ou** and **iu**

yōu	to worry
liū	to slide
yóu	oil
líu	to stay
yǒu	to have

liǔ	willow
yòu	right
liù	six

3. ie and üe

jiéchū	outstanding
juédìng	to decide
qiē	to cut
quē	to lack
xiě	to write
xuě	snow

4. an and en

gān	liver
gēn	root
bān	class
bēn	to run

5. ang and eng

lǎng	bright
lěng	cold
máng	blind, busy
língméng	lemon

LESSON 6

A. DAYS AND MONTHS

xīngqīyī	Monday
xīngqīèr	Tuesday

xīngqīsān	Wednesday
xīngqīsì	Thursday
xīngqīwǔ	Friday
xīngqīliù	Saturday
xīngqītiān/	
xīngqīrì	Sunday
yīyuè	January
èryuè	February
sānyuè	March
sìyuè	April
wǔyuè	May
lùyuè	June
qīyuè	July
bāyuè	August
jiǔyuè	September
shíyuè	October
shíyīyuè	November
shíèryuè	December

B. NUMBERS 1–10

yī	one
èr	two
sān	three
sì	four
wǔ	five
liù	six
qī	seven
bā	eight
jiǔ	nine
shí	ten
Yī jiā yī děngyú èr.	One and one are two. (*lit.,* One plus one equals two.)
Yī jiā èr děngyú sān.	One and two are three.

Èr jiā èr děngyú sì.	Two and two are four.
Èr jiā sān děngyú wǔ.	Two and three are five.
Sān jiā sān děngyú liù.	Three and three are six.
Sān jiā sì děngyú qī.	Three and four are seven.
Sì jiā sì děngyú bā.	Four and four are eight.
Sì jiā wǔ děngyú jiǔ.	Four and five are nine.
Wǔ jiā wǔ děngyú shí.	Five and five are ten.

C.   COLORS

hóngsè	red
lánsè	blue
lǜsè	green
hēisè	black
báisè	white
huángsè	yellow
kāfēisè	brown (coffee)
lìsè	brown (chestnut)
huīsè	gray
chéngsè	orange
zǐsè	purple

D.   SEASONS AND DIRECTIONS

chūntiān	spring
xiàtiān	summer
qiūtiān	autumn
dōngtiān	winter
dōng	east
nán	south
xī	west
běi	north

E. MORNING, NOON, AND NIGHT; TODAY, YESTERDAY, TOMORROW

shàngwǔ	morning
zhōngwǔ	noon
xiàwǔ	afternoon
wǎnshàng	evening, night
jīntiān	today
zuótiān	yesterday
míngtiān	tomorrow
Jīntiān shì xīngqīwǔ.	Today is Friday.
Zuótiān shì xīngqīsì.	Yesterday was Thursday.
Míngtiān shì xīngqīliù.	Tomorrow is Saturday.

QUIZ 1

Match the Chinese words in the left column with their English translations in the right column.

1.	*xīngqīwǔ*	a.	January
2.	*qiūtiān*	b.	summer
3.	*xīngqīsì*	c.	June
4.	*chūntiān*	d.	winter
5.	*bā*	e.	October
6.	*yīyuè*	f.	white
7.	*dōngtiān*	g.	autumn
8.	*lǜsè*	h.	Sunday
9.	*liùyuè*	i.	eight
10.	*xiàtiān*	j.	spring
11.	*xīngqīyī*	k.	west
12.	*sì*	l.	Thursday
13.	*shíyuè*	m.	four
14.	*xīngqītiān*	n.	ten
15.	*xī*	o.	red

16. *hóngsè*		p. black
17. *hēisè*		q. green
18. *shí*		r. Friday
19. *báisè*		s. gray
20. *huīsè*		t. Monday

ANSWERS

1—r; 2—g; 3—l; 4—j; 5—i; 6—a; 7—d; 8—q; 9—c; 10—b; 11—t; 12—m; 13—e; 14—h; 15—k; 16—o; 17—p; 18—n; 19—f; 20—s.

F.   WORD STUDY

bān	class
kěguān	considerable
qūbié	difference
yuánsù	element
guāngróng	glory
xíngdòng	action, operation
māma	mother
bàba	father

LESSON 7

A.   GREETINGS

ZĂOSHÀNG	IN THE MORNING
zǎo	morning
ān	good, well
Zǎoān.	Good morning.
Lǐ	Li
xiānsheng	Mr.

Lǐ xiānsheng, zǎoān.	Mr. Li, good morning.[1]
nín	you *(fml.)*[2]
hǎo	good
ma	question particle
Nín hǎo ma?	How are you *(fml.)*?
	(*lit.,* You are good?)
nǐ	you *(infml.)*
hǎo	good, well
ma	question particle
Nǐ hǎo ma?	How are you *(infml.)*?
hěn	very
hǎo	well
Hěn hǎo.	Very well.
xièxie	thank you, thanks
Hěn hǎo, xièxie.	Very well, thank you.
nín	you
ne	how about (question particle)
Nín ne?	How about you? *(fml.)*
Nǐ ne?	How about you? *(infml.)*
hǎo	fine (*lit.,* good)
Hǎo, xièxie.	Fine, thank you.

NOTE:

Nǐ and *nín* both mean "you." *Nǐ* is an informal form and *nín* is a formal form. *Nín* is used with people one does not know well, with people older than oneself, and with people who have greater authority than oneself (e.g., teachers, parents, supervisors). When you speak to a person to whom you should show respect, use *nín* even if the occasion is not formal. But you don't use *nín* to speak to a waiter even if the occasion is formal.

---

[1] The greeting usually follows a person's name.
[2] *fml.* stands for "formal"; *infml.* stands for "informal."

XIÀWÚ	IN THE AFTERNOON
nín	you *(fml.)*
hǎo	good, well
Nín hǎo.	Good afternoon. (*lit.,* You're good.)[3]
Lǐ tàitai, nín hǎo.	Good afternoon, Mrs. Li.
nǐ	you *(infml.)*
hǎo	good, well
Zhāng xiānsheng, nǐ hǎo.	Good afternoon, Mr. Zhang.
nín	you *(fml.)*
hǎo	good, well
ma	particle
Nín hǎo ma?	How are you? (*lit.,* You're good?)
Hái hǎo.	So-so. (*lit.,* fairly good)
Hái hǎo, nín ne?	So-so, and how about you?
hái	still
shì	to be
yí yàng	same
Hái shì yí yàng, xièxie.	Same as usual, thanks.
WǍSHÁNG	IN THE EVENING
WǍSHÁNG	AND AT NIGHT
nín	you *(fml.)*
hǎo	good, well
Chén xiáojie, nín hǎo.	Good evening, Miss Chen.
hěn	very
hǎo	good

[3] In Chinese, there are no exact equivalents of English "good afternoon" or "good evening." Instead, one can use the expressions *nín hǎo (fml.)* or *nǐ hǎo (infml.),* or the questions *nín hǎo ma (fml.)?* or *nǐ hǎo ma (infml.)?* to greet a person.

| Yībō, nǐ hǎo. | Good evening, Yi Bo. |
| Měilì, nǐ hǎo. | Good evening, Mei Li. |

RÈNHÉ SHÍJIĀN	AT ANY TIME OF DAY
Nǐ hǎo.	Hello./Hi.
Zàijiàn.	Good-bye.

NOTE:
Xiāngsheng (sir, Mr.), *tàitai* (Ma'am, Mrs.) and *xiáojie* (Miss)
are general terms of address. They're used in combination
with the person's last name, which they follow. During formal introduction, a person's full name is announced, as in:
Chén Měilì xiáojie (Miss Mei Li Chen). Because the last
name is more important than the first name in the Chinese
culture, it has to be mentioned before the first name.

B.   HOW'S THE WEATHER?

Tiānqì zěnmeyàng?	How's the weather?,
	What's the weather like?
Hěn lěng.[4]	It's (very) cold.
Hěn rè.	It's (very) hot.
Hěn hǎo.	It's (very) nice.
Yǒu fēng.	It's windy. (*lit.*, There is wind.)
Qíngtiān.	It's sunny.
Xiàyǔ.	It's raining.
Xiàxuě.	It's snowing.
Fēicháng rè!	What heat! (*lit.*, Extremely hot!)
Qīngpéndàyǔ.	It's raining cats and dogs. (*lit.*,
	pouring rain)

---

[4] Monosyllabic adjectives, such as *lěng*, are commonly preceded by adverbs *hěn*
(very) or *tǐng* (quite).

NOTE:

Note that there is no *tā* (it) in Chinese weather expressions. The same is true of expressions of time and distance (see Lessons 8 and 14).

QUIZ 2

Match the Chinese words in the left column with their English translations in the right column.

1. *zǎo*	a. How about you?
2. *tàitai*	b. How are you? *(infml.)*
3. *Nín hǎo ma?*	c. What's the weather like?
4. *Hěn hǎo.*	d. morning
5. *Zǎoān.*	e. Thank you.
6. *Nǐ hǎo.*	f. Mrs.
7. *Nǐ hǎo ma?*	g. It's very hot.
8. *Hái shì yí yàng.*	h. Sir/Mr.
9. *Xièxie.*	i. fine
10. *Hěn rè.*	j. Good morning.
11. *Tiānqì zěnmeyàng?*	k. in the evening.
12. *Nǐ ne?*	l. How are you? *(fml.)*
13. *hǎo*	m. Very well.
14. *xānsheng*	n. Same as usual.
15. *wǎnshang*	o. Good evening./Good night.

ANSWERS

1—d; 2—f; 3—l; 4—m; 5—j; 6—o; 7—b; 8—n; 9—e; 10—g; 11—c; 12—a; 13—i; 14—h; 15—k.

Supplemental Vocabulary 1: Weather

weather	*tiānqì*
It's raining.	*Xiàyǔ.*
It's snowing.	*Xiàxuě.*
It's hailing.	*Xiàbáo.*
It's windy.	*Yǒu fēng.*
It's very hot.	*Hěn rè.*
It's very cold.	*Hěn lěng.*
It's sunny.	*Qíngtiān.*
It's cloudy.	*Duōyún.*
It's very beautiful.	*Hěn měilì.*
storm	*fēngbào*
wind	*fēng*
sun	*tàiyáng*
thunder	*léi*
lightning	*shǎndiàn*
hurricane	*jùfēng*[5]
temperature	*wēndù*
degree	*dù*
rain	*yǔ*
snow	*xuě*
cloud	*yún*
fog	*wù*
smog	*yānwù*
umbrella	*yǔsǎn*

[5] Some regions of China have a typhoon in the summer. The Chinese word for "typhoon" is *táifēng*.

LESSON 8

A. WHERE IS...?

nǎli[6]	where
yǒu	there is, are
Nǎli yǒu...?	Where is there...?
lǚguǎn	a hotel[7]
Nǎli yǒu lǚguǎn?	Where's there a hotel?
hǎo	good
cānguǎn	restaurant
Nǎli yǒu hǎo de cānguǎn?[8]	Where's there a good restaurant?
nǎli	where
zài	at
Zài nǎli?	Where is it? (*lit.*, where is?)
Diànhuà zài nǎli?	Where's the telephone?
Cānguǎn zài nǎli?	Where's the restaurant?
Huǒchēzhàn zài nǎli?	Where's the train station?
Jīchǎng zài nǎli?	Where's the airport?
Xǐshǒujiān zài nǎli?	Where's the bathroom?

B. CAN YOU TELL ME...?

nín kěyǐ	can you
gàosu wǒ	tell me
Nín kěyǐ gàosu wǒ...?	Can you tell me...?
Nín kěyǐ gàosu wǒ nǎli yǒu lǚguǎn ma?	Can you tell me where there is a hotel?

[6] In addition to *nǎli*, Chinese has two other words for "what"—*nǎr* and *shénme dìfang*.

[7] There is no equivalent for the English indefinite article "a" in Chinese (see Summary of Chinese Grammar).

[8] *De* is a particle used to separate an adjective from a noun.

Nín kěyǐ gàosu wǒ nǎli yǒu hǎo de cānguǎn ma?	Can you tell me where there is a good restaurant?
Nín kěyǐ gàosu wǒ diànhuà zài nǎli ma?	Can you tell me where the telephone is?
Nín kěyǐ gàosu wǒ huǒchēzhàn⁹ zài nǎli ma?	Can you tell me where the train station is?
Nín kěyǐ gàosu wǒ jīchǎng zài nǎli ma?	Can you tell me where the airport is?

NOTE:
Yǒu has two meanings: "there is/are" and "to have." When a location word precedes it, *yǒu* means "there is/are." The negative form of *yǒu* is *méiyǒu*.

Huǒchēzhàn yǒu diànhuà.	There are phones in the train station.
Huǒchēzhàn méiyǒu diànhuà.	There are no phones in the train station.

QUIZ 3

Match the Chinese words in the left column with their English translations in the right column.

1. *Nǎli yǒu lǚguǎn?*   a. Where's the telephone?
2. *Nǎli yǒu diànhuà?*   b. Can you tell me where the train station is?
3. *Nín kěyǐ gàosù wǒ…?* c. Can you tell me…?

---

⁹ *Huǒchē* means "railroad train" and *dìtiě* means "underground train."

4. *Nín kěyǐ gàosù*   d. the airport
   wǒ huǒchēzhàn
   zài nǎlǐ ma?

5. *jīchǎng*   e. Where is there a hotel?

ANSWERS
1—e; 2—a; 3—c; 4—b; 5—d.

C.   DO YOU HAVE...?

Nín yǒu...?	Do you have...?
qián	money
xiāngyān	cigarettes
huǒchái	matches
yī liàng chē	a/one car
Wǒ yào...	I need...
yìxiē[10] zhǐ	some paper
qiānbǐ[11]	a pencil
bǐ	a pen
yóupiào	a postage stamp
féizào	soap
yágāo	toothpaste
máojīn	a towel
Wǒ kěyǐ zài nǎli mǎi...?	Where can I buy...?
Zhōngwén zìdiǎn	a Chinese dictionary
yóukè zhǐnán	a tourist guidebook
yìxiē yīngwén shū	some books in English
yīfu	clothes

[10] *Yìxiē* means "some" and "a few."
[11] Note that there is no exact equivalent in Chinese of the English indefinite article "a." The number "one" can be used in front of the Chinese noun with a similar function; see p. 34.

D. IN A RESTAURANT

zǎocān	breakfast
wǔcān	lunch
wǎncān	dinner
wǎncān	supper

NOTE:

In China, a late snack or dessert, called *yèxiāo,* is often taken later in the evening, after the dinner.

Nín yào shénme?	What will you have? (*lit.,* What do you want?)
gěi wǒ	give me
càidān	the menu
qǐng nǐ	please *(infml.)*
Qǐng nǐ gěi wǒ càidān.	May I have a menu, please?
Gěi wǒ...	Bring me...
miànbāo	bread
miànbāo hé niúyóu	bread and butter
tāng	soup
ròu	meat
niúròu	beef
niúpái	a steak
huótuǐ	ham
yú	fish
jī	chicken
jīdàn	eggs
cài	vegetables
tǔdòu	potatoes
shālā	salad
kuàngquánshuǐ	mineral water
jiǔ	wine

píjiǔ	beer
niúnǎi	milk
kāfēi jiā nǎi	coffee with milk
táng	sugar
yán	salt
hújiāo	pepper
shuǐguǒ	fruit
tiándiǎn	dessert
Gěi wǒ...	Bring me...
yì bēi kāfēi	a cup of coffee
yì bēi chá	a cup of tea
yì tiáo cānjīn	a napkin
yí gè gēngchí	a spoon
yí gè xiǎo gēngchí	a teaspoon
yì bǎ dāo	a knife
yí gè pánzi	a plate
yí gè bēizi	a glass
Wǒ xiǎng yào...	I would like...
yìxiē shuǐguǒ	some fruit
yì píng jiǔ	a bottle of wine
yì píng hóng jiǔ	a bottle of red wine
yì píng bái jiǔ	a bottle of white wine
zài lái yì píng jiǔ	another bottle of wine
zài lái yìdiǎnr nà ge	a little more of that
zài lái yìdiǎnr miànbāo	a little more bread
zài lái yìdiǎnr ròu	a little more meat
Qǐng nǐ jiézhàng.	The check, please. (*lit.*, Please settle the bill.)

QUIZ 4

Match the Chinese words in the left column with their English translations in the right column.

1.	*ròu*	a.	fish
2.	*tǔdòu*	b.	water
3.	*shuǐ*	c.	vegetables
4.	*Nín yào shénme?*	d.	I need soup.
5.	*dàn*	e.	The check, please.
6.	*jī*	f.	breakfast
7.	*yú*	g.	a spoon
8.	*yì píng jiǔ*	h.	coffee
9.	*Wǒ yào tāng.*	i.	What will you have?
10.	*Géi wǒ yì xiē miànbāo.*	j.	dessert
11.	*kāfēi*	k.	meat
12.	*táng*	l.	a knife
13.	*cài*	m.	eggs
14.	*yì bēi chá*	n.	Bring me some bread.
15.	*zài lái yì xiē miànbāo*	o.	chicken
16.	*yì bǎ dāozi*	p.	a cup of tea
17.	*tiándiǎn*	q.	some more bread
18.	*zǎocān*	r.	sugar
19.	*yí gè gēngchí*	s.	a bottle of wine
20.	*Qǐng nǐ jiézhàng.*	t.	potatoes

ANSWERS

1—k; 2—t; 3—b; 4—i; 5—m; 6—o; 7—a; 8—s; 9—d; 10—n; 11—h; 12—r; 13—c; 14—p; 15—q; 16—l; 17—j; 18—f; 19—g; 20—e.

SUPPLEMENTAL VOCABULARY 2: FOOD

food	*shíwù*
dinner	*wǎncān*
lunch	*wǔcān*
breakfast	*zǎocān*
meat	*ròu*

chicken	*jī*
beef	*niúròu*
pork	*zhūròu*
fish	*yú*
shrimp	*xiā*
lobster	*lóngxiā*
bread	*miànbāo*
egg	*dàn*
cheese	*nǎilào*
rice (cooked)	*fàn*
vegetable	*cài*
lettuce	*shēngcài*
tomato	*fānqié*
carrot	*húluóbo*
cucumber	*huángguā*
pepper	*làjiāo*
fruit	*shuǐguǒ*
apple	*píngguǒ*
orange	*júzi*
banana	*xiāngjiāo*
pear	*lí*
grapes	*pútao*
drink	*yǐnliào*
water	*shuǐ*
milk	*niúnǎi*
juice	*guǒzhī*
coffee	*kāfēi*
tea	*chá*
wine	*jiǔ*
beer	*píjiǔ*
soft drink/soda	*qìshuǐ*
salt	*yán*
pepper	*hújiāo*
sugar	*táng*

honey	*fēngmì*
hot/cold	*rè/lěng*
sweet/sour	*tián/suān*

LESSON 9

The next several lessons contain some important information on Chinese grammar. Read each section of these lessons carefully until you understand every point. As you continue with the course, try to notice grammatical constructions you have mastered. Refer back to the grammar explanations in these lessons as often as you find it necessary. Eventually, you will gain a good grasp of the basic features of Chinese grammar without any deliberate memorization of "rules." Be sure to refer to the Summary of Chinese Grammar at the end of this book if you need more information.

A. VERBS: TO SPEAK: *SHUŌ*

1. I speak

wǒ shuō	I speak
nǐ shuō	you speak *(infml.)*
tā shuō	he speaks
tā shuō	she speaks
wǒmen shuō	we speak
nǐmen shuō	you speak *(pl.)*[12]
nín shuō	you speak *(fml.)*
tāmen shuō	they speak

---

[12] *pl.* refers to the plural form.

2. Study these examples:

Wǒ shuō Zhōngwén.	I speak Chinese.
Lǐ Měi shuō Yīngwén.	Li Mei speaks English.
Wǒ hé Lǐ Měi shuō Zhōngwén.	Li Mei and I speak Chinese. (*lit.,* I and Li Mei speak Chinese.)

NOTE:

The form of the verb remains the same, regardless of which pronoun it is used with. There is no verb conjugation in Chinese. Later, you will learn about different suffixes, which are added to verbs to indicate the time and completion of the action.

The pronoun *wǒ* "I" comes first when combined with another pronoun or a personal name.

B. MEASURE WORDS

In English, a noun can be modified by a numeral or a demonstrative pronoun, which directly precedes it, e.g., *one book* or *this book*. In Chinese, a "measure word" must be placed between the number and the demonstrative pronoun and the noun. Some common types of measure words are discussed below. You can find a more complete list of measure words in the Summary of Chinese Grammar.

1. Nature of the object

Different measure words are used for different categories of objects. For a book, *běn* is used. For something that can be held in a hand, *bǎ* is used. For utensils and most animals, *zhī* is used. For machines, *tái* is used. For a person, *gè* is used.

...u	one/a book
...a yǔsǎn	one/an umbrella
yì bǎ yǐzi	one/a chair
yì zhī jī	one/a chicken
yì zhī māo	one/a cat
yì zhī bēi	one/a cup/glass
yì zhī wǎn	one/a bowl
yì tái diànnǎo	one/a computer
yí ge rén	one/a person

2. Shape of the object

For something with a flat surface, *zhāng* is used. For something pointed and thin, *zhī* is used. For something long and thin, *tiáo* is used. For something round and flat, *pán* is used.

yì zhāng zhǐ	one/a paper
yì zhāng zhàopiàn	one/a photo
yì zhāng chuáng	one/a bed
yì zhī bǐ	one/a pen
yì tiáo lù	one/a road
yì pán cídài	one/an audiotape

3. More examples

A word denoting a container can be used as a measure word.

yì bēi shuǐ	one/a cup of water
yì dài píngguǒ	one/a bag of apples
yì xiāng lājī	one/a box of rubbish

4. Collective measure words

yì shuāng/duì xiézi	one/a pair of shoes
yì shuāng/duì yǎnjing	one/a pair of eyes
yì dá jīdàn	one/a dozen eggs

C. SINGULAR AND PLURAL NOUNS

1. There is no distiction between the singular and the plural forms of most nouns in Chinese. For example, *shū* can mean both "a book" and "books."

2. The use of *men*

The ending *men* can be added to human nouns to denote plural.

wǒ	I/me
wǒmen	we/us
lǎoshī	teacher
lǎoshīmen	teachers
xiānsheng	sir
xiānshengmen	gentlemen[13]
nǚshì	lady
nǚshìmen	ladies

If the noun is qualified by a numeral and a measure word, *men* cannot be used.

3. *yí* "one," *yìxiē* "some, a few," or *jǐ* "several"

yí ge nánháir	a/one boy
yí ge nǚháir	a/one girl
yìxiē nánháir	some/a few boys
yìxiē nǚháir	some/a few girls
jǐ ge nánháir	several boys
jǐ ge nǚháir	several girls

---

[13] *Xiānshengmen* and *nǚshìmen* are commonly used to address an audience.

NOTE:

Yì in *yìxiē* "some, a few" can be replaced by a demonstrative pronoun to form *zhèxiē* "these" or *nàxiē* "those." Between *jǐ* "several" or *yí* "one" and the noun being modified, a measure word is needed.

QUIZ 5

Match the Chinese words in the left column with their English translations in the right column.

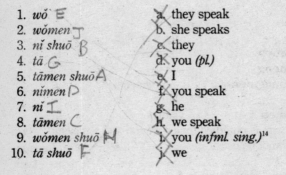

1. *wǒ* E   a. they speak
2. *wǒmen* J   b. she speaks
3. *nǐ shuō* B   c. they
4. *tā* G   d. you *(pl.)*
5. *tāmen shuō* A   e. I
6. *nǐmen* D   f. you speak
7. *nǐ* I   g. he
8. *tāmen* C   h. we speak
9. *wǒmen shuō* H   i. you *(infml. sing.)*[14]
10. *tā shuō* F   j. we

ANSWERS

1—e; 2—j; 3—f; 4—g; 5—a; 6—d; 7—i; 8—c; 9—h; 10—b.

D. POSSESSIVE "DE"

Possessive meaning is expressed with the particle *de*, placed between two nouns. *De* corresponds to English "possessive *'s*" or "of."

---

[14] *sing.* refers the singular form.

Zhāng xiānsheng *de* shū   Mr. Zhang's book
wǒmen *de* shū   our book

E. ASKING QUESTIONS

1. To ask a simple question in Chinese, add the question particle *ma* at the end of the sentence, without making any changes in the word order.

Nín shuō Zhōngwén.   You speak Chinese.
Nín shuō Zhōngwén ma?   Do you speak Chinese?

2. You can also ask a simple question by adding a negative particle before the verb and duplicating the verb.

Nín huì shuō Zhōngwén.   You know (how) to speak Chinese.
Nín huì *bu huì* shuō Zhōngwén?   Do you know (how) to speak Chinese or not?

3. Chinese has no equivalent of the verb "to be" in equational sentences. (Equational sentences are sentences such as "Chinese is easy.") When a question is formed from an equational sentence, the adjective follows the noun directly, followed by the question particle *ma*.

Zhōngwén róngyì ma?   Is Chinese easy?

F. NOT

The Chinese word for "not" is *bù*. *Bù* is placed before the verb.

Wǒ *bù* shuō Yīngwén.   I don't speak English.

REVIEW QUIZ 1

1. *Zhén xiānsheng,*____ (good afternoon).
    a. *zǎo*
    b. *nín hǎo*
    c. *wǎn'ān*

2. *Nín kěyǐ gàosu wǒ*_____ (where) *yǒu fàndiàn ma?*
    a. *nǎli*
    b. *zài*
    c. *yào*

3. _____ (bring me) *yìxiē shuǐguǒ.*
    a. *Wǒ xiǎng*
    b. *Qǐng nǐ*
    c. *Gěi wǒ*

4. *Kāfēi jiā*_____ (milk).
    a. *ròu*
    b. *jiǔ*
    c. *nǎi*

5. *Zài lái*_____ (a little) *miànbāo.*
    a. *yìdiǎnr*
    b. *jǐ ge*
    c. *yì píng*

6. *Wǒ shuō*_____ (Chinese).
    a. *Wǒmen*
    b. *Zhōngwén*
    c. *Yīngwén*

7. _____ shì "September."
    a. sānyuè
    b. liùyuè
    c. jiǔyuè

8. Nín _____ (good) ma?
    a. xièxie
    b. hǎo
    c. rè

9. Lí xiānsheng _____ (speaks) Yīngwén.
    a. mǎi
    b. shuō
    c. yǒu

10. Nǐ yǒu _____ (wine) ma?
    a. nǎi
    b. jiǔ
    c. zhǐ

ANSWERS
1—b; 2—a; 3—c; 4—c; 5—a; 6—b; 7—c; 8—b; 9—b;
10—b.

LESSON 10

A.   MAY I INTRODUCE…?

Zǎoān.	Good morning.
zǎo	morning
Nín zǎo.	Good morning. (fml.)
Nǐ zǎo.	Good morning. (infml.)

Xiānsheng, zǎo.	Good morning, sir.
Nín hǎo ma?	How are you?
Hěn hǎo, xièxie. Nín ne?	Very well, thanks. How about you?
Nín shì cóng Měiguó lái de ma?[15]	Are you from the United States?
Shì.	Yes.
Nín huì shuō Zhōngwén ma?	Do you speak Chinese? (*lit.*, Do you know how to speak Chinese?)
Yì diǎndiǎn.	A little.
wǒ lái jièshào	let me introduce (*fml.*)
zhè shì	this is
wǒ péngyou	my friend
Wáng Xiǎo Lì	Xiao Li Wang
Wǒ lái jièshào, zhè shì wǒ péngyou, Wáng Xiǎo Lì.	Let me introduce to you my friend, Xiao Li Wang.
hěn gāoxìng	much pleasure
rènshi nín	to meet you (*lit.*, to know you)
Hěn gāoxìng rènshi nín.	I'm glad to meet you.
rènshi nín	to meet you
wǒ yě hěn	I am also
Rènshi nín, wǒ yě hěn gāoxìng.	I'm also glad to meet you.
ràng wǒ	let me
zìwǒ jièshào	introduce myself
wǒ jiào Hé Péng	my name is Peng He (*lit.*, I am called)

---

[15] The structure *shì...de* is used to emphasize the place where the action is taking place. (See more in the Summary of Chinese Grammar.)

shì lái fúwù nín de	at your service (*lit.*, is to serve you)
Wǒ zìwǒ jièshào, wǒ jiào Hé Péng, shì lái fúwù nín de.	Let me introduce myself, my name is Peng He, at your service.
Wǒ shì Hé Péng.	I'm Peng He.
ràng wǒ	let me
géi nǐ jièshào	introduce to you
zhè shì wǒ péngyou	this is my friend
Ràng wǒ géi nǐ jièshào, zhè shì wǒ péngyou, Wú Wén yīshēng.	Let me introduce to you my friend Dr. Wen Wu.
hěn	very
gāoxìng	glad
rènshi nín	meeting you
Hén gāoxìng rènshi nín, Wú yīshēng.	It's such a pleasure to meet you, Dr. Wu.

B. HOW ARE THINGS?

Xiǎo Qīng, nǐ hǎo!	Hello, Xiao Qing.
Qiáng Shēng, nǐ hǎo!	Hello, Qiang Sheng.
Kànjiàn nǐ zhēn hǎo!	It's really nice to see you!
Zuìjìn zěnme yàng?	How have you been recently?
Zuìjìn hǎo ma?	Have you been well recently?
Hái hǎo, nǐ ne?	Fairly well, and how about you?
chī	eat
le	verb suffix (completed action)
méiyǒu	not have

Chī le ma?	Have you eaten yet?
Chī le.	I have eaten.
Hái méiyǒu.	Not yet.
méiyǒu	not have
shénme	what
tèbié	particular
Méiyǒu shénme tèbié.	Nothing in particular.
zuìjìn	recently
máng	busy
bù máng	not busy
Zuìjìn máng bu máng?	Have you been busy recently?
Máng bù máng?	Are you busy?
búshì	not
tài	too/excessive
máng	busy
Búshì tài máng.	Not too busy.

NOTE:

Chī le ma? (Have you eaten yet?) is a common greeting in Chinese. The speaker doesn't expect a literal reply to a question. In order to ask whether someone has already had food, use *Nǐ chī le fàn méiyǒu?* "Have you eaten yet?" (*lit.* Have you eaten cooked rice yet?).

C. GOOD-BYE

Zàijiàn.	Good-bye.
xià	lower
cì	time
jiàn	see
Xià cì jiàn.	See you next time.
Zàijiàn. Xià cì jiàn.	Good-bye. See you next time.
děng	wait

yìhuír	a while
jiàn	see
Děng huìr jiàn.	See you later.
huítóu	after a short while
jiàn	see
Huítóu jiàn.	See you soon.
Wǎn'ān.	Good night./Sleep well.
nǐ	you (*infml.*)
hǎo	good
Nǐ hǎo.	Good evening.
Míngtiān jiàn.	See you tomorrow.

QUIZ 6

Match the Chinese words in the left column with their English translations in the right column.

1. *Nǐ hǎo ma?*   a. Nothing in particular.
2. *Děng huìr jiàn.*   b. Allow me to introduce
                                      you to my friend.
3. *Wǎn'ān.*   c. See you later.
4. *Nǐ hǎo, Xiǎo Qīng.*   d. Hello, Xiao Qing.
5. *Méiyǒu shénme*   e. It's nice to meet
   tèbié.   you.
6. *Ràng wǒ gěi nǐ*   f. How are you?
   jièshào wǒ péngyou.
7. *Huítóu jiàn.*   g. Good night.
8. *zuìjìn*   h. to know you
9. *Hěn gāoxìng rènshi*
   nín.   i. recently
10. *rènshi nǐ*   j. See you later.

ANSWERS
1—f; 2—c; 3—g; 4—d; 5—a; 6—b; 7—j; 8—i; 9—e; 10—h.

SUPPLEMENTAL VOCABULARY 3: PEOPLE

people	*rén*
person	*rén*
man	*nánrén*
woman	*nǚrén*
adult	*dàren/chéngrén*
child	*xiǎoháir/xiǎopéngyǒu*
boy	*nánháir/nánháizi*
girl	*nǚháir/nǚháizi*
teenager	*qīngshàonián*
tall/short	*gāo/ǎi*
old/young	*lǎo/niánqīng*
fat/thin	*pàng/shòu*
friendly/unfriendly	*yǒushàn/bùyǒushàn*
happy/sad	*kuàilè/shāngxīn*
beautiful/ugly	*měilì/nánkàn*
sick/healthy	*yǒubìng/jiànkāng*
strong/weak	*qiáng/ruò*
famous	*yǒumíng*
intelligent	*cōngming*
talented	*yǒu cáinéng*

LESSON 11

A. TO BE OR NOT TO BE: *SHÌ, BÚ SHÌ*

1. SHÌ

wǒ shì	I am
nǐ shì	you are
tā shì	he/she is
wǒmen shì	we are

| nǐmen shì | you are *(pl.)* |
| tāmen shì | they are |

2. BÚ SHÌ

wǒ bú shì	I am not
nǐ bú shì	you are not
tā bú shì	he/she is not
wǒmen bú shì	we are not
nǐmen bú shì	you are not *(pl.)*
tāmen bú shì	they are not

3. Study the following examples. Notice that *shì*, unlike English "to be," is not used in equational sentences that contain an adjective.

Tā *shì* yīshēng.	He's a doctor.
Tā *shì* Zhōngguórén.	He's a Chinese./He's Chinese.
Tā hěn niánqīng.	She's very young.
Tā hěn cōngmíng.	She's intelligent.
Shì wǒ.	It's me.
Nǐ *shì* cóng nǎli lái de?	Where are you from? (*lit.,* Where do you come from?)
Wǒ *shì* cóng Zhōngguó lái de.	I'm from China.
Zhè *shì* mùtóu zuò de ma?	Is it made of wood? (*lit.,* Is this made of wood?)
Zhè *shì* shéi de?	Whose is this?
Zhè *shì* tā de.	This is his.
Xiànzài *shì* yīdiǎn.	It's one o'clock. (*lit.,* Now is one o'clock.)
Zhè *shì* bìxū de.	It's necessary. (*lit.,* This is necessary.)

Study additional examples where the English verb "to be" doesn't correspond to Chinese *shì*.

Tā zài nàbianr.	He's over there.
Tā zài Shànghǎi.	He's in Shanghai.
Shū zài nǎli?[16]	Where's the book?
Zài zhuōzi shàng.	It's on the table.
Wǒ hěn lèi.	I'm very tired.
Wǒ zhǔnbèi hǎo le.[17]	I'm ready.
Kāfēi lěng le.[18]	The coffee is cold. (*lit.*, The coffee has become cold.)
Zhè ge hěn míngxiǎn.	It's very clear./It's very obvious.
Chuānghu dǎkāi le.	The window is open.
Chuānghu guān le.	The window is shut.

B.   ADJECTIVES

yí ge hěn gāo de nánhái	a very tall boy
yí ge hěn gāo de nǚhái	a very tall girl
yíxiē hěn gāo de nánhái	some (a few) tall boys
yíxiē hěn gāo de nǚhái	some (a few) tall girls
Tā hěn gāo.	He is very tall.
Tā bù gāo.	He is not tall.
Tā bú shì hěn gāo.	He is not very tall.

---

[16] There is no article "the" in Chinese. However, the position of a noun with respect to a verb indicates whether the noun is definite or indefinite. When a noun is placed before a verb, it has definite reference, as in this example. Compare this example with *Nǎli yǒu shū?* (Where's there a book?), where the noun comes after the verb and it is indefinite. See more details in the Summary of Chinese Grammar.

[17] In Chinese, a verb is used to translate the English adjective "ready."

[18] When placed at the end of a sentence, *le* denotes a change of state.

NOTE:

1. An adjective usually precedes a noun in Chinese. Adjectives are often preceded by degree adverbs, like *hěn* "very." *De* is added after an adjective when it modifies a noun.

2. As mentioned earlier, *shì* "to be" is not used in equational sentences with adjectives. The negative form of an equational sentence with an adjective is formed by adding *bù* before the adjective if the adjective is not modified by a degree adverb. *Bú shì* is placed before the adjective if the adjective is modified by a degree adverb.

QUIZ 7

Match the Chinese words in the left column with their English translations in the right column.

1. *Tā hěn cōngmíng.*
2. *Kāfēi lěng le.*
3. *Tā shì yīshēng.*
4. *Wǒ shì.*
5. *Xiànzài shì yìdiǎn.*
6. *wǒmen shì*
7. *Zhè shì mùtóu zuò de.*
8. *Nǐ shì cóng nǎli lái de?*
9. *Tā zài nàbianr.*
10. *Shì wǒ.*
11. *Wǒ hěn lèi.*
12. *Tāmen shì.*
13. *Zhè shì shéi de?*
14. *Zhè shì bìxū de.*
15. *Tā shì Zhōngguórén.*

a. Whose is this?
b. Where are you from?
c. they are
d. He's a doctor.
e. It's me.
f. He's a Chinese.
g. He's very intelligent.
h. The coffee is cold.
i. I am.
j. It's one o'clock.
k. It's made of wood.
l. we are
m. He's over there.
n. I'm very tired.
o. It's necessary.

ANSWERS
1—g; 2—h; 3—d; 4—i; 5—j; 6—l; 7—k; 8—b; 9—m; 10—
e; 11—n; 12—c; 13—a; 14—o; 15—f.

C.   IT IS

The English expression "it is..." is usually translated as
"this is..." in Chinese.

Zhè shì...	This is.../It is...
Zhè shì zhēn de.	It's true.
Zhè bú shì zhēn de.	That isn't true./That isn't so.
Jiù shì zhèyàng le.	It's so./That's the way it is.
Zhè shì kěndìng de.	It's certain.
Hěn dà.	It's very big.
Hěn xiǎo.	It's very small.
Hěn guì.	It's very expensive.
Hěn piányi.	It's very cheap.
Zhè shì wú jiàzhí de dōngxi.	It's worthless./It's junk.
Hěn bèn.	It's very silly./It's very stupid.
Hěn nán.	It's very difficult.
Hěn róngyi.	It's very easy.
Yì rú fǎn zhǎng!	It's easy! (*lit.,* It's as easy as flipping the hand!)
Yǒu yìdiǎnr.	It's a little./It's not much.
Hěn shǎo.	It's very little.
Hěn duō.	It's a lot.
Gòu le.	It's enough.
Bú gòu.	It's not enough.
Zhè shì nǐ de.	It's yours.

Zhè shì wǒ de.	It's mine.
Zhè shì wǒmen de.	It's ours.
Zhè shì gěi nǐ de.	It's for you.
Hěn wǎn le.	It's very late.
Hěn zǎo.	It's very early.
Méi guānxi./Bú yàojǐn.	It's all right. (*lit.*, No relation/Not important)
Zhè yàng bù hǎo.	It's not all right. (*lit.*, It's not good in this way.)
Zāogāo.	It's bad.
Zhēn zāogāo.	It's very bad.
Hěn jìn.	It's very near.
Hěn yuǎn.	It's very far.
Jiù zài zhèr.	It's here.
Jiù zài nàr.	It's there.
Hěn shímáo.	It's very chic./It's in style.

QUIZ 8

Match the Chinese words in the left column with their English translations in the right column.

1. *Hěn duō.*	a. It's enough.
2. *Hěn róngyi.*	b. That isn't true.
3. *Hěn jìn.*	c. It's bad.
4. *Gòu le.*	d. It's very near.
5. *Zhè bú shì zhēn de.*	e. It's mine.
6. *Zāogāo.*	f. It's true.
7. *Hěn xiǎo.*	g. It's here.
8. *Zhè shì zhēn de.*	h. It's very small.
9. *Zhè shì wǒ de.*	i. It's very easy.
10. *Jiù zài zhèr.*	j. It's a lot.

ANSWERS
1—j; 2—i; 3—d; 4—a; 5—b; 6—c; 7—h; 8—f; 9—e;
10—g.

D.   TO HAVE AND HAVE NOT: *YŎU* AND *MÉIYŎU*

1. I have

wǒ yǒu	I have
nǐ yǒu	you have
tā yǒu	he has
wǒmen yǒu	we have
nǐmen yǒu	you have (*pl.*)
tāmen yǒu	they have

2. I don't have

wǒ méiyǒu	I don't have
nǐ méiyǒu	you don't have
tā méiyǒu	he doesn't have
wǒmen méiyǒu	we don't have
nǐmen méiyǒu	you don't have (*pl.*)
tāmen méiyǒu	they don't have

3. Study these phrases:

Wǒ yǒu shíjiān.	I have time.
Wǒ shénme shíjiān yě méiyǒu.	I do not have any time.
Tā shénme qián yě méiyǒu	She/He does not have any money.
Nǐ yǒu xiāngyān ma?	Do you have a cigarette?

E.   WORD STUDY

xǐjù	comedy
búbiàn	constant/no change
xiāngfǎn	contrary
yuànwàng	wish
cháng	long
běi	north
qìguān	organ
jiǎndān	simple
tānfàn	vendor

LESSON 12

A.   I ONLY KNOW A LITTLE CHINESE

Ní huì shuō Zhōngwén ma?	Do you speak Chinese? (*lit.*, Do you know how to speak Chinese?)
Huì shuō yīdiǎnr.	Yes, a little.
Yī diǎndiǎnr.	Very little.
Bú tài hǎo.	Not very well.
Wǒ huì shuō Zhōngwén.	I speak Chinese.
Wǒ shuō de bù hǎo.	I speak it poorly.
Wǒ shuō de bú tài hǎo.	I don't speak it very well. (*lit.*, I speak not very well.)
Wǒ zhǐ huì shuō jǐgè dāncí.	I only know a few/several words.
Wǒ huì shuō yīxiē Zhōngwén dāncí.	I can say some words in Chinese.

Nǐ péngyou huì shuō Zhōngwén ma?	Does your friend speak Chinese?
Wǒ péngyou bú huì shuō Zhōngwén.	No, my friend doesn't speak Chinese.
Nǐ dǒng Zhōngwén ma?	Do you understand Chinese?
Wǒ dǒng Zhōngwén.	Yes, I understand Chinese.
Wǒ dǒng, kěshì wǒ bú huì shuō.	I understand it but I don't speak it.
Wǒ huì kàn, kěshì wǒ bú huì shuō.	I can read it but I don't speak it.
Wǒ bù dǒng Zhōngwén.	No, I don't understand Chinese.
Wǒ bù tài dǒng Zhōngwén.	I don't understand Chinese very well.
Wǒ fāyīn fā de bú tài hǎo.	I don't pronounce it very well.
Wǒ yào duō liànxí.	I need to practice more.
Nǐ tīng de dǒng ma?	Do you understand me?
Wǒ tīng de dǒng.	I understand you.
Wǒ tīng de bú tài dǒng.	I don't understand you very well.
Nǐ shuō shénme?	What did you say?
Nǐ jiǎng shénme?	What did you say?
Nǐ shuō de tài kuài.	You speak too fast./ You're speaking too fast.
Bú yào shuō zhème kuài.	Don't speak so fast.
Shuō màn yīdiǎnr.	Speak more slowly.
Qǐng shuō zài màn yīdiǎnr.	Please speak a little more slowly.
Qǐng zài shuō yí biàn.	Please repeat. (*lit.,* Please speak again.)

Qǐng zài shuō yí cì. Please repeat it. (*lit.*, Please speak again.)

Nǐ xiànzài míngbai le ma? Do you understand me now? (*lit.*, Have you understood now?)

È, wǒ míngbai le. Oh, now I understand.

Zhè ge shì shénme yìsi? What does this mean?

"Thanks" Zhōngwén zěnme shuō? How do you say "thanks" in Chinese?

Zhège zì zěnme xiě? How do you write this word?

Qǐng nǐ xiě gěi wǒ. Please write it down for me.

B. DO YOU SPEAK CHINESE?

Xiānsheng, nín zǎo. Good morning, sir.

Nín zǎo. Good morning.

Nín huì shuō Zhōngwén ma ? Do you speak Chinese?

Wǒ huì. Yes, I speak Chinese.

Wǒ bú huì shuō Yīngwén. I don't speak English.

Nín shì cóng Běijīng lái de ma? Are you from Beijing?

Shì. Wǒ shì cóng Běijīng lái de. Yes, I'm from Beijing.

Nín zài Měiguó duō jiǔ le? How long have you been in the United States?

Sān gè yuè. Three months.

Nín hěn kuài jiǔ huì xuéhuì Yīngwén. Nā bú shì tài nán. You'll soon learn English. It's not very hard.

Bǐ nín xiǎngxiàng de yào nán. It's harder than you think.

Nín kěnéng shuō de duì. Duì wǒmen lái shuō, wǒmen xué Zhōngwén bǐ nǐmen xué Yīngwén róngyì.	You're probably right. Chinese is easier for us to learn than English is for you.
Nín shuō Zhōngwén shuō de hěn hǎo.	You speak Chinese very well.
Wǒ zài Běijīng zhù le hǎo jǐ nián.	I lived in Beijing for several years.
Nín de fāyīn fēicháng hǎo.	You have an excellent pronunciation.
Xièxie. Dànshì wǒ yào duō liànxí.	Thank you. I need practice though. (*lit.*, Nevertheless, I need to practice more.)
Wǒ xiànzài yào zǒu le. Wǒ de huǒchē yào kāi le.	I'll have to leave now. My train's about to leave. (*lit.*, My train has to start.)
Yílùshùnfēng.	Good luck and a pleasant trip. (*lit.*, Have a favorable wind through the whole journey.)
Nín yě shì.	The same to you. (*lit.*, You are as well.)
Zàijiàn.	Good-bye.

QUIZ 9

Match the Chinese words in the left column with their English translations in the right column.

1. *Wǒ dǒng, kěshì wǒ bú huì shuō.*
2. *Nǐ xiànzài míngbai le ma?*
3. *Wǒ shuō de bú tài hǎo.*
4. *Nǐ shuō de tài kuài.*
5. *Zhège zì zěnme xiě?*
6. *Nǐ huì shuō Zhōngwén ma?*
7. *Wǒ yào duō liànxí.*
8. *yìdiǎnr*
9. *Qǐng zài shuō yí cì.*
10. *Wǒmen yóu qián.*
11. *Shuō màn yìdiǎnr.*
12. *Wǒ shuō de bù hǎo.*
13. *Nǐ shuō shénme?*
14. *"Thanks" Zhōngwén zěnme shuō?*
15. *Yílùshùnfēng.*

a. Do you speak Chinese?
b. I need to practice more.
c. a little
d. What did you say?
e. Please repeat it.
f. We have money.
g. I am thirsty.
h. I understand it but I don't speak it.
i. Speak more slowly.
j. I don't speak it very well.
k. How do you say "Thanks" in Chinese?
l. You speak too fast.
m. Do you understand me now?
n. How do you write this word?
o. I speak it poorly.

ANSWERS

1—h; 2—m; 3—j; 4—l; 5—n; 6—a; 7—b; 8—c; 9—e; 10—f; 11—i; 12—o; 13—d; 14—k; 15—g.

C.   EXCUSE ME AND THANK YOU

Duìbuqǐ.	Pardon me./Excuse me./ I beg your pardon.
Bùhǎoyìsi.	I'm sorry./Excuse me./ Allow me.
Qǐng nǐ zài zuò yí cì.	Please repeat.
Méi wèntí.	No problem.
Bú yòng kèqi.[19]	You are welcome. (*lit.,* You don't need to be polite.)
Bú kèqi.	Don't mention it. (*lit.,* Don't be polite.)
Wǒ kěyǐ zěnme bāng nǐ?	What can I do for you? (*lit.,* What can I help you with?)
Nǐ hěn hǎo.	You're very kind.
Nǐ zhēn hǎo.	That's really kind of you.
Xièxie.	Thanks.
Xièxie nǐ.	Thank you.
Duō xiè.	Thanks a lot.
Fēicháng gǎnxie.	Thanks a lot.
Zhēn de hěn xièxie nǐ.	Thanks very much.
Bié kèqi.	You're welcome. (*lit.,* Don't be polite.)
Búyòng xiè.	You're welcome. (*lit.,* You don't need to thank.)
Bú yàojǐn.	Never mind. (*lit.,* It's not important.)
Méishénme	It's nothing.
Dāngrán.	Of course.

---

19 *Bú yòng kèqi, bú kèqi* and *bié kèqi* have closely related meanings.

NOTE:

Bú yòng kèqi is used as a reply to someone's thanks and to express graditude for someone's offer. It's habitual to say "thank you" using *xièxie nǐ* instead of *xièxie nín.*

D.   WORD STUDY

liànzi	chain
xìn	letter
wánquán	complete/entire
nǎiyóu	cream
yǒnghéng	eternal
pēnquán	fountain
guānyuán	officer
xìtǒng	system

LESSON 13

A.   THIS AND THAT

1. Demonstrative pronouns

Gěi wǒ zhège.[20]	Give me this one.
Gěi wǒ zhèxiē.	Give me these.
Gěi wǒ nàge.	Give me that one.
Gěi wǒ nàxiē.	Give me those.
Gěi wǒ nàbiānr nàge.	Give me that one over there.
Gěi wǒ nàbiānr nàxiē.	Give me those over there.

[20] Because there is no context, the general measure word *ge* is used here.

NOTE:
When *zhè* and *nà* are followed by measure words or numerals, they are pronounced as *zhèi* and *nè/nèi*, e.g., *zhèige* and *nèige*.

2. Demonstrative adjectives

When a demonstrative adjective precedes a noun, a measure word is placed between the demonstrative and the noun. Remember that different measure words are used with different nouns.

zhège nánháir	this boy
zhèwèi nǔshì	this lady
nàwèi nǔshì	that lady
zhè běn shū	this book
nàbiānr nàwèi xiānsheng	that gentleman over there
nàbiānr nàxiē línjū	those neighbors over there

QUIZ 10

Match the Chinese words in the left column with their English translations in the right column.

1. *Gěi wǒ zhèxiē.*   a. Give me those over there.

2. *Zhège.*   b. That one over there.

3. *Gěi wǒ nàge.*   c. This lady.

4. *Zhège nánháir.*   d. This one.

5. *Nàge.*   e. That gentleman over there.

6. *Nàbiānr nàxiē línjū.*   f. This boy.

7. *Gěi wǒ nàbiānr nàxiē.*   g. Give me these.

8. *Nàbiānr nàge.*	h. That one.
9. *Zhèwèi nǔshì.*	i. Those neighbors over there.
10. *Nàbiānr nàwèi xiānsheng.*	j. Give me that one.

ANSWERS

1—g; 2—d; 3—j; 4—f; 5—h; 6—i; 7—a; 8—b; 9—c; 10—e.

B. MORE OR LESS

1. More

gèng màn	slower (*lit.,* even slower)
gèng nán	more difficult
gèng róngyì	easier
gèng yuǎn	farther
gèng jìn	nearer
bǐ zhège gèng	more than that
chāoguò yì nián	more than a year (*lit.,* exceed one year)

NOTE:

Gèng means "(even) more." When placed in front of an adjective, it forms a comparative form of an adjective or adverb.

2. Less

méiyǒu zhème màn	less slow (*lit.,* not so slow)
méiyǒu zhème nán	less difficult (*lit.,* not so difficult)
méiyǒu zhème róngyì	less easy (*lit.,* not so easy)

méiyǒu zhème yuǎn	less far/not so far
méiyǒu zhème jìn	less near/not so near
bǐ zhège shǎo	less than that (*lit.*, less than this)
bú gòu yì nián	less than a year (*lit.*, not enough [for] a year)

C.   AND, OR, BUT

1. *hé* "and"

Jiā Míng hé Jiā Qiáng shì xiōngdì.	Jia Ming and Jia Qiang are brothers.
Xiǎo Líng hé Xiǎo Méi shì jiěmèi.	Xiao Ling and Xiao Mei are sisters.
Mǔqin hé nǚ'ér.	Mother and daughter.

NOTE:
The conjunction *hé* is used to connect nouns, noun phrases and gerunds, but not clauses.

2. *huòzhě* "or" and *háishì* "or"
Huòzhě is used in statements.

Wǔ kuài huòzhě liù kuài.	Five or six dollars.
Wǒ gēn wǒ dìdi huòzhě mèimei qù.	I'm going with my younger brother or (with) my younger sister.

Háishì is used in questions.

Nǐ qù háishì tā qù?	You go or he goes?
Wǔdiǎn háishì qīdiǎn?	Five o'clock or seven o'clock?
Nán háishì nǚ?	Male or female?

NOTE:
Special words are used to address or talk about different family members. For example, *dìdi* means "younger brother," *gēge* means "elder brother," *mèimei* means "younger sister," and *jiějie* means "elder sister."

3. *kěshì* "but"

Wǒ xiǎng qù, kěshì wǒ bù zhīdào shénme shíhou.	I want to go but I don't know when.
Wǒ xiǎng qù, kěshì wǒ bù néng qù.	I want to go but I can't.
Wǒ qù kěshì tā bú qù.	I'm going but she isn't going.

D.   WORD STUDY

yuèduì	band
sījī	chauffeur/driver
chéngfèn	composition
liángxīn	conscience
zhuāngshì	decoration
rènwu	mission/task
shùzì	numeral
pǔtōng	common
dìqū	region

QUIZ 11

Match the Chinese words in the left column with their English translations in the right column.

1. *Yīngwén*
2. *hé*

a. five or six days
b. I want to go but I

		don't know when.
3. *dànshì*	c.	male or female
4. *nǚ'ér*	d.	English
5. *dìdi*	e.	but
6. *wǔ tiān huòzhě liù tiān*	f.	tomorrow
7. *shénme shíhou*	g.	daughter
8. *Wǒ xiǎng qù kěshì wǒ bù zhīdào shénme shíhou.*	h.	and
9. *míngtiān*	i.	when
10. *nán háishì nǚ*	j.	younger brother

ANSWERS
1—d; 2—h; 3—e; 4—g; 5—j; 6—a; 7—i; 8—b; 9—f;
10—c.

REVIEW QUIZ 2

1. _____ (This) *nánháir*.
   a. *Nàge*
   b. *Zhège*
   c. *Zhèxiē*

2. _____ (Those) *shū*.
   a. *Nàxiē*
   b. *Nàge*
   c. *Zhèxiē*

3. _____ (Give) *nàxiē shū*.
   a. *Qù*
   b. *Gěi*
   c. *Gē*

4. _____ (Less) *màn.*
   a. *Méiyǒu*
   b. *Bú gòu*
   c. *Méiyǒu zhème*

5. _____ (Less than) *yì nián.*
   a. *Bú gòu*
   b. *Méiyǒu*
   c. *Méiyǒu zhème*

6. *Wǒ de* _____ (younger sister).
   a. *jiějie*
   b. *mèimei*
   c. *érzi*

7. _____ (More) *nán.*
   a. *Gèng*
   b. *Hěn*
   c. *Bù*

8. _____ (But) *wě bù zhīdào.*
   a. *Háishì*
   b. *Kěshì*
   c. *Huòzhě*

9. *Wǔdiǎn* _____ (or) *qīdiǎn.*
   a. *háishì*
   b. *hé*
   c. *huòzhě*

10. *Nǚ'er* _____ (or) *érzi.*
    a. *háishì*
    b. *huòzhě*
    c. *hái*

ANSWERS
1—b; 2—a; 3—b; 4—c; 5—a; 6—b; 7—a; 8—b; 9—a;
10—b.

SUPPLEMENTAL VOCABULARY 4: AT HOME

at home	*zài jiā lǐ*
house	*fángzi*
apartment	*fángzi/gōngyù*
room	*fángjiān*
living room	*kètīng*
dining room	*fàntīng*
kitchen	*chúfáng*
bedroom	*wòfáng/wòshì*
bathroom	*yùshì*
hall	*méntīng*
closet	*bìchú/yīguì*
window	*chuānghu*
door	*mén*
table	*zhuōzi*
chair	*yǐzi*
sofa/couch	*shāfā/chángshāfā*
curtain	*chuānglián*
carpet	*dìtǎn*
television	*diànshì*
CD player	*guāngdiéjī*
lamp	*dēng*
dvd player	*dvd jī*
sound system	*yīnxiǎng*
painting/picture	*huà/túhuà*
shelf	*jiàzi*
stairs	*lóutī*
ceiling	*tiānhuābǎn*
wall	*qiáng*

floor	*dìbǎn*
big/small	*dà/xiǎo*
new/old	*xīn/jiù*
wood/wooden	*mùtóu/mùzhìde*
plastic/made of plastic	*sùjiāo/sùjiāo*
	zuò de

LESSON 14

A. WHERE?

Nǎr?	Where?
Zài nǎr?	Where is (it)?
Zhèr.	Here.
Nàr.	There.
Zài yòubianr.	To the right.
Zài zuǒbianr.	To the left.
Zài Jiěfànglù.	It's on Jiefang Street. (*lit.*, on Jiefang Street)
Zài Tiān'ānmén Guǎngchǎng.	It's on Tiananmen Square.
Zài Běijīng Dàdào	It's on Beijing Avenue.
Nǎbianr?	Which way?
Zhèbianr.	This way.
Nàbianr.	That way.
Nǐ zěnme qù nàli?	How do you get there?
Nǐ shuō de dìfang zài nǎr?	Where's the place you're talking about?
Zài zhèlǐ.	It's here.
Zài nàli.	It's there.
Nà běn shū zài nǎli?	Where's the book?
Zài zhèlǐ.	It's here.

Nǐ zài nǎr?[21]	Where are you?
Wǒ lái le.[21]	Here I am. (*lit.*, I have come.)
Nímen zài nǎli?	Where are you *(pl.)*?
Wǒmen dào le.	Here we are. (*lit.*, We have arrived.)

B. HERE AND THERE

Jiù zài zhèr.	It's here. (*lit.*, It's at here.)/ Here it is.
Jiù zài zhèr.	It's right here.
Jiù zài nàr.	It's there.
Jiù zài nàr.	It's over there.
Tā zài zhèr.	Here he is./ He's here.
Tā zài nàr.	He's there.
Tā dào nàr qù le.	There he goes.
Tā zài nàr.	He's somewhere over there.
Fàng zài zhèr.	Put it here.
Fàng zài nàr.	Put it there.
Zài zhèr děng wǒ.	Wait for me here.
Zài nàr děng wǒ.	Wait for me there.
Lái zhèbianr.	Come here.
Tā lái le.	Here he comes.
Qù nàbianr.	Go there.
Zài hěn yuǎn nàbianr.	Way over there.
Jiù zài fùjìn.	Around here./Near here.
Zài Zhōngguó.	Over there in China.
Zài Měiguó.	Here in America.
Zài lǐbianr.	In there./Inside.

---

[21] The particle *le* indicates a completed action.

Zài wàibianr.	Out there./Outside.
Tā zhù zài nǎr?	Where does he live?
Tā zhù zài nàr.	He lives there.
Wǒ yuē le tā zài nàli jiàn.	I expect to see him there. (*lit.,* I made an appointment with him to meet there.)
Tā zài nàli.	She's there.
Jiā Míng shì bú shì zhù zài zhèr?	Does Jia Ming live here?/Is this where Jia Ming lives?
Shì.²²	This is the place./It's here.
Tā bú shì zhù zài zhèr.²³	It's not here. (*lit.,* He doesn't live here.)
Tā zhù zài nàr.	It's there. (*lit.,* He lives there.)
Zòu zhèbianr.	Go this way.
Zòu nàbianr.	Go that way.
Cóng zhèbianr jìnlái.	Come in this way.
Cóng nàbianr chūqù.	Go out that way.

NOTE:

Both *zhèr* and *zhèlǐ* mean "here." Both *nàr* and *nàli* mean "there." *Zhèr* and *nàr* are more commonly used in colloquial conversation.

Zài is a preposition placed before pronouns *zhèr* and *nàr* in locative expressions. For example, *Wǒ zài zhèr* "I am here" (*lit.,* I am at here).

Zhèr and *nàr* are placed after nouns to form locative noun phrases. For example, *Tā zài lǎoshī nàr* "She is at the teacher's place." *Zhèr* and *nàr* cannot be used with nouns denoting place names.

---

²² *Shì* is a positive answer to the question "Is this where Jia Ming lives?"

²³ A negative answer to the question *Zhèlǐ shì bú shì Jiā Míng de fángzi?* "Is this Jia Ming's apartment?" is *Zhèlǐ bú shì* (*lit.,* here is not).

C.   TO THE RIGHT, ETC.

Wǎng yòu zhuǎn.	To the right. (*lit.,* Turn towards the right.)
Wǎng zuǒ zhuǎn.	To the left. (*lit.,* Turn towards the left.)
Zài lùkǒu.	On the corner.
Yīzhí zǒu.	Straight ahead. (*lit.,* Walk straight.)
Yīzhí wǎng qián zǒu.	Go straight ahead. (*lit.,* Walk straight ahead.)
Xiàng yòu zǒu.	Turn (to your) right. (*lit.,* Turn right to walk.)
Xiàng zuǒ zǒu.	Turn (to your) left. (*lit.,* Turn left to walk.)

NOTE:

Both *wǎng* and *xiàng* mean "toward." *Wǎng* is preferred in such expressions as *Wǎng xià kàn* "Look down" and *Wǎng shàng kàn* "Look up."

D.   NEAR AND FAR

Zài fùjìn.	It's nearby.
Lí zhèr hěn jìn.	Near here. (*lit.,* Very near away from here.)
Hěn jìn.	Very near.
Lí zhèr jǐ bù.	A few steps from here. (*lit.,* Away from here a couple of steps.)
Kàojìn chéngshì.	Near the town.
Kàojìn gōngyuán.	Near the park.
Zài jiàotáng pángbiānr.	Next to the church.

Lí zhèr jìn ma?	Is it near here? (*lit.,* Is it near away from here?)
Yuǎn ma?	Is it far?
Lí zhèr yuǎn ma?	Is it far from here?
Hěn yuǎn.	It's very far.
Búshì tài yuǎn.	It's not too far.
Lí zhèr búshì tài yuǎn.	It's not too far away from here.
Gèng yuǎn.	It's farther.
Yǒu diǎnr yuǎn.	It's a little farther.
Cóng zhèr dào nàr yǒu duō yuǎn?	How far is it from here to there?
Lí zhèr yǒu liǎng ge lùkǒu.	It's two blocks from here.
Lí zhèr yǒu yì lǐ.	It's a mile from here.

NOTE:

Jìn is an adjective and *kàojìn* is a verb.

Yǒu duō yuǎn means "How far?"—e.g., *Cóng Shànghǎi dào Běijīng yǒu duō yuǎn?* "How far is it from Shanghai to Beijing?" This question can also be answered by replacing *duō yuǎn* with the specified distance, e.g., *Cóng Shànghǎi dào Běijīng yǒu liǎng bǎi gōnglǐ?* "It is two hundred kilometers from Shanghai to Beijing?"

The expression *cóng X dào Y* means "from X to Y." *Lí X* means "away from X."

QUIZ 12

Match the Chinese words in the left column with their English translations in the right column.

1. *Zài nǎr?*
a. I expect to see him there.

2. *Zài zhèr děng wǒ.*	b. Which way?
3. *Zhèr.*	c. To the left.
4. *Wǎng yòu zhuǎn.*	d. It's very far.
5. *Nàr.*	e. Here.
6. *Jiùshì zài zhèr.*	f. Wait for me here.
7. *Wǒ yuē le tā zà zhèr jiàn.*	g. Straight ahead.
8. *Wǎng zuǒ zhuǎn.*	h. To the right.
9. *Hěn yuǎn.*	i. There.
10. *Nǎbianr?*	j. Out there.
11. *Tā zài zhèr.*	k. Go that way.
12. *Hěn jìn.*	l. It's right here.
13. *Zài wàibianr.*	m. Where is it?
14. *Cóng nàbianr zǒu.*	n. He's somewhere around here.
15. *Yìzhí zǒu.*	o. It's very near.

ANSWERS

1—m; 2—f; 3—e; 4—h; 5—i; 6—l; 7—a; 8—c; 9—d; 10—b; 11—n; 12—o; 13—j; 14—k; 15—g.

LESSON 15

A. I, YOU, HE, ETC. (SUBJECT PRONOUNS)

SINGULAR

wǒ	I
nǐ	you *(infml.)*
nín	you *(fml.)*
tā	he
tā	she
tā	it

PLURAL

wǒmen	we
zánmen	we
nǐmen[24]	you
tāmen	they

NOTE:

No distinction in pronunciation exists between *tā* "he," *tā* "she," and *tā* "it." However, the distinction exists in writing where different Chinese characters are used to represent each pronoun.

Both *zánmen* and *wǒmen* translate as "we" in English. However, *zánmen* refers to the speaker and the listener(s) (inclusive meaning), while *wǒmen* usually exludes the listener(s) (exclusive meaning). *Zánmen* is always used as a subject pronoun.

B. IT'S ME, YOU, HIM, ETC.

Shì wǒ.	It's me.
Shì nǐ.	It's you *(infml.)*.
Shì nín.	It's you *(fml.)*.
Shì tā.	It's him.
Shì tā.	It's her.
Shì wǒmen.	It's us.
Shì nǐmen.	It's you.
Shì tāmen.	It's them.

C. IT AND THEM (DIRECT OBJECT PRONOUNS)

Nǐ yǒu qián ma?	Do you have the money?
Wǒ yǒu.	Yes, I have it.

---

[24] The plural form of the formal pronoun *nín* doesn't exist. (See Summary of Chinese Grammar.)

Nǐ yǒu xìn ma?	Do you have the letter?
Wǒ yǒu.	Yes, I have it.
Nǐ yǒu méiyǒu jiàn[25] **guò Jiāmíng hé Dà Wéi?**	Did you see Jia Ming and Da Wei?
Wǒ jiàn guò tāmen.	Yes, I saw them.
Nǐ yǒu méiyǒu jiàn guò Měilì hé Xiǎoqīng?	Did you see Mei Li and Xiao Qing?
Wǒ jiàn guò tāmen.	Yes, I saw them.

NOTE:

There is no distinction between subject and object personal pronouns in Chinese.

Tā (it) is normally used to refer to an animal. *Tāmen,* the plural form of *tā,* is very rarely used in everyday language. When *tā* refers to an inanimate object, it is usually omitted from the sentence, whether it is used as a subject or as an object.

LESSON 16

A. MY, YOUR, HIS, ETC. (POSSESSIVE PRONOUNS/ADJECTIVES)

1. Singular

Possessive pronouns and adjectives are formed by adding the particle *de* after the pronoun.

[25] When *yǒu měiyǒu* is placed before a verb in a question, it means "Did (someone) do X?" It is usually combined with a particle *guò* in such usage. You can answer this type of question with the structure *"verb + guò"* for a positive answer, and *"měi + verb + guò"* for a negative answer.

wǒ de	my (mine)
nín de	your (yours) *(fml.)*
nǐ de	your (yours) *(infml.)*
tā de	his, her, its
	(his, hers, its)

2. Plural

men is added to form plural possesive pronouns and adjectives.

wǒmen de	our (ours)
zánmen de	our (ours)
nǐmen de	your (yours)
tāmen de	their (theirs)

3. Study the following examples:

SINGULAR

wǒ (de) péngyou	my friend
nǐ (de) péngyou	your friend
tā (de) péngyou	his, her friend
wǒmen de péngyou	our friend (exclusive)
zánmen de péngyou	our friend (inclusive)
nǐmen de péngyou	your friend
tāmen de péngyou	their friend

PLURAL

wǒ (de) péngyou	my friends
nǐ (de) péngyou	your friends
tā (de) péngyou	his, her friends
wǒmen de péngyou	our friends (exclusive)
zánmen de péngyou	our friends (inclusive)
nǐmen de péngyou	your friends
tāmen de péngyou	their friends, your friends

NOTE:

In expressions denoting close personal relationships, *de* is used optionally between the possessor and the possessed nouns.

As mentioned earlier, *men* can be added to a noun referring to a human being to change it into a plural form. Such a noun is always definite, e.g., *péngyoumen* "the friends." However, *men* cannot attach to a noun preceded by a possessive adjective.

SINGULAR

wǒ de màozi	my hat
nǐ de qúnzi	your dress
tā de wàitào	his/her coat
wǒmen de péngyou	our friend
wǒmen de māma	our mom
nǐ de érzi	your son
nǐ de nǚ'er	your daughter

PLURAL

wǒ zhèxiē màozi	my hats (*lit.,* my these hats)
nǐ nàxiē qúnzi	your dresses (*lit.,* your those dresses)
tā nàxiē wàitào	their coats (*lit.,* their those coats)
wǒmen zhèxiē péngyou	our friends (*lit.,* our these friends)
wǒmen de māma	our mothers
nǐmen de érzi	your sons
nǐmen de nǚ'er	your daughters

NOTE:

When a noun is preceded by a possessive adjective, demonstrative plural pronouns *zhèxiē* "these" or *nàxiē* "those" can be added between the possessive pronoun and the noun in order to turn it into a plural form, e.g., *wǒ zhèxiē màozi* "my hats."

When human nouns "mothers," "sons," and "daughters" follow plural possessive pronouns, their number is understood from the context.

4. Other Examples:

SINGULAR

Wǒ de gēge zài nǎr?	Where is my elder brother?
Nǐ de dìdi zài nǎr?	Where is your younger brother?
Tā de dìdi zài nǎr?	Where is his/her younger brother?
Wǒmen de gēge zài nǎr?	Where is our elder brother?
Tāmen de dìdi zài nǎr?	Where is their younger brother?
Wǒ de mèimei zài nǎr?	Where is my younger sister?
Nǐ de jiějie zài nǎr?	Where is your elder sister?
Tā de jiějie zài nǎr?	Where is his/her elder sister?
Wǒmen de mèimei zài nǎr?	Where is our younger sister?
Nǐmen de jiějie zài nǎr?	Where is your elder sister?
Tāmen de jiějie zài nǎr?	Where is their elder sister?

PLURAL

Wǒ nàxiē shū zài nǎr?	Where are my books?
Nǐ nàxiē shū zài nǎr?	Where are your books?
Tā nàxiē shū zài nǎr?	Where are his (her) books?
Wǒmen nàxiē shū zài nǎr?	Where are our books?
Nǐmen nàxiē shū zài nǎr?	Where are your books?
Tāmen nàxiē shū zài nǎr?	Where are their books?
Wǒ nàxiē xìn zài nǎr?	Where are my letters?
Nǐ nàxiē xìn zài nǎr?	Where are your letters?
Tā nàxiē xìn zài nǎr?	Where are his/her letters?
Wǒmen nàxiē xìn zài nǎr?	Where are our letters?
Nǐmen nàxiē xìn zài nǎr?	Where are your letters?
Tāmen nàxiē xìn zài nǎr?	Where are their letters?

B. ITS, MINE, YOURS, HIS, ETC. (POSSESSIVE PRONOUNS)

Possessive pronouns are formed by adding *de* after personal pronouns, e.g., *wǒ de* "mine."

wǒ de	mine
nín de	yours *(fml.)*
nǐ de	yours *(infml.)*
tā de	his, hers, its

1. With verb *yǒu*

Tā yǒu wǒ de.	He has mine.
Tā yǒu nǐ de.	He has yours.
Tā yǒu tā de.	He has his/hers.
Tā yǒu wǒmen de.	He has ours.
Tā yǒu nǐmen de.	He has yours.
Tā yǒu tāmen de.	He has theirs

2. With demonstrative pronouns

Zhè shì wǒ de./Zhèxiē shì wǒ de.	This is mine./These are mine.
Zhè shì nǐ de./Zhèxiē shì nǐ de.	This is yours./These are yours.
Zhè shì tā de./Zhèxiē shì tā de.	This is his/hers./These are his/hers.
Zhè shì wǒmen de./Zhèxiē shì wǒmen de.	This is ours./These are ours.
Zhè shì nǐmen de./Zhèxiē shì nǐmen de.	This is yours./These are yours.
Zhè shì tāmen de./Zhèxiē shì tāmen de.	This is theirs./These are theirs.

NOTE:
Shéi de? is used to mean "whose?"

3. Other examples:

Wǒ de péngyou hé nǐ de.	My friends and yours.
Tā de shū bǐ wǒ de hǎo.	His book is better than mine.
Zhè shì shéi de xìn?	Whose letter is this?—
Zhè shì tā de xìn.	It's his letter.
Zhè fēng xìn shì shéi de?	Whose is this letter?—
Zhè fēng xìn shì tā de.	It's his.

C. PRONOUNS WITH PREPOSITIONS

Personal pronouns keep the same form when used after prepositions.

wèile wǒ	for me
wèile nǐ de lìyì	for your sake
gēn tā	with him
gěi tā	(give it) to her
wèile tā	for you
méiyǒu wǒmen	without us
gēn nǐ	with you
wèile tāmen	for them
nǐ de	of, about you
Wǒ zài shuō nǐ.	I'm speaking about you.
Jiā Qiáng bú gēn wǒmen yìqǐ qù.	Jia Qiang is going without us.
Tā xiǎng gēn wǒ yìqǐ qù.	He wants to go with me. (*lit.,* He wants to go with me together.)
Tā zài shuō tā.	He/she is speaking about him.

D. DIRECT AND INDIRECT OBJECT PRONOUNS

Chinese personal pronouns do not change in form depending on the function they have in the sentence, as they do in English. For example, *wǒ* means either "I" or "me," depending on the context.

1. Jia Qiang understands me.

Jiā Qiáng míngbai wǒ. Jia Qiang understands me.
Jiā Qiáng míngbai nǐ. Jia Qiang understands you.
                                   (infml.)

Jiā Qiáng míngbai nín.	Jia Qiang understands you. *(fml.)*
Jiā Qiáng míngbai tā.	Jia Qiang understands him/her.
Jiā Qiáng míngbai wǒmen.	Jia Qiang understands us.
Jiā Qiáng míngbai nǐmen.	Jia Qiang understands you. *(pl.)*
Jiā Qiáng míngbai tāmen.	Jia Qiang understands them.

2. He told me.

Tā gàosu wǒ.	He/she told me.
Tā gàosu nǐ.	He/she told you *(infml.)*.
Tā gàosu nín.	He/she told you *(fml.)*.
Tā gàosu tā.	He/she told her/him.
Tā gàosu wǒmen.	He/she told us.
Tā gàosu nǐmen.	He/she told you *(pl.)*.
Tā gàosu tāmen.	He/she told them.

3. I'm speaking to you.

Wǒ zài gēn nǐ shuōhuà.	I'm speaking to you *(infml.)*.
Wǒ zài gēn nín shuōhuà.	I'm speaking to you *(fml.)*.
Wǒ zài gēn tā shuōhuà.	I'm speaking to him/her.
Tā zài gēn wǒ shuōhuà.	He/she is speaking to me.
Wǒ zài gēn nǐmen shuōhuà.	I'm speaking to you *(pl.)*.
Támen zài gēn wǒmen shuōhuà.	They are speaking to us.
Wǒ zài gēn tāmen shuōhuà.	I'm speaking to them.

Nǐ zěnme la?	What's the matter with you?
Wǒ gěi nǐ zhè běn shū.	I give you the/this book.
Wǒ gěi tā zhè běn shū.	I give her/him the/this book.
Wǒ gěi tā zhè běn shū.	I give the/this book to him/her.
Wǒ gěi nǐ zhè běn shū.	I give the/this book to you.
Wǒ xǐhuān zhè běn shū.	I like the/this book.

When there are two object pronouns in a sentence, the indirect object pronoun precedes the direct object pronoun and both follow the verb.

Tā gāosu wǒ zhège.	He/she told this to me.
Tā gāosu nǐ zhège.	He/she told this to you *(infml.)*.
Tā gāosu nín zhège.	He/she told this to you *(fml.)*.
Tā gāosu tā zhège.	He/she told this to him/her.
Tā gāosu wǒmen zhège.	He/she told this to us.
Tā gāosu nǐmen zhège.	He/she told this to you *(pl.)*.
Tā gāosu tāmen zhège.	He/she told this to them.

E. MYSELF, YOURSELF, HIMSELF, ETC. (REFLEXIVE PRONOUNS)

1. The reflexive pronoun *zìjǐ* "self," used in the object position, can refer to any person or number. Its actual meaning, e.g., "myself," "yourself," "himself," etc., depends on the subject of the sentence in which it is used.

Wǒmen zài jìngzili kànjiàn *zìjǐ*.	We see ourselves in the mirror. (*lit.,* We in the mirror see ourselves.)

Nǐ bié guài *zìjǐ*.	Don't blame yourself.
Nǐ duì *zìjǐ* yào yǒu xìnxīn.	You must have confidence in yourself. (*lit.,* You towards yourself must have confidence.)

2. *Zìjǐ* "self" can also be added after a personal pronoun to emphasize it, e.g., *wǒ zìjǐ* "you yourself."

Nǐ zìjǐ cái zhīdào.	Only you yourself know it.
Tā juéde tā zìjǐ zuì piàoliang.	She thinks she herself is the prettiest.
Wǒ zìjǐ yǒu xǐyījī.	I myself have a washing machine.

3. The verb to "to wash oneself," as in "I wash myself," does not exist in Chinese. Instead, one must say something like "I wash *by* myself."

Nǐ zìjǐ xǐ.	You wash yourself. (*lit.,* You wash by yourself.)
Wǒ zìjǐ lái.[26]	Let me do it by myself.
Tā zìjǐ qù kàn diànyǐng.	He goes to watch a movie by himself.

F. WORD STUDY

fāzhǎn	development
zhuǎnxiàng	diversion
yètǐ	liquid
yìwù	obligation

[26] This is an idiomatic expression. *Lái* means "to come."

zhíyè	occupation
cāngbái	pale
liúxíng	popular, fashionable, trendy
gùtǐ	solid
jùyuàn	theater
hángxíng	voyage

QUIZ 13

1. *Wǒ zìjǐ yǒu xǐyījī.*
2. *Wǒ zìjǐ qù kàn diànyǐng.*
3. *Wǒ zìjǐ xǐshǒu.*
4. *Tā zìjǐ gēpò le shǒuzhǐ.*
5. *Nǐ bié guài zìjǐ.*
6. *Wǒ zìjǐ xǐ.*
7. *Nǐ duì zìjǐ yào yǒu xìnxīn.*
8. *Tā juéde tā zìjǐ zuì hǎo.*
9. *Tā zài jìngzilǐ kànjiàn zìjǐ.*
10. *Tā zìjǐ qù.*

a. Don't blame yourself.
b. He goes by himself.
c. She saw herself in the mirror.
d. You must have confidence in yourself.
e. I wash myself.
f. I wash my hands.
g. He thinks he himself is the best.
h. She cut her fingers.
i. I'm going to watch a movie by myself.
j. I (myself) have a washing machine.

ANSWERS

1—j; 2—i; 3—f; 4—h; 5—a; 6—e; 7—d; 8—g; 9—c; 10—b.

REVIEW QUIZ 3

1. *Shì* _____ (she).
   a. *wǒ*

      b. *tā*
      c. *nǐ*

2. *Shì* _____ (us).
      a. *tāmen*
      b. *nín*
      c. *wǒmen*

3. *Zhè shì* _____ (his) *shū*.
      a. *tā de*
      b. *tā*
      c. *tāmen*

4. *Nà shì* _____ (her) *bízi*.
      a. *tā de*
      b. *tā*
      c. *wě de*

5. *Nàxiē shì* _____ (our) *qián*.
      a. *wó de*
      b. *wǒmen de*
      c. *nǐmen de*

6. _____ (My) *shū zài nǎr?*
      a. *Nǐ de*
      b. *Wǒ de*
      c. *Tāmen de*

7. *Zhè běn shū shì* _____ (ours).
      a. *nǐmen de*
      b. *wǒmen de*
      c. *tā de*

8. *Wǒ gāosu* _____ (you).

    a. *nǐ*
    b. *tā*
    c. *tāmen*

9. *Dùi* _____ (us) *lái shuō.*
    a. *nǐmen*
    b. *wǒmen*
    c. *tāmen*

10. *Wǒ zìjǐ qù kàn* _____ (movie).
    a. *diànshì*
    b. *diànyǐng*
    c. *fēijī*

11. *Gēn* _____ (with me) *lái.*
    a. *nǐ*
    b. *nín*
    c. *wǒ*

12. *Wǒ zìjǐ* _____ (wash hands).
    a. *xǐ shǒu*
    b. *xǐ tóu*
    c. *xǐ wèi*

13. *Tā zìjǐ* _____ (has cut) *tā de liǎn.*
    a. *gāosu*
    b. *shuō le*
    c. *gēpò le*

14. *Bié* _____ (blame) *zìjǐ.*
    a. *gùtǐ*
    b. *guài*
    c. *hángxíng*

15. *Wǒ* _____ (leaving, going away) *le*.
    a. *zǒu*
    b. *chī*
    c. *shuō*

ANSWERS
1—b; 2—c; 3—a; 4—a; 5—b; 6—b; 7—b; 8—a; 9—b;
10—b; 11—c; 12—a; 13—c; 14—b; 15—a.

SUPPLEMENTAL VOCABULARY 5:
THE HUMAN BODY

the human body	*réntǐ*
head	*tóu*
face	*liǎn*
forehead	*étóu*
eye	*yǎngjing*
eyebrow	*méimao*
eyelashes	*jiémáo*
ear	*ěrduo*
nose	*bízi*
mouth	*zuǐ/kǒu*
tooth	*yáchǐ*
tongue	*shétou*
cheek	*liǎnjiá*
chin	*xiàba*
hair	*tóufa*
neck	*bózi*
chest	*xiōngkǒu*
breast	*xiōngbù*
shoulders	*jiānbǎng*
arm	*shǒubì*
elbow	*zhǒu*
wrist	*shǒuwànr*
hand	*shǒu*

stomach/abdomen	*wèi/fù*
penis	*yīnjīng*
vagina	*yīndào*
leg	*tuǐ*
knee	*xīgài*
ankle	*huái*
foot	*jiǎo*
finger	*shǒuzhǐ*
toe	*jiǎozhǐ*
skin	*pífū*
blood	*xuè*
brain	*nǎo*
heart	*xīn*
lungs	*fèi*
bone	*gǔtou*
muscle	*jīròu*
tendon	*jiàn*

LESSON 17

A.   SOME ACTION PHRASES

Wǒ lái le!	I'm coming!
Wǒ mǎshàng lái!	I'm coming right away!
Mǎshàng.	Immediately.
Wǒ xiànzài jiù lái.	I'm coming immediately.
Zánmen zǒu ba!	Let's go!
Kuài diǎn lái!	Come quickly!
Kuài yìdiǎnr!	Hurry up! (*lit.*, More quick!)
Kuài yìxiē!	Hurry up! (*lit.*, More quick!)
Bú yòng gǎn.	Don't rush. (*lit.*, Don't need to be rushed.)

Bié jíjímángmáng.	Don't rush.
Wǒ zài gǎn shíjiān.	I'm in a hurry. (*lit.*, I am rushing time.)
Wǒ bú gǎn shíjiān.	I'm not in a hurry.
Kuài diǎnr!	Quickly!
Màn diǎnr.	Slower.
Xiànzài.	Right now.
Děng yíhuìr!	One moment!/Just a minute! (*lit.*, Wait a moment!)
Hěn kuài.	Very soon.
Mǎshàng.	Immediately.
Bù jiǔ.	Sooner.
Hòulái.	Later.
Tūrán.	Suddenly.
Xiǎoxīn!	Watch out! (*lit.*, Be careful.)

QUIZ 14

Match the Chinese words in the left column with their English translations in the right column.

1. *Xiǎoxīn!*	a. Slower.
2. *Wǒ zài gǎn shíjiān.*	b. Right now.
3. *Děng yíhuìr!*	c. Come right away.
4. *Bù jiǔ.*	d. I'm coming right away!
5. *Mǎshàng.*	e. Watch out!
6. *Hòulái.*	f. Later.
7. *Màn diǎnr.*	g. I'm in a hurry.
8. *Wǒ xiànzài jiù lái!*	h. One moment!
9. *Mǎshàng lái.*	i. Immediately.
10. *Xiànzài.*	j. Soon.

ANSWERS

1—e; 2—g; 3—h; 4—j; 5—i; 6—f; 7—a; 8—d; 9—c; 10—b.

B.   CAN YOU TELL ME?

Wǒ kěyǐ wèn nǐ yí ge wèntí ma?	May I ask you a question?
Qǐng wèn…?	May I ask (you)…?
Nǐ kěyǐ gàosù wǒ ma?	Can you tell me?
Nǐ kěyǐ gàosù wǒ ma?	Could you tell me?
Nǐ huì gàosù wǒ ma?	Will you tell me?
Qǐng nǐ gàosù wǒ.	Tell me, please.
Qǐng nǐ gàosù wǒ, kěyǐ ma?	Could you please tell me?
Nǐ zhè jù huà shì shénme yìsi?	What do you mean? (*lit.,* What do you mean by this sentence?)
Wǒ de yìsi shì shuō…	I mean that…
Nà ge shì shénme yìsi?	What does that mean?
Nà ge shì…	That means…

C.   WORD STUDY

zhàng'ài	barrier
xìnggé	character
hàoqí	curious
hàoqí	curiosity
zìdiǎn	dictionary
chéngdù	degree
jūnduì	army
jīngcháng	often
guānfāng	official
yíhàn	pity

LESSON 18

A.   NUMBERS

1. One through one thousand

yī	one
èr	two
sān	three
sì	four
wú	five
liù	six
qī	seven
bā	eight
jiǔ	nine
shí	ten
shí yī	eleven
shí èr	twelve
shí sān	thirteen
shí sì	fourteen
shí wǔ	fifteen
shí liù	sixteen
shí qī	seventeen
shí bā	eighteen
shí jiǔ	nineteen
èrshí	twenty
èrshí yī	twenty-one
èrshí èr	twenty-two
èrshí sān	twenty-three
sānshí	thirty
sānshí yī	thirty-one
sānshí èr	thirty-two
sānshí sān	thirty-three
sìshí	forty

sìshí yī	forty-one
sìshí èr	forty-two
sìshí sān	forty-three
wǔshí	fifty
wǔshí yī	fifty-one
wǔshí èr	fifty-two
wǔshí sān	fifty-three
liùshí	sixty
liùshí yī	sixty-one
liùshí èr	sixty-two
liùshí sān	sixty-three
qīshí	seventy
qīshí yī	seventy-one
qīshí èr	seventy-two
qīshí sān	seventy-three
bāshí	eighty
bāshí yī	eighty-one
bāshí èr	eighty-two
bāshí sān	eighty-three
jiǔshí	ninety
jiǔshí yī	ninety-one
jiǔshí èr	ninety-two
jiǔshí sān	ninety-three
yìbǎi	one hundred
yìbǎi líng yī	a hundred and one
yìbǎi líng èr	a hundred and two
yìbǎi líng sān	a hundred and three
yìqiān	one thousand
yìqiān líng yī	a thousand and one
yìqiān líng èr	a thousand and two
yìqiān líng sān	a thousand and three

B. MORE NUMBERS

1.

yìbǎi èrshí	one hundred twenty
yìbǎi èrshí èr	one hundred twenty-two
yìbǎi sānshí	one hundred thirty
yìbǎi sìshí	one hundred forty
yìbǎi wǔshí	one hundred fifty
yìbǎi liùshí	one hundred sixty
yìbǎi qīshí	one hundred seventy
yìbǎi qīshí yī	one hundred seventy-one
yìbǎi qīshí bā	one hundred seventy-eight
yìbǎi bāshí	one hundred eighty
yìbǎi bāshí èr	one hundred eighty-two
yìbǎi jiǔshí	one hundred ninety
yìbǎi jiǔshí bā	one hundred ninety-eight
yìbǎi jiǔshí jiǔ	one hundred ninety-nine
èrbǎi	two hundred
sānbǎi èrshí sì	three hundred twenty-four
wǔbǎi wǔshí wǔ	five hundred fifty-five
bābǎi qīshí wǔ	eight hundred seventy-five
jiǔbǎi sānshí èr	nine hundred thirty-two

2. First, second, third

dìyī	first
dìèr	second
dìsān	third
dìsì	fourth
dìwǔ	fifth
dìliù	sixth
dìqī	seventh
dìbā	eighth
dìjiǔ	ninth
dìshí	tenth

3. Two and two

èr jiā èr shì sì.	Two and two are four.
èr èr dé sì.	Two and two are four.
Sì jiā èr shí liù.	Four and two are six.
Shí jiǎn èr shì bā.	Ten minus two is eight.

QUIZ 15

Match the Chinese words in the left column with their English translations in the right column.

1. *yìqiān*		a.	1,002
2. *shí yī*		b.	32
3. *yìbǎi*		c.	102
4. *shí qī*		d.	324
5. *sānshí*		e.	11
6. *èrshí*		f.	1,000
7. *liùshí*		g.	60
8. *sānbǎi èrshí sì*		h.	71
9. *sānshí èr*		i.	17
10. *yìbǎi líng èr*		j.	875
11. *bābǎi qīshí wǔ*		k.	83
12. *qīshí yī*		l.	93
13. *yìqiān líng èr*		m.	20
14. *jiǔshí sān*		n.	30
15. *bāshí sān*		o.	100

ANSWERS

1—f; 2—e; 3—o; 4—i; 5—n; 6—m; 7—g; 8—d; 9—b;
10—c; 11—j; 12—h; 13—a; 14—l; 15—k.

C. WORD STUDY

juéduì	absolute
fāngmiàn	aspect
jiǔbā	bar
jiāohuàn	exchange
kěndìng	certain
jiéhé	combination
tàidù	manner
wēixiǎn	danger

LESSON 19

A. HOW MUCH?

Zhège yào duōshǎo qián?	How much does this cost?
Zhège yào sì máo qián.	It costs forty cents.
Yī gōngjīn kāfēi duōshǎo qián?	How much is a kilo of coffee?
Yào liǎng kuài qián yī gōngjīn.	It costs two dollars a kilo.

NOTE:

Both *èr* and *liǎng* mean "two." *Liǎng* is used to quantify a noun, e.g., *liǎng kuài* "two dollars." *Èr* is used in counting.

B. IT COSTS...

Zhège yào...	It costs... (*lit.,* This costs...)
Zhè běn shū yào sānqiān kuài qián.	This book costs three thousand dollars.
Tā yòng le yīwàn	He bought a car for ten

kuài qián mǎi le yī liàng chē.	thousand dollars.
Wǒ chǔcún le qīshí èr kuài qián mǎi le yī tiáo liánshēnqún.	I've saved seventy-two dollars to buy a dress.
Tā zài liùyuè zhuàn le sānwàn wǔqiān bābǎi èrshí èr kuài qián.	He made 35,822 dollars in the month of June.
Zhège zhǐ yǐ gōngjīn lái mài, yī gōngjīn mài yìbǎi kuài.	It's sold only by the kilo and costs one hundred dollars per kilo.

NOTE:
Notice that the word for "ten thousand" is *wàn*, not *shíqiān* as expected.

C.   MY ADDRESS IS...

Wǒ zhù zài Jiěfànglù èrbǎi wǔshí hào.	I live at 250 Jiefang Road.
Wǒ zhù zài Dōngdàménjiē sānbǎi hào.	She lives at 300 Dongdamen Street.
Nà jiā shāngdiàn zài Wángfǔjǐngdàjiē sānbǎi èrshí liù hào.	The store is at 326 Wangfujing Avenue.
Tāmen bān dào Běijīng Guǎngchǎng jiǔbǎi èrshí yī hào qù le.	They moved to 921 Beijing Plaza.

NOTE:
In addresses, the name of the street is followed by the house or building number.

D. MY TELEPHONE NUMBER IS...

Wǒ de diànhuà hàomǎ   My telephone number
shì sì-yī-wǔ-sān   is 415-3288.
-èr-bā-bā.

E. THE NUMBER IS...

Hàomǎ shì...   The number is...
Wǒ de hàomǎ shì...   My number is...
Wǒ de fángjiān hàomǎ   My room number is 30.
shì sānshí hào.

Wǒ zhù zài sānshí hào   I live in room 30.
fángjiān.

Wǒ de ménpái hàomǎ   My house number
shì yīqiān sānbǎi èrshí   is 1322.
er hào.

Wǒ zhù zài   I live at 332 Dongfang
Dōngfāngdàjiē sānbǎi   Avenue, Fifth Floor.
sānshí èr hào, wǔ lóu.

LESSON 20

A. WHAT'S TODAY?

Jīntiān shì xīngqī jǐ?   What's today? (*lit.*, What
day of the week is
today?)

Jīntiān shì xīngqī jǐ?   What day is today?
Xīngqīyī.   Monday.
Jīntiān shì jǐ yuè   What date is it today? (*lit.*,
jǐ hào?   What's the month and the
the number of today?)

Jīntiān shì jǐ hào?	What is today's date? (*lit.*, What's the number of today?)
Xīngqīliù shì jǐ hào?	What is Saturday's date?
Èrshí hào.	It's the 20th.
Wǔyuè yī hào.	The 1st of May./May 1st.
Sìyuè shí yī hào.	The 11th of April.
Qīyuè sì hào.	The 4th of July.
Jiǔyuè shí wǔ hào.	The 15th of September.
Liùyuè èrshí yī hào.	The 21st of June.
Shíèryuè èrshí wǔ hào.	The 25th of December.
Shíyīyuè shí qī hào.	The 17th of November.
Èryuè shísān hào.	The 13th of February.
Bāyuè èrshí bā hào.	The 28th of August.

B.   SOME DATES

Hóng Lóu Mèng shì zài yī-qī-wǔ-sì nián chūbǎn de.	"Dream of the Red Mansion" was published in 1754.
Lǐbǎi zài qī-liù-èr nián qùshì de.	Li Bai died in 762.
Tā de bàba shì èr-líng-líng-sān nián guòshì de.	His father died in 2003.
Zài yī-jiǔ-jiǔ-liù nián huòzhě shì yī-jiǔ-jiǔ-qī nián wǒmen zài nàr.	We were there in 1996 or in 1997.
Zài èr-líng-líng-sān nián fāshēng le shénme shì?	What happened in 2003? (*lit.*, What thing happened in 2003?)

Zhōngguó zài èr-líng-líng-sān nián shíyuè shíwǔ hào dì yí cì sòng tàikōngrén shàng tàikōng.	China sent an astronaut into space on October 15, 2003, for the first time.

C. WORD STUDY

zǒngjié	conclusion
qíngkuàng	condition
kǎolù	consideration
juédìng	decision
qíngjǐng	scene/sight/circumstances
jìjié	season
rén	person
xìnhào	signal

QUIZ 16

Match the Chinese words in the left column with their English translations in the right column.

1. *Shì xīngqīyī.*	a. The 25th of June.
2. *Shì jǐ hào?*	b. The 28th of February.
3. *Qīyuè yi hào.*	c. The 13th of August.
4. *Jīntiān shì jǐ hào?*	d. 1605.
5. *Sìyuè shí yī hào.*	e. It's Monday.
6. *Èryuè èrshí bā hào.*	f. What day of the month is it?
7. *Liùyuè èrshí wǔ hào.*	g. Date (*lit.,* number).

8.	*Yī-liù-líng-wǔ.*	h.	The first of July.
9.	*Bāyuè shí sān hào.*	i.	The 11th of April.
10.	*Hào.*	j.	What's today's date?
11.	*Jīntiān shì xīngqī jǐ*	k.	She died in 1985.
12.	*Jīntiān shì xīngqīsì.*	l.	Today is Monday, the 30th.
13.	*Tā shì zài yī-jiǔ-bā-wǔ nián qùshì de.*	m.	I live at 30 Dalu Street.
14.	*Jīntiān shì xīngqīyī sānshí hào.*	n.	Today is Thursday.
15.	*Wǒ zhù zài Dàlùjiē sānshí hào.*	o.	What day is today?

ANSWERS

1—e; 2—f; 3—h; 4—j; 5—i; 6—b; 7—a; 8—d; 9—c;
10—g; 11—o; 12—n; 13—k; 14—l; 15—m.

LESSON 21

A.   WHAT TIME IS IT?

Fēnzhōng	minute
Xiǎoshí	hour
Diǎn	o'clock
Xiànzài jǐ diǎn?	What time is it?
Yī diǎn.	It's 1:00.
Yī diǎn líng wǔ fēn.	It's 1:05.
Yī diǎn shí fēn.	It's 1:10.
Yī diǎn shí wǔ fēn.	It's 1:15.
Yī diǎn yí kè.	It's 1:15.
Yī diǎn bàn.	It's 1:30.
Yī diǎn wǔshí fēn.	It's 1:50.

Liǎngdiǎn.	It's 2:00.
Sāndiǎn.	It's 3:00.
Sìdiǎn.	It's 4:00.
Wǔdiǎn.	It's 5:00.
Liùdiǎn.	It's 6:00.
Qīdiǎn.	It's 7:00.
Bādiǎn.	It's 8:00.
Jiǔdiǎn.	It's 9:00.
Shídiǎn	It's 10:00.
Shí yī diǎn.	It's 11:00.
Sāndiǎn shí fēn.	It's 3:10.
Liùdiǎnbàn.	It's 6:30.
Yīdiǎn sānkè.	It's a quarter to two.
Hái méi dáo sìdiǎn	It's not four yet.
Zhōngwǔ shíèrdiǎn.	It's 12:00./It's noon.
Bànyè shíèrdiǎn.	It's 12:00 midnight./ It's midnight.
Nǐ de shǒubiǎo shí jǐdiǎn?	What time do you have? (*lit.,* What time does your watch have?)
Wǒ de shǒubiǎo shí wǔdiǎn.	It's five o'clock by my watch. (*lit.,* My watch shows five o'clock.)

NOTE:
Liǎngdiǎn is used for "two o'clock" and *liǎngdiǎn èrshífēn* for "2:20."

B.   AT WHAT TIME?

Jǐdiǎn?	At what time?
Huǒchē jǐdiǎn kāi?	What time does the train leave?
Zhǔnshíde jiǔdiǎn zhèng.	At nine o'clock sharp.

Dàyuē jiǔdiǎn.	About nine o'clock.
Jiǔdiǎn zuǒyòu.	Around nine o'clock.
Xiàwǔ liǎngdiǎn sìshífēn	At 2:40 P.M.
Xiàwǔ liùdiǎn.	At 6 P.M.

NOTE:
Shàngwǔ or *bànyè* is added after a time expression for "A.M." and *xiàwǔ* or *wǎnshang* for "P.M."

Zǎoshang bādiǎn. **Shàngwǔ bādiǎn.**	It's eight o'clock in the morning./It's 8:00 A.M.
Xiàwǔ liǎngdiǎn.	It's two o'clock in the afternoon./It's 2:00 P.M.
Wǎnshang jiǔdiǎn.	It's nine in the evening./It's 9:00 P.M.
Bànyè sāndiǎn.	It's three in the middle of night./It's 3:00 A.M.
Wǒ shàngwǔ qīdiǎn shàngbān.	I go to work at 7:00 A.M.
Wǒ wǎnshang bādiǎn qù cāntīng.	I'm going to the restaurant at 8:00 P.M.

NOTE:
Wǎnshang means "evening" or "night" and begins at 6:00 P.M. For the period from 12:00 A.M. to 3:00 A.M., *bànyè* is usually used. To say "2:00 P.M.," use *xiàwǔ liǎngdiǎn*, not *liǎngdiǎn xiàwǔ*. Also, note that the time expression is placed after the main verb.

C.   IT'S TIME

Shì shíhou le.	It's time.
Shì shíhou zuò le.	It's time to do it.

Shì shíhou zǒu le.	It's time to leave.
Shì wǒmen huíjiā de shíhou le.[27]	It's time for us to go home.
Wǒ yǒu hěnduō shíjiān.	I have a lot of time.
Wǒ shénme shíjiān yě méiyǒu.	I haven't any time.
Tā zài làngfèi tā de shíjiān.	He's wasting his time.
Tā bùshí de lái.	He comes from time to time.

D. TIME EXPRESSIONS

liǎng fēnzhōng yǐqián	two minutes ago
sān ge zhōngtóu yǐqián	three hours ago
guò bàn ge zhōngtóu	in half an hour
bādiǎn yǐhòu	after eight
jiǔdiǎn zhīqián	before nine
zhǔnshí	on time
zǎo	early
chí/wǎn	late

QUIZ 17

Match the Chinese words in the left column with their English translations in the right column.

1. *Shì shíhou zòu le.*	a. He comes from time to time.
2. *Xiànzài jǐdiǎn?*	b. It's nine.
3. *Yīdiǎn.*	c. At what time?

[27] *Shì shíhou wǒmen huíjiā le* can also be used here.

4. *Sāndiǎn.*	d. It's time to do it.
5. *Jiǔdiǎn.*	e. It's two.
6. *Bànyè.*	f. It's one.
7. *Jǐdiǎně*	g. I haven't any time.
8. *Wǒ shénme shíjiān yě méiyǒu*	h. It's 2:40 p.m.
9. *Yīdiǎn yīkè.*	i. It's noon.
10. *Sìdiǎn.*	j. It's three.
11. *Liǎngdiǎn.*	k. It's 1:05.
12. *Tā bùshí de lái.*	l. It's four.
13. *Zhōngwǔ.*	m. What time is it?
14. *Yīdiǎn líng wǔfēn.*	n. It's 1:15.
15. *Liǎngdiǎn sìshífēn.*	o. It's midnight.

ANSWERS

1—d; 2—m; 3—f; 4—j; 5—b; 6—o; 7—c; 8—g; 9—n; 10—l; 11—e; 12—a; 13—i; 14—k; 15—h.

LESSON 22

A. YESTERDAY, TODAY, TOMORROW, ETC.

GUÒQÙ	XIÀNZÀI	WÈILÁI
zuótiān	**jīntiān**	**míngtiān**
yesterday	today	tomorrow
zuótiān	**jīntiān**	**míngtiān**
zǎoshang	**zǎoshang**	**zǎoshang**
yesterday morning	this morning	tomorrow morning
zuóyè/	**jīnwǎn**	**míngtiān**
zuówǎn		**wǎnshang**
last evening	this evening	tomorrow evening

zuóyè/	jīnwǎn	míngtiān
zuówǎn		wǎnshang
last night	tonight	tomorrow
		night

B. MORNING, NOON, NIGHT, ETC.

Jīntiān zǎoshang.	This morning.
Zuótiān zǎoshang.	Yesterday morning.
Míngtiān zǎoshang.	Tomorrow morning.
Jīntiān zhōngwǔ.	This noon./Noon today.
Zuótiān zhōngwǔ.	Yesterday noon.
Míngtiān zhōngwǔ.	Tomorrow noon.
Jīntiān wǎnshang.	This evening.
Zuótiān wǎnshang.	Yesterday evening.
Míngtiān wǎnshang.	Tomorrow evening.
Jīntiān wǎnshang.	Tonight.
Zuótiān wǎnshang.	Last night.
Míngtiān wǎnshang.	Tomorrow night.

C. THIS WEEK, NEXT MONTH, IN A LITTLE WHILE, ETC.

Zhège xīngqī.	This week.
Shàngyíge xīngqī.	Last week.
Xiàyíge xīngqī.	Next week.
Guò liǎng ge xīngqī.	In two weeks.
Liǎng ge xīngqī yǐqián.	Two weeks ago.
Zhège yuè.	This month.
Shàngyíge yuè.	Last month.
Xiàyíge yuè.	Next month.
Guò liǎng ge yuè.	In two months.
Liǎng ge yuè yǐqián.	Two months ago.

Qián ge yuè.	The month before last.
Jīnnián.	This year.
Qùnián.	Last year.
Míngnián.	Next year.
Xiàyī'nián.	Next year.
Guò liǎngnián.	In two years.
Liǎngnián qián.	Two years ago.
Duōjiǔ yǐqián?	How long ago?
Gāngcái.	A moment ago.
Hěnjiǔ yǐqián.	A long time ago.
Xiànzài.	Now.
Mùqián.	This very moment./ For the time being.
Zài zhège shíhou.	At this moment.
Zài rènhé shíhou.	At any moment.
Guò yīzhènzi	In a short time.
Guò yīhuìr.	In a little while.
Bùshí.	From time to time.
Duōshǎo cì?	How many times?
Yí cì.	Once.
Měi cì.	Each time.
Liǎng cì.	Twice.
Bùcháng.	Very seldom./Not often.
Jīngcháng.	Very often.
Yǒushí.	Sometimes.
Ǒu'ěr.	Once in a while.
Yǒushí.	Now and then./From time to time.
Qīngzǎo/yídàzǎo.	Early in the morning.
Zài wǎnshang.	In the evening.
Dìèrtiān.	On the following day.
Yìrì.	On the following day.

Cóng jīntiān kāishǐ liáng ge xīngqīng yǐhòu.	Two weeks from today.
Cóng jīntiān kāishǐ yī ge xīngqīng yǐhòu.	A week from today.
Cóng míngtiān kāishǐ yī ge xīngqīng yǐhòu.	A week from tomorrow.
Guò yī ge xīngqīng.	In a week.
Xiàyíge xīngqīngsān.	Next Wednesday.
Shàngyíge xīngqīngyī.	Monday a week ago.
Zhège yuè wǔ hào.	The fifth of this month.
Shàngyíge yuè wǔ hào.	The fifth of last month.
Sānyuè chū.	At the beginning of March.
Yuèdǐ.	At the end of the month.
Niánchū.	In the early part of the year.
Niándǐ.	Toward the end of the year.
Fāshēng zài bānián qián.	It happened eight years ago.

QUIZ 18

Match the Chinese words in the left column with their English translations in the right column.

1. *Míngtiān zǎoshang.*	a. Last year.
2. *Jīntiān xiàwǔ.*	b. Last night.
3. *Míngtiān xiàwǔ.*	c. Today at noon.
4. *Zuòwǎn.*	d. Now.
5. *Xiàyíge yuè.*	e. In two weeks.
6. *Xiànzài.*	f. In a little while.
7. *Shàngyíge xīngqī.*	g. Tomorrow morning.
8. *Qùnián.*	h. From time to time.

9. *Jīntiān zhōngwǔ.*	i. It happened eight years ago.
10. *Guò yíhuìr.*	j. This afternoon.
11. *Zhège xīngqī.*	k. Sometimes.
12. *Fāshēng zài bā'nián qián.*	l. Within a week.
13. *Niándǐ.*	m. Tomorrow afternoon.
14. *Liǎng ge yuè yǐqián.*	n. Next month.
15. *Yuèdǐ.*	o. Last week.
16. *Yí ge xīngqī zhīnèi*	p. Each time.
17. *Bùshí.*	q. About the end of the month.
18. *Yǒushí.*	r. Towards the end of the year.
19. *Guò liǎng ge xīngqī.*	s. This week.
20. *Měicì.*	t. Two months ago.

ANSWERS

1—g; 2—j; 3—m; 4—b; 5—n; 6—d; 7—o; 8—a; 9—c; 10—f; 11—s; 12—i; 13—r; 14—t; 15—q; 16—l; 17—h; 18—k; 19—e; 20—p.

REVIEW QUIZ 4

1. *Wǒ yòng le* _____ (four thousand) *kuài qián mǎi le yí liàng qìchē.*

     a. *sānqiān*

     b. *sìwàn*

     c. *sìqiān*

2. *Wǒ de diànhuà hàomǎ shì* _____ (845-0860).

     a. *bā, sì, wǔ, líng, bā, jiǔ, líng*

     b. *bā, sān, yī, líng, bā, liù, líng*

     c. *bā, sì, wǔ, líng, bā, liù, líng*

3. *Jīntiān shì* _____ (date)?
   a. *jǐtiān*
   b. *xīngqíjǐ*
   c. *jǐhào*

4. _____ (Today) *shì xīngqíjǐ?*
   a. *Xiànzài*
   b. *Jīntiān*
   c. *Shénme*

5. *Shièryuè* _____ (17) *hào.*
   a. *shíqī*
   b. *qī*
   c. *qīshí*

6. _____ (1:10).
   a. *yīdiǎn yīkè*
   b. *yīdiǎn shífēn*
   c. *shídiǎn sìfēn*

7. _____ (7:00).
   a. *qīdiǎn*
   b. *jiǔdiǎn*
   c. *sìdiǎn*

8. _____ (12:00 noon).
   a. *bànyè shíèrdiǎn*
   b. *zhōngwǔ shíèrdiǎn*
   c. *yīdiǎn*

9. _____ (2:40).
   a. *liǎngdiǎn sānkè*
   b. *liǎngdiǎn sìshífēn*
   c. *liǎngdiǎn shísìfēn*

10. _____ (Yesterday) *shì xīngqītiān.*
    a. *Jīntiān*
    b. *Zuótiān*
    c. *Míngtiān*

11. *Shàngyíge* _____ (week).
    a. *xīngqī*
    b. *tiān*
    c. *yuè*

12. _____ (In a little while).
    a. *Bùshí*
    b. *Xiànzài*
    c. *Yíhuìr*

13. *Liǎng* ____ (years) *yǐqián.*
    a. *xīngqī*
    b. *nián*
    c. *tiān*

14. *Xiàyíge* _____ (Wednesday).
    a. *xīngqīliù*
    b. *xīngqīyī*
    c. *xīngqīsān*

15. *Nián* _____ (end).
    a. *dǐ*
    b. *chū*
    c. *nián*

ANSWERS
1—c; 2—c; 3—c; 4—b; 5—a; 6—b; 7—a; 8—b; 9—b;
10—b; 11—a; 12—c; 13—b; 14—c; 15—a.

D. WORD STUDY

jìnzhǎn	(an) advance
yínháng	bank
zhāng	chapter
nèiróng	content
kěkǒu	delicious
dírén	enemy
shuǐguǒ	fruit
bǎiwàn	million
yǒnghéng	permanence, eternity
fùyù	rich

LESSON 23

A. NO, NOTHING, NEVER, NOBODY

The Chinese word for "not"—*bù*—is always placed before the verb. If the verb has two syllables, *bù* is inserted between them.

Wǒ kàn *bú* jiàn.	I don't see. (*lit.,* I cannot see.)
Nǐ kàn *bú* jiàn.	You don't see.
Wǒ *bú* qù.	I don't go.

Remember that the negative form of the verb "to have" is *méiyǒu* "not to have."

Wǒ méiyǒu qián.	I don't have money.

"Nothing" is *méiyǒu shénme*, "never" is *yǒngyuǎn búhuì*, and "nobody" is *méiyǒu rén*.

Wǒ shénme yě méi (yǒu) kànjiàn.[28]	I see nothing./I don't see anything. (*lit.*, I didn't see anything.)
Wǒ méi kànjiàn shénme.	I see nothing./I don't see anything. (*lit.*, I didn't see anything.)
Wǒ yǒngyuǎn yě búhuì qù.	I never go. (*lit.*, I will not go forever.)
Méiyǒu rén lái le.	No one is coming here./ Nobody comes here.
Shénme rén yě bù lái le.	No one is coming.
Shì, xiānsheng.[29]	Yes, sir.
Bù, xiānsheng.	No, sir.
Tā shuō shì.	He says yes.
Tā shuō bù.	He says no.
Wǒ xiǎng shì ba.	I think so.
Bù hǎo.	It's not good.
Bú cuò.	It's not bad.
Bú shì nàyàng.	It's not that.
Tā bú zà zhèr.	He's not here.
Shì zhèr le.	It's here.
Búshì hěnduō.	It's not a lot/much.
Bú gòu.	It's not enough.
Gòu le.	It's enough.
Méiyǒu nàme kuài.	Not so fast.
Búshì jīngcháng.	Not so often.
Shénme yě méiyǒu.	It's nothing. (*lit.*, Not anything.)

[28] Chinese verbs of perception, e.g., *kànjiàn* "to see," are always expressed as completed actions. *Wǒ méi kànjiàn*, literally "I didn't see," translates into English as "I don't see."

[29] "Yes" and "no" do not have direct equivalents in Chinese. The kind of expression one uses depends on the question. In response to certain questions, *shì* and *bù* can be used. See Summary of Chinese Grammar for more details.

Méi shénme.	That's nothing.
Búshì hěn zhòngyào.	It's not very important.
Wǒ méiyǒu shíjiān.	I have no time.
Wǒ bù zhīdào shì zěnmeyàng huòzhě shì shénme shíhou.	I don't know how or when.
Wǒ bù zhīdào shì nǎr.	I don't know where.
Wǒ shénme yě bù zhīdào.	I don't know anything.
Wǒ shénme yě bú yào.	I don't want anything.
Wǒ bú yào shénme dōngxi.	I don't want anything.
Búyàojǐn.	It doesn't matter./It's not important.
Wǒ bù zàihu.	I don't care./It makes no difference to me.
Wǒ cái bù zàihu ne.[30]	I don't care at all./It doesn't make the slightest difference to me.
Bú yào shuō.	Don't say.
Nǐ bú yào shuō!	You don't say!
Wǒ méiyǒu shénme hǎo shuō.	I've nothing to say.
Wǒ yǒngyuǎn yě búhuì shuō.	I'll never say it.
Méiyǒu fāshēng shénme shì.	Nothing happened.
Wǒ méiyǒu shénme shì zuò.	I have nothing to do.
Wǒ cóng bù jiàn tā.	I never see him.

---

[30] *Ne* is a particle used at the end of statements for emphasis.

Wǒ yǐqián cónglái méiyǒu jiàn guò tā.	I've never seen him before.
Wǒ cóng wèi jiàn guò tā.	I've never seen him before.
Tā cóng bù lái.	He never comes.
Tā cóng wèi lái guò.	He has never come.
Wǒ cóng bù qù.	I never go.

B.   NEITHER, NOR

Yě bù/yě méiyǒu.	Nor.
Wǒ yí jù huà yě méiyǒu jiǎng.	I haven't said a word.
Jì bù ... yě bù.	Neither ... nor.
Gāng gāng hǎo.	Just so (*lit.*, neither more nor less)./Just right.
Zhège hé nàge dōu búshì.	Neither one nor the other./ Neither this one nor that one over there.
Bú tài duō yě bú tài shǎo.	Neither too much nor too little.
Bú tài hǎo yě bú tài huài.	It's so-so./It's not too good and not too bad.
Wǒ bùnéng qù yě bùxiǎng qù.	I can't go and I don't want to.
Wǒ shíjiān hé qián dōu méiyǒu.	I have neither the time nor the money.
Kàn hé xiě tā dōu bùxíng.	He can neither read nor write.
Xiāngyān hé huǒchái wǒ dōu méiyǒu.	I don't have any cigarettes or matches.

C.   WORD STUDY

jiǎo	angle
pǐnzhì	quality
yuányīn	cause
dìngzuì	conviction
jùlí	distance
xiàoguǒ	effect
lìjí	instant
fèijiě	obscure
suǒyǒurén	proprietor

LESSON 24

A.   ISN'T IT? AREN'T THEY? ETC.

Duì ma?	Is it?
Duì búduì?	Isn't it?
Zhōngwén hěn róngyì, duì búduì?	Chinese is very easy, isn't it?
Zhèr de rén dōu hěn hǎo, duì búduì?	The people here are very nice, aren't they?
Nǐ méiyǒu bǐ, duì ma?	You don't have a pencil, do you?
Nǐ zhīdào zhège dìfang, duì búduì?	You know this place, don't you?
Nǐ rènshi Wáng xiānsheng, duì búduì?	You know Mr. Wang, don't you?
Nǐ yǒu tiáogēng hé cānjīn, duì búduì?	You have a spoon and a napkin, don't you?
Nǐ zài zhèr búshì tài jiǔ, duì ma?	You haven't been here very long, have you?

Nǐ huì lái de, duì ma?	You'll come, won't you?
Hěn lěng, duì búduì?	It's very cold, isn't it?
Tài hǎo le! Duì búduì?	How nice! Isn't it? (*lit.*, Too good! Isn't it?)
Tài kěài le! Duì búduì?	How cute! Isn't it? (*lit.*, Too adorable! Isn't it?)
Kěyǐ, duì búduì?	It's all right, isn't it?

B.   SOME, ANY, A FEW

Nǐ yǒu qián ma?	Do you have any money? (*lit.*, Do you have money?)
Wǒ yǒu yìxiē.	Yes, I have some.
Wǒ yìdiǎnr yě méiyǒu.	No, I don't have any. (*lit.*, I don't even have a little bit.)
Tā yǒu qián ma?	Does he have any money?
Tā yìdiǎnr yě méiyǒu.	He doesn't have any.
Nǐ hái yǒu qián ma?	Do you have money left? (*lit.*, Do you still have money?)
Nǐ yǒu duōshǎo běn shū?	How many books do you have?
Wǒ yǒu yìxiē.	I have some.
Nǐ yào yìxiē shuǐguǒ ma?	Do you want some fruit?
Gěi wǒ jǐge.	Give me a few.
Gěi wǒ yìxiē.	Give us some.
Gěi tā yìxiē.	Give him some.
Wǒ yìxiē péngyou.	Some of my friends.

QUIZ 19

Match the Chinese words in the left column with their English translations in the right column.

1. *Wǒ kàn bú jiàn.*
2. *Shénme yě méiyǒu.*
3. *Wǒ yǒngyuǎn yě búhuì shuō.*
4. *Wǒ cóng bù qù.*
5. *Wǒ méi kànjiàn Xiǎoqīng.*
6. *Wǒ jué de búshì.*
7. *Méiyǒu nàme kuài.*
8. *Wǒ shénme yě bù zhīdào.*
9. *Wǒ méi kànjiàn shénme.*
10. *Wǒ cónglái méiyǒu jiàn guò tā.*
11. *Wǒ bù lǐ.*
12. *Méiyǒu fāshēng shénme shì.*
13. *Tā cóng bù lái.*
14. *Bú cuò.*
15. *Wǒ yǒngyuǎn yě búhuì qù*
16. *Tā búzài zhèr.*
17. *Méiyǒu rén lái.*
18. *Zhège hé nàge dōu búshì.*
19. *Búyào gàosu tā.*
20. *Wǒ méiyǒu shíjiān.*

a. Neither this one nor that one over there.
b. I have no time.
c. Don't tell it to him.
d. Nothing happened.
e. I don't see.
f. I don't know anything.
g. I've never seen him.
h. I don't see Xiaoqing.
i. I'll never say it.
j. He never comes.
k. I see nothing.
l. I'll never go.
m. It's nothing.
n. He's not here.
o. I don't think so.
p. It's not bad.
q. I don't care.
r. Not so fast.
s. I never go.
t. No one comes.

ANSWERS

1—e; 2—m; 3—i; 4—s; 5—h; 6—o; 7—r; 8—f; 9—k; 10—g; 11—q; 12—d; 13—j; 14—p; 15—l; 16—n; 17—t; 18—a; 19—c; 20—b.

C. LIKE, AS, HOW

hǎoxiàng	like/as
Hǎoxiàng wǒ.	Like me.
Hǎoxiàng zhèyàng.	Like that. (*lit.,* Like this.)
Hǎoxiàng wǒmen.	Like us.
Hǎoxiàng qítāde.	Like the others.
Zhège búxiàng nàge.	This one isn't like that one.
Jiùshì zhè yàngzi.	That's how it is./That's the way it is.
Rǔ nǐ suǒ yuàn.	As you wish.
Hǎoxiàng jiā yíyàng.	It's like (being) home.
Tā búxiàng tā bàba.	He's not like his father.
Wǒ bù zhīdào zěnyàng jiěshì.	I don't know how to explain it.
Zhège xiàng shénme?	What does it look like?
Zhège xiàng xuě yíyàng de bái.	It's as white as snow.
Hǎo dà de yǔ!	What a rain!
Shénme?	What?/What did you say?/ What do you mean?
Wèishénme bùkěyǐ?	Why not?/Yes, of course.

QUIZ 20

Match the Chinese words in the left column with their
English translations in the right column.

1. *Rǔ nǐ suǒ yuàn.*	a. He's not like his father.
2. *Hǎoxiàng qítāde.*	b. What?/What did you say?
3. *Hǎoxiàng zhège.*	c. Give him a few.
4. *Tā yǒu qián ma?*	d. Why not?

5. *Wǒ yìxiē péngyou.*

6. *Tā búxiàng tā bàba*

7. *Shénme?*

8. *Gěi tā jǐge.*

9. *Wèishénme bùkěyǐ?*

10. *Nǐ yào yìxiē shuǐguǒ ma?*

e. Do you want some fruit?

f. As you wish.

g. Does he have any money?

h. Like the others.

i. Like this.

j. Some of my friends.

ANSWERS

1—f; 2—h; 3—i; 4—g; 5—j; 6—a; 7—b; 8—c; 9—d; 10—e.

LESSON 25

Let's review some expressions used to greet people and to make introductions.

A. HAVE YOU TWO MET?

Nín rènshi wǒ de péngyou ma?	Do you know my friend?
Wǒ xiāngxìn wǒmen yǐqián jiàn guò.	I believe we've met before.
Wǒ xiǎng wǒ méiyǒu nàme róngxìng jiàn guò nín.	I don't believe I've had the pleasure. (*lit.*, I think I was not so honored to meet you.)
Wǒ méiyǒu nàme róngxìng jiàn guò nín.	I haven't had the pleasure of meeting you. (*lit.*, I was not so honored to meet you.)

Ní rènshi wǒ de péngyou ma?	Do you know my friend *(infml.)*?
Dāngrán!	Of course!
Wǒ jué de nǐmen yǐjing rènshi le.	I think you already know one another.
Wǒmen dāngrán shì rènshi de.[31]	Of course we know one another.
Wǒ méiyǒu zhège róngxìng.	I haven't had the pleasure. (*lit.*, I don't have this honor.)
Wǒ hěn róngxìng rènshi tā.	I've already had the pleasure of meeting him. (*lit.*, I'm very honored to know him.)
Wǒ xiǎng gěi nǐ jièshào Xiǎoqīng.	I'd like to introduce you to Xiaoqing. (*lit.*, I want to introduce you to Xiaoqing.)
Ràng wǒ gěi nǐ jièshào wǒ de péngyou, Wáng Dàwéi.	Allow me to introduce you to my friend Dawei Wang.

B. HELLO, HOW ARE YOU?

Zǎo.	Morning.
Zǎoān.	Good morning.
Nǐ hǎo!	Hello!/Hi!
Bié lái wú yàng ba?	Everything is fine *(infml.)*?
Zuìjìn zěnme yàng?	How have you been recently?
Hái hǎo. Nín ne?	So-so. And you *(infml.)*?
Zuìjìn hǎo ma?	How are you recently?
Méiyǒu shénme tèbié.	Nothing much. (*lit.*, Nothing special.)
Méiyǒu shénme.	Nothing much.

---

[31] *Rènshi* functions as an adjective in this sentence, not a verb.

Nǐ hǎo ma?	How are you *(infml.)*?
Wǒ hěn hǎo.	I'm fine. (*lit.,* I'm very well.)
Zuìjìn máng ma?	Have you been busy recently?
Zhè jǐ tiān wǒ yìzhí zài máng.	I've been very busy these days.
Yǒukòng gěi wǒ yí ge diànhuà.	Give me a ring when you're free.
Wǒ huì zài zhè jǐ tiān gěi nǐ diànhuà.	I'll phone you one of these days.
Nǐ wèishénme bù lái jiàn wǒmen?	Why don't you come to see us?
Wǒ xià ge xīngqī huì zhèngshì yāoqǐng nǐ.	I'll come to visit you next week.
Xiànzài bú yào wàng le nǐ de chéngnuò.	Now don't forget your promise.
Xià ge xīngqī jiàn.	Until next week, then. (*lit.,* See you next week.)

SUPPLEMENTAL VOCABULARY 6: TRAVEL AND TOURISM

travel and tourism	*lǚyóu jí lǚyóuyè*
tourist	*guānguāngkè*
hotel	*lǚguǎn*
youth hostel	*qīngnián lǚguǎn*
reception desk	*jiēdàitái*
to check in	*bànlǐ dēngjì shǒuxù*
to check out	*fùzhàng hòu líkāi lǚguǎn*
reservation	*yùdìng*
passport	*hùzhào*
tour bus	*lǚyóuchē*
guided tour	*lǚxíngtuán*
camera	*zhàoxiàngjī*
information center	*xìnxī zhōngxīn*
map	*dìtú*
brochure	*xiǎocèzi*

monument	*jìniànbēi*
to go sight-seeing	*qù guānguāng*
to take a picture	*qù pāizhào*
Can you take our picture?	*Nǐ kěyǐ bāng wǒmen pāizhào*
(*lit.*, Can you help to take	*ma?*
our picture?)	

LESSON 26

A. GLAD TO HAVE MET YOU

Hěn gāoxìng rènshi nǐ.	Glad/Happy to have met you. (*lit.*, Glad to know you.)
Wǒ xīwàng bùjiǔ néng zài jiàn dào nǐ.	Hope to see you again soon.
Wǒ yě xīwàng.	I hope so too.
Zhè shì wǒ de zhùzhǐ hé diànhuà hàomǎ.	Here's my address and telephone number.
Nǐ yǒu wǒ de zhùzhǐ ma?	Do you have my address?
Méiyǒu. Gěi wǒ, hǎo ma?	No. Give it to me, okay?
Nǐ de diànyóu dìzhǐ shì shénme?	What's your e-mail address?
Jiùshì zhège.	Here it is.
Xièxie.	Thanks.
Hěn wǎn le.	It's getting late.
Shì shíhou huíqù le.	It's time to get back.
Wǒmen míngtiān zǒu.	We're leaving tomorrow.
Wǒ shénme shíhou kěyǐ gěi nǐ diànhuà?	When can I phone you?
Zǎoshang.	In the morning.

Wǒ huì děng nǐ de diànhuà.	I'll be expecting your call.

B. SO LONG

Děng huìr jiàn.	See you later.
Děng yíxià jiàn.	See you later.
Dài huìr jiàn.	See you later.
Xiàyícì jiàn.	See you next time.
Míngtiān jiàn.	See you tomorrow.
Xīngqīliù jiàn.	See you on Saturday.
Xià ge xīngqī jiàn.	See you next week./Till next week.
Zàijiàn.	Good-bye.

QUIZ 21

Match the Chinese words in the left column with their English translations in the right column.

`1. *Xīwàng bùjiǔ néng zài jiàn dào nǐ.*
2. *Zàijiàn.*
3. *Hěn gāoxìng rènshi nǐ.*
4. *Nǐ yǒu wǒ de zhùzhǐ ma?*
5. *Zǎoshang.*
6. *Nǐ rènshi wǒ de péngyou ma?*
7. *Míngtiān jiàn.*
8. *Zuìjìn zěnmeyàng?*

a. Do you have my address?
b. See you tomorrow.
c. How have you been recently?
d. Saturday.
e. Do you know my friend?
f. Glad to have met you.
g. Thanks a lot.
h. Hope to see you soon.

9. *Xièxie*.   i. In the morning.
10. *Xīngqīliù*.   j. Good-bye.

ANSWERS
1—h; 2—j; 3—f; 4—a; 5—i; 6—e; 7—b; 8—c; 9—g; 10—d.

C.   VISITING SOMEONE

Wáng Qiáng xiānsheng zhù zài zhèr ma?	Does Mr. Qiang Wang live here?
Tā zhù zài zhèr.	Yes, he does. (*lit.*, Correct. He lives here.)
Nǎ yì lóu?	On what floor?/Which floor?
Zuǒbiānr sānlóu.	Third floor, left.
Chén xiānsheng zài ma?	Is Mr. Chen at home (*lit.*, here)?
Xiānsheng, tā búzài. Tā chūqù le.	No, sir. He's gone out.
Tā shénme shíhou huílái?	What time will he be back?
Wǒ bùnéng gàosù nǐ.	I can't tell you.
Nǐ yào liú ge kǒuxìn gěi tā ma?	Do you want to leave him a message?
Yào. Wǒ yǒu shìqing yào gàosù tā.	Yes, I need to tell him something. (*lit.*, Yes, I have things to tell him.)
Wǒ liú ge biàntiáo gěi tā, nǐ kěyǐ jiè wǒ yì zhī bǐ hé yì zhāng zhǐ ma?	I'll leave him a note if I may borrow a pencil and a sheet of paper from you? (*lit.*, … can I borrow …)
Wǒ děng yíxià huílái.	I'll come back later.
Wǒ wǎnshang zài lái.	I'll come back again at night.

Wǒ míngtiān zài lái.	I'll come back tomorrow.
Wǒ gǎitiān zài lái.	I'll come back another day.
Wǒ huì zhěngtiān	
zài jiā lǐ.	I'll be at home all day.
Wǒ xiànzài qù	I'm going to the post office.
yóuzhèngjú.	
Zài nǎr mǎi yóupiào?	Where are stamps sold?
	(*lit.,* Where [does one] buy
	stamps?)
Nǐ yǒu yóupiào ma?	Do you have stamps?
Wǒ yào yì zhāng	I need an airmail stamp.
hángkōng yóupiào.	
Zhèr yǒu yìxiē	Here are some stamps.
yóupiào.	
Máfan nǐ, yì zhāng	A special delivery stamp,
ytèbié tóudì	please.
yóupiào.	
Yóutǒng zài nǎr?	Where is the mailbox?

QUIZ 22

Match the Chinese words in the left column with their English translations in the right column.

1. *Zuǒbiānr sān lóu.*   a. I'll be at home all day.
2. *Wǒ děng yíxià huílái.*   b. He's gone out.
3. *Wáng xiānsheng zhù*   c. I'll come back tonight.
   zài zhèr ma?
4. *Wǒ xiànzài qù*   d. I can't tell you.
   yóuzhèngjú.
5. *Wǒ wǎnshang zài lái.*   e. What floor?
6. *Tā chūqù le.*   f. I'll leave him a note.
7. *Nǎ yì lóu?*   g. I'm going to the post office.
8. *Wǒ huì liú ge.*   h. Does Mr. Wang live here?

    biàntiáo gěi tā.
9. *Wǒ zhěngtiān zài*   i. Third floor, left.
   jiā lǐ.
10. *Wǒ bùnéng gàosù nǐ.*   j. I'll come back later.

ANSWERS
1—i; 2—j; 3—h; 4—g; 5—c; 6—b; 7—e; 8—f; 9—a;
10—d.

D.   WORD STUDY

bàofù	ambition
huīhuáng	brilliant
shǒudū	capital
jiéchù	contact
bùmén	department
māma	mom, mommy
jìniànbēi	monument
zhàng'ài	obstacle
zuìjìn	recent

SUPPLEMENTAL VOCABULARY 7: IN THE OFFICE

in the office	*zài bàngōngshì lǐ*
office	*bàngōngshì /bàngōnglóu*
desk	*xiězìtái/bàngōng zhuō*
computer	*diànnǎo/diànzǐ jìsuànjī*
telephone	*diànhuà*
fax machine	*chuánzhēnjī*
bookshelf	*shūjià*
file cabinet	*wénjiànguì*
file	*wénjiàn*
boss	*lǎobǎn*
colleague	*tóngshì*
employee	*gùyuán*

staff	*gōngzuò rényuán*
company	*gōngsī*
business	*mǎimài/shāngyè*
factory	*gōngchǎng*
meeting room	*huìyìshì*
meeting	*huìyì*
appointment	*yuēhuì*
salary	*xīnjīn*
job	*gōngzuò*
busy	*máng*
to work	*shāngbān*
to earn	*zhuàn*

LESSON 27

A.   PLEASE

Máfan nǐ.	Please. (*lit.*, I'm troubling you.)
Qǐng.	Please. (*lit.*, Have the goodness.)
Qǐng jìnlái.	Please come in.
Qǐng nǐ ná zhège.	Please carry this.
Qǐng guòlái.	Please come.
Qǐng jìn.	Please come in.
Qǐng děng yíxià.	Will you please wait a short while? (*lit.*, Please wait a little bit.)
Qǐng jiào yíbù chūzūchē.	Will you please call a taxi? (*lit.*, Please call a taxi.)
Qǐng gàosù wǒ chēzhàn zài nǎr.	Please tell me where the station is.
Nǐ de chēpiào, xièxie.	Your ticket, please.

Qǐng zuò zài zhèr.[32]	Please sit here.
Xièxie.	Please.
Qǐng jǐnkuài zuò.	Please do it as soon as possible.
Qǐng gàosù wǒ túshūguǎn zài nǎr.	Please tell me where the library is.

B. EXCUSE ME, I'M SORRY

Qǐng zài shuō yíbiàn.	Pardon me./Excuse me. (*lit.,* Please say it again.)
Duìbuqǐ.	Pardon me./Excuse me./ Sorry.
Bù hǎoyìsi.	Excuse me. (*lit.,* Be shamed.)
Hěn duìbuqǐ.	I'm so sorry.
Wǒ tì tā nánguò.	I feel sorry for him.
Duìbuqǐ wǒ chí le.	Sorry I'm late.

QUIZ 23

Match the Chinese words in the left column with their English translations in the right column.

1. *Qǐng zuò zài zhèr.*   a. Sorry I'm late.
2. *Qǐng guòlái.*   b. Excuse me./Pardon me.
3. *Qǐng jiào yíbù chūzūchē.*   c. Please come.
4. *Duìbuqǐ wǒ chí le.*   d. Please carry this.
5. *Qǐng zài shuō yíbiàn.*   e. Please tell me where the library is.
6. *Qǐng jìnlái.*   f. I'm sorry.
7. *Qǐng gàosù wǒ chēzhàn zài nǎr.*   g. Will you please call a taxi?

---

[32] The verb *qǐng zuò* can be used when no specific location is mentioned.

8. *Qǐng ná zhège.*	h. Please come in.
9. *Duìbuqǐ.*	i. Please tell me where the station is.
10. *Qǐng gàosù wǒ túshūguǎn zài nǎr.*	j. Please sit here.

ANSWERS
1—j; 2—c; 3—g; 4—a; 5—b; 6—h; 7—i; 8—d; 9—f; 10—e.

C. SOME USEFUL VERBAL EXPRESSIONS

1. *Gāng(gāng)* means "to have just" and it is usually combined with a verb suffix *guò*.

Tā gānggāng lái guò.	He just came.
Wǒ gānggāng wánchéng le wǒ de gōngzuò.	I've just finished my work.
Wǒ lái de shíhou, Xiǎoqīng gānggāng chūqù le.	Xiaoqing had just gone out when I came/arrived.

2. *Yào* means "to have to."

Wǒ yào qù.	I have to go.
Wǒ yào zǒu le.	I have to leave.
Nǐ yào xuéxí	You have to study.
Wǒmen yào chī!	We have to eat!

3. *Yǒu* means "there is" or "there are."

| **Zhèr yǒu hěnduō rén.** | There are a lot of people here. |

Zhèr fùjìn yǒu yì jiā lǚguǎn.	There is a hotel near here.

4. *Wǒ xiǎng* means "I would like to."

Wǒ xiǎng zuò zài zhèr.	I would like to sit here.
Wǒ xiǎng gěi nǐ jièshào...	I'd like to introduce you to...
Wǒ xiǎng qù kěshì wǒ bùnéng.	I'd like to go, but I can't.

REVIEW QUIZ 5

1. *Huáng xiānsheng* _____ (at home, house) *ma?*
    a. *zěn*
    b. *shǎo*
    c. *zài*

2. *Wǒ kěyǐ gěi tā liú ge* _____ (message)?
    a. *fàn*
    b. *kǒuxìn*
    c. *kǒubù*

3. *Duìbuqǐ, wǒ* _____ (lateness) *le.*
    a. *chǐ*
    b. *chī*
    c. *chí*

4. _____ (I need) *gàosù tā.*
    a. *Wǒ bù*
    b. *Wǒ yào*
    c. *Wǒ qù*

5. *Méiyǒu* _____ (nothing/what).
   a. *zěnme*
   b. *shénme*
   c. *qián*

6. *Méiyǒu* _____ (person).
   a. *rén*
   b. *rì*
   c. *shén*

7. *Tā búhuì kàn* _____ (nor) *xiě*.
   a. *bù*
   b. *yě búhuì*
   c. *búyào*

8. *Zhōngwén hěn róngyì,* _____ (isn't it)?
   a. *qù búqù*
   b. *hǎo bùhǎo*
   c. *duì búduì*

9. *Qǐng nǐ* _____ (tell) *chēzhàn zài nǎr.*
   a. *xiě*
   b. *gàosù*
   c. *gěi*

10. *Qǐng* _____ (come in).
    a. *chūqù*
    b. *jìnlái*
    c. *duì*

11. _____ (Please) *jǐnkuài qù bàn.*
    a. *Qǐng*
    b. *Xièxie*
    c. *Gěi*

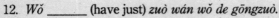

12. *Wǒ* _____ (have just) *zuò wán wǒ de gōngzuò.*
     a. *gēn*
     b. *gāng*
     c. *gěi*

13. *Wǒ* _____ (would like) *qù kěshì wǒ bùnéng.*
     a. *xiǎng*
     b. *yào*
     c. *huì*

14. *Wǒ* _____ (have to) *qù.*
     a. *huì*
     b. *yào*
     c. *xiǎng*

15. *Wǒ tì tā* _____ (feel sorry).
     a. *nánguò*
     b. *nán*
     c. *duìbuqǐ*

ANSWERS

1—c; 2—b; 3—c; 4—b; 5—b; 6—a; 7—b; 8—c; 9—b;
10—b; 11—a; 12—b; 13—a; 14—b; 15—a.

D. WORD STUDY

qiú	ball
zhàngdān	check
gōngmín	citizen
jiàoyù	education
nǔlì	effort
luójì	logical
zhuōzi	table
shěnglüè	omission
yè	page

LESSON 28

A. WHO? WHAT? WHEN? ETC.

1. *Shéi?* "Who?"

Tā shì shéi?	Who is he (she)?
Wǒ bù zhīdào tā shì shéi.	I don't know who he is.
Tāmen shì shéi?	Who are they?
Shéi shuō de?	Who said it?
Shéi zhèyàng shuō?	Who said so?
Shéi zuò de?	Who did it?
Zhè shì shéi de qiānbǐ?	Whose pencil is this?
Zhège shì wèile shéi?	Who is this for?
Nǐ xiǎng yào jiàn shéi?	Whom do you wish to see?
Shéi zhīdào?	Who knows?

2. *Shénme?* "What?"

Zhège shì shénme?	What's this?
Nàge shì shénme?	What's that?
Shénme shì?	What's the matter?
Yǒu shénme shì ma?	What's the matter?
Fāshēng le shénme shì?	What happened?
Nǐ jué de zěnmeyàng?	What do you think? (*lit.,* How do you think?)
Nàxiē shì shénme dōngxi?	What are they? (*lit.,* What things are those?)
Nǐ yǒu shénme?	What do you have?
Jǐdiǎn?	What time is it?
Nǐ zài shuō shénme?	What are you saying?

Nǐ shuō le shénme?	What did you say?
Nǐ zài shuō xiē shénme?	What are you talking about?
Zhège shì zěnme huí shì?	What's it all about?
Nǐ yào shénme?	What do you want?
Wǒ kěyǐ tì nǐ zuò xiē shénme?	What can I do for you?
Nǐ jiào shénme (míngzi)?	What is your name? (*lit.,* What [name] are you called?)
Tā jiào shénme (míngzi)?	What is his name?

3. *Wèishénme?* "Why?"

Wèishénme zhèyàng?	Why so?
Wèishénme bù kěyǐ?	Why not?
Shénme yuányīn?	For what reason?
Nǐ wèishénme zhèyàng shuō?	Why do you say that? (*lit.,* Why did you say [it] in this way?)
Nǐ wèishénme zhème máng?	Why are you in such a hurry?
Nǐ wèishénme zhèyàng zuò?	Why did you do it? (*lit.,* Why did you do in this way?)

4. *Zěnme(yàng)?* "How?"

Zhège Zhōngwén zěnme shuō?	How do you say this in Chinese?
Zhège zěnme xiě?	How is that written?

5. *Duōshǎo?* "How much?"/"How many?"

Nǐ yào duōshǎo qián? How much money do
you need?

Yǒu duōshǎo běn shū? How many books are there?

6. *Nǎge?* "Which?"

Nǐ yào nǎge?	Which (one) do you want?
Nǐ yào nǎge, zhège háishì nàge?	Which (one) do you want, this or that one?
Nǎ yìzhī qiānbǐ shì nǐ de?	Which one of these pencils is yours?
Zhè liǎng tiáo lù nǎ tiáo shì qù Běijīng de?	Which of these two roads leads to Beijing?

7. *Nǎr/Nǎli?* "Where?"

Nǐ de péngyou zài nǎr?	Where is your friend?
Tā zhù zài nǎr?	Where does he live?
Nǐ zài nǎr?	Where are you?
Gōngchēzhàn zài nǎr?	Where is the bus stop?

8. *Shénme shíhou?* "When?"

Nǐ de dìdi shénme shíhou lái?	When will your younger brother come?
Shì shénme shíhou fāshēng de?	When did that happen?
Nǐ shénme shíhou zǒu?	When are you going (leaving)?

Wǒ bù zhīdào (shénme shíhou).	I don't know when.
Duō jiǔ?	How long?/How soon?
Wǒ bù zhīdào duō jiǔ.	I don't know how long.
Shénme shíhou?	When?/What time?
Zhǐyào nǐ xǐhuan.	As soon as you like.
Cóng shénme shíhou?	Since when?
Wèishénme?	How come?

QUIZ 24

Match the Chinese words in the left column with their English translations in the right column.

1.	*Nǐ jiào shénme míngzi?*	a.	When did that happen?
2.	*Yǒu duōshǎo běn shū?*	b.	Since when?
3.	*Zhège Zhōngwén zěnme shuō?*	c.	Who knows?
4.	*Nǐ zài shuō shénme?*	d.	Where does he live?
5.	*Shì shénme shíhou fāshēng de?*	e.	What's your name?
6.	*Cóng shénme shíhou?*	f.	What are you saying?
7.	*Shéi zhīdào?*	g.	Why not?
8.	*Wèishénme bù kěyǐ?*	h.	How is this written?
9.	*Tā zhù zài nǎr?*	i.	How many books are there?
10.	*Zhège zěnme xiě?*	j.	How do you say this in Chinese?

ANSWERS

1—e; 2—i; 3—j; 4—f; 5—a; 6—b; 7—c; 8—g; 9—d; 10—h.

B. WHAT A SURPRISE! WHAT A PITY! HOW AWFUL! HOW NICE!

Duōme yìxiǎngbúdào!	What a surprise!
Hǎo!	Good!
Duōme kěxī!	What a pity!
Hěn kěxī.	It's a pity. (*lit.,* Very pity.)
Xiūxiǎng!	No way! (*lit.,* Don't think about it!)
Duō bèn![33]	How stupid!/What stupidity!
Fèihuà!	What nonsense! (*lit.,* Nonsense!)
Duō fán!	What a drag!
Duōme xìngyùn!	How lucky!/What luck!
Duōme zǒuyùn!	What unbelievable luck!
Duōme búxìng!	How unfortunate!/What a misfortune!
Duōme zāogāo!	How awful!/What a horror!
Duō hǎo/duō bàng!	How nice!
Duō měi!	How pretty!/How nice!
Duō piàoliang!	How pretty!
Duōme měilì!	How beautiful!

REVIEW QUIZ 6

1. *Duō* _____ (unfortunate)*!*
    a. *xìngyùn*
    b. *búxìng*
    c. *yùnqì*

---

[33] *Duō* is used with monosyllabic adjectives. With polysyllabic adjectives, either *duō me* or *duō* can be used.

2. *Duō* _____ (nice)*!*
   a. *hǎo*
   b. *měi*
   c. *bèn*

3. *Zhèr* _____ (there is) *yǒu yì jiā fàndiàn.*
   a. *yīn*
   b. *yào*
   c. *yǒu*

4. *Wǒ yǒu* _____ (some).
   a. *yìxiē*
   b. *yìkuài*
   c. *hěnduō*

5. *Gěi wǒ* _____ (a few).
   a. *yíge*
   b. *jǐgè*
   c. *liǎngge*

6. *Gěi wǒ* _____ (some) *shuǐguǒ?*
   a. *yíge*
   b. *hěnduō*
   c. *yìxiē*

7. _____ (Give me) *yìxiē.*
   a. *Gěi wǒ*
   b. *Wǒ yào*
   c. *Gěi tā*

8. *Zhè jǐtiān wǒ yìzhí zài* _____ (busy).
   a. *hǎo*
   b. *máng*
   c. *xīn*

9. *Nǐ* _____ (know) *tāmen ma?*
    a. *rèn*
    b. *rènshi*
    c. *rén*

10. *Shéi* _____ (do) *de?*
    a. *zuò*
    b. *yǒu*
    c. *shuō*

11. *Zhèshì wǒ de* _____ (address) *hé diànhuà hàomǎ.*
    a. *rì*
    b. *fángzi*
    c. *zhùzhí*

12. *Wǒ bù zhīdào shénme* _____ (time).
    a. *shíhou*
    b. *jiàn*
    c. *míngtiān*

13. *Děng* _____ (later) *jiàn.*
    a. *míngtiān*
    b. *yíxià*
    c. *jīntiān*

14. *Nǐ zài shuō* _____ (what)?
    a. *shéi*
    b. *shénme shíhou*
    c. *shénme*

15. *Nǐ* _____ (why) *zhèyàng shuō?*
    a. *shénme*
    b. *wèishénme*
    c. *zěnmeyàng*

16. *Zhège Zhōngwén* _____ (how) *xiě?*
    a. *zěnyàng*
    b. *wèishénme*
    c. *shénme*

17. *Nǐ yào* _____ (how much)*?*
    a. *shénme*
    b. *duōshǎo*
    c. *hěnduō*

18. _____ (Who) *zhīdào?*
    a. *Shéi*
    b. *Duōshǎo*
    c. *Shénme*

19. *Nǐ de péngyou zài* _____ (where)*?*
    a. *nǎr*
    b. *nàlǐ*
    c. *nǎge*

20. _____ (When) *fāshēng de?*
    a. *Shéi*
    b. *Shíhou*
    c. *Shénme shíhou*

ANSWERS

1—b; 2—a; 3—c; 4—a; 5—b; 6—c; 7—a; 8—b; 9—b;
10—a; 11—c; 12—a; 13—b; 14—c; 15—b; 16—a; 17—b;
18—a; 19—a; 20—c.

C. WORD STUDY

yōulù	anxious
zhǔyào	chief, major
kùnnan	difficulty
yīshēng	doctor

jí	episode
jiānglái	future
guāngróng	glorious
jǐnzhāng	nervous
shíqī	period

SUPPLEMENTAL VOCABULARY 8: AT SCHOOL

at school	*zài xuéxiào*
school	*xuéxiào*
university	*dàxué*
classroom	*jiàoshì*
course	*kèchéng*
teacher	*lǎoshī/jiàoshī/xīan shēng*
professor	*jiàoshòu*
student	*xuésheng*
subject	*xuékē*
notebook	*bǐjìběn*
textbook	*jiàokēshū*
math	*shùxué*
history	*lìshǐ*
chemistry	*huàxué*
biology	*shēngwùxué*
literature	*wénxué*
language	*yǔyán*
art	*yìshù*
music	*yīnyuè*
gym	*tǐyùguǎn*
recess	*xiǎoxiū/kèjiān xiūxí*
test	*cèyàn*
grade	*jíbié*
report card	*chéngjìdān*
diploma	*bìyè zhèngshū/wénpíng*
degree	*xuéwèi*

difficult/easy	*kùnnan/róngyì*
to study	*xuéxí*
to learn	*xué*
exam	*kǎoshì*
to pass	*kǎoshì jígé*
to fail	*kǎoshì bùjígé*

LESSON 29

A.   IT'S GOOD

Hǎo.	Good.
Hěn hǎo.	Very good./It's very good./ It's excellent.
Tài bàng le.	It's excellent./It's wonderful.
Fēicháng de hǎo.	It's excellent./It's admirable.
Wánměi.	It's perfect.
Hǎo.	It's all right.
Bú cuò.	It's not bad. (*lit.*, Not incorrect.)
Hǎo bù hǎo?	Is it all right?
Shífēn hǎo!	Very well!/Very good!/Perfect!
Tā hěn piàoliang.	She's very beautiful.
Tā hěn měi.	She's very pretty.
Tā hěn yǒu mèilì.	He's charming. (*lit.*, He has a lot of charisma.)
Tā shì yíge hǎo rén!	He's a good guy!

B.   IT'S NOT GOOD

Bùhǎo.	It's not good./It's no good./ It's bad.
Búshì tài hǎo.	It's not very good.

Nàge bù hǎo.	That's no good.
Zhèyàng bú duì.	It's not right./This isn't right./This isn't proper./This is wrong. (*lit.*, It's not correct in this way.)
Zhèyàng bù hǎo.	That's bad. (*lit.*, It's bad in this way.)
Tā hěn huài.	He's very bad.
Zhèyàng hěn bù hǎo.	That's very bad./That's awfully bad. (*lit.*, It's very bad in this way.)
Zhège tài huài.	That's too bad.
Tā zhēnde hěn huài.	He's really very bad.
Hěn bèn!	It's very silly./It's very stupid.
Wǒ bù guǎn.	I don't care for it.
Zhège wú jiàzhí.	That's worthless. (*lit.*, This is worthless.)
Wú guān tòngyǎng.	It's not worth the trouble./It's not worth it. (*lit.*, It's not worth the pain.)
Háo wú jiàzhí.	It's worthless./It's good for nothing.
Duō kěxī!	What a pity!
Duō dǎoméi!	How unfortunate!
Duō zāogāo!	How awful!

QUIZ 25

Match the Chinese words in the left column with their English translations in the right column.

1. *Hǎo.*	a. It's excellent./It's wonderful.
2. *Hěn hǎo.*	b. She's very pretty.
3. *Tài bàng le.*	c. That's worthless!
4. *Búcuò.*	d. He's a good guy!
5. *Zhèyàng bù hǎo.*	e. That's very bad!
6. *Tā shì yíge hǎorén!*	f. It's wonderful!
7. *Tā hěn piàoliang.*	g. It's all right.
8. *Zhège wú jiàzhí.*	h. That's bad.
9. *Zhèyàng hěn bù hǎo!*	i. Very well.
10. *Hěn hǎo.*	j. It's not bad.

ANSWERS

1—g; 2—i; 3—a; 4—j; 5—h; 6—d; 7—b; 8—c; 9—e; 10—f.

C. I LIKE IT

Wǒ xǐhuan…	I like…
Wǒ xǐhuan tā.	I like him/her.
Wǒ hěn xǐhuan tā.	I like him/her very much.
Wǒ fēicháng xǐhuan tā.	I like him/her very much.
Wǒ xǐhuan zhège.	I like that. (*lit.,* I like this.)
Wǒ xǐhuan tā.	I like her.
Wǒ shífēn xǐhuan tāmen.	I like them a lot.
Nǐ xǐhuan ma?	Do you like it?
Nǐ xǐhuan shuǐguǒ ma?	Do you like fruit?
Wǒ xǐhuan.	Yes, I like fruit.
Nǐmen xǐhuan qiǎokèlì ma?	Do you (*pl.*) like chocolate?
Nǐ xǐhuan Měiguó ma?	Do you like America/the United States?

Nǐ xǐhuan Zhōngguó cài?	Do you like Chinese food?
Nǐ xǐhuan Zhōngguó ma?	Do you like China?
Nǐ yǐqián xǐhuan Zhōngguó ma?	Did you like China?
Wǒ yǐqián xǐhuan Zhōngguó.	I liked China.
Nǐ xǐhuan ma?	Do you like it?
Nǐ xǐhuan zhèxiē ma?	Do you like them? (*lit.*, Do you like these?)
Nǐ xǐhuan lǚyóu ma?	Do you like to travel?
Nǐ jué de tāmen huì xǐhuan zhè suǒ wūzi ma?	Do you think they'll like the house?
Nǐmen jué de wǒ de fángzi zěnmeyàng?	How do you (*pl.*) like my apartment? (*lit.*, What do you think about my apartment?)
Wǒ xǐhuan.	I like it.
Wǒ hěn xǐhuan.	I like it very much.
Rúguǒ nǐ xǐhuan.	If you like it.
Nǐ xǐhuan, shénme shíhou dōu xíng.	Whenever you like.
Nǐ xǐhuan tiàowǔ ma?	Do you like to dance?

NOTE:
The object "it" in *wǒ xǐhuan* "I like (it)" is not expressed when it can be understood from the context. If specific mention is necessary, one can say *wǒ xǐhuan zhège* "I like this" or *wǒ xǐhuan nàge* "I like that."

D.   I DON'T LIKE IT

Wǒ bù xǐhuan.	I don't like it.
Wǒ gēnběn bù xǐhuan.	I don't like it at all.
Wǒ bù xǐhuan nàxiē.	I don't like those.
Nǐ bù xǐhuan ma?	Don't you like it?
Wǒ bù xǐhuan zhège gēr ma?	Don't I like this song?
Wǒ bù xǐhuan tiàowǔ!	I don't like to dance!
Wǒ bù guǎn.	I don't care for it. It doesn't interest me.

E.   I HAD A GOOD TIME!

Wǒ wán de hěn gāoxìng.	I had a good time. (*lit.*, I played very happily.)
Wǒ wán de hěn kāixīn.	I had a good time.
Wǒmen wán de hěn gāoxìng!	We had a good time!
Tāmen wán de hěn gāoxìng.	They had a good time.
Wán de kāixīn diǎn!	Have a good time! (*lit.*, Enjoy happily.)

QUIZ 26

Match the Chinese words in the left column with their English translations in the right column.

1. *Nǐ xǐhuan Zhōngguó cài ma?*	a. I don't like it at all.
2. *Nǐ xǐhuan nàxiē ma?*	b. How do you like my room?
3. *Wǒ hěn xǐhuan.*	c. Did you like China?
4. *Nǐ xǐhuan shuǐguǒ ma?*	d. If you like it.

5. *Nǐ xǐhuan, shéme shíhou dōu xíng.* e. Don't you like it?

6. *Nǐ xǐhuan Zhōngguó ma?* f. I like it very much.

7. *Nǐ bù xǐhuan ma?* g. Do you like them?

8. *Rúguǒ nǐ xǐhuan.* h. Whenever you like.

9. *Wǒ gēnběn bù xǐhuan.* i. Do you like Chinese food?

10. *Nǐ jué de wǒ de fángjiān zěnmeyàng?* j. Do you like fruit?

ANSWERS

1—i; 2—g; 3—f; 4—j; 5—h; 6—c; 7—e; 8—d; 9—a; 10—b.

SUPPLEMENTAL VOCABULARY 9: SPORTS AND RECREATION

sports and recreation	*yùndòng jí yúlè*
soccer	*zúqiú*
basketball	*lánqiú*
baseball	*bàngqiú*
American football	*Měishìzúqiú*
hockey	*qūgùnqiú*
tennis	*wǎngqiú*
game	*yóuxì*
team	*duì/qiúduì/yùndòng duì/xiǎo zǔ*
stadium	*yùndòngchǎng*
coach	*jiàoliàn*
player	*yùndòngyuán*
champion	*guànjūn*
ball	*qiú*
to go hiking	*yuǎnzú*
to go camping	*yěyíng*

to play a sport	*zuò yùndòng*
to play a game	*wán yóuxì*
to win	*yíng*
to lose	*shū*
to draw/tie	*dǎchéng píngjú*
(*lit.,* The match was	
drawn/tied.)	
cards	*kǎ*
pool/billiards	*luòdài táiqiúxì/dànzǐ yóuxì*

LESSON 30

A.   IN, TO, FROM, ETC.

Study the uses of these prepositions.

1. With places

Wǒ qù guò Běijīng.	I've been in Beijing.
	(*lit.,* I have gone to Beijing
	before.)
Wǒ xiànzài qù	I'm going to Beijing.
Běijīng.	
Wǒ cóng Nánjīng lái.	I come from Nanjing.
Wǒ shì cóng Nánjīng.	I'm from Nanjing.
lái de.	
Wǒ xiànzài qù Xī'ān	I'm leaving for Xian.
Wǒ xiě le xìn gěi tā.	I wrote letter to him.
Wǒ zài túshūguǎn	I'm in the library.
(lǐ).[34]	

---

[34] *Lǐ* is not used with the names of the cities or countries.

Cóng Nánjīng qù Shànghǎi yào yíge zhōngtóu.	It takes one hour from Nanjing to Shanghai.
Tā xiànzài wǎng Shànghǎi qù.	He's going toward Shanghai.
Wǒ zuì yuǎn dào le Lánzhōu.	I got as far as Lanzhou. (*lit.*, The furthest I arrived was Lanzhou.)

2. "to," "by," "at," "on," "in"

Zhuǎn yòu.	To the right.
Zhuǎn zuǒ.	To the left. (*lit.*, Turn left.)
Liǎngge liǎngge.	Two by two.
Yìdiǎnr yìdiǎnr.	Little by little.
Zǒulù.	On foot. (*lit.*, To walk.)
Yòngshǒu.	By hand. (*lit.*, To use hands.)
(Zài) zhōngwǔ.	At noon.
(Zài) wǔyè.	At midnight.
Tāmen zài zhuōzi pángbiān zuò xià lái.	They sat down at the table. (*lit.*, They sat down next to the table.)
Wǒ yǐqián zǒulù shàngxué.	I used to walk to school.
Yòng Zhōngguó fāngfǎ.	In the Chinese manner.
Zài.	Again.

NOTE:
Zài can be translated as "in," "at," or "on" in English. It is optional when it refers to time. When it refers to a location, it may not be omitted.

3. "with"

Kāfēi jiā nǎi.	Coffee with milk. (*lit.,* Coffee plus milk.)
Wǒ gēn Xiǎobō qù le.	I went with Xiaobo.
Tā yòng qiānbǐ xiě le.	He wrote it with a pencil.
Tā hé Měilì yìqǐ lái.	He's coming with Meili.
Tā gēn wǒ yìqǐ lái.	He's coming with me.

4. "of," "from"

Zhè shì wǒ gēge jì lái de.	It's from my elder brother. (*lit.,* This is sent by my elder brother.)
Wǒ cóng Běijīng lái.	I come from Beijing.
Zhè shì yòng mùtou zuò de.	It's made of wood.
Wūzi de chuānghu.	The window of the house.

5. "in"

Wǒ zài Zhōngguó zhù le jǐ nián.	I lived in China for several years.
Wǒ sì tiān zhīhòu jiù zǒu le.	I'm leaving in four days. (*lit.,* After four days, then I leave.)
Ér búshì...	Instead of...

6. "up to," "until"

Yìzhí dào Shànghǎi.	Up to/as far as Shanghai.
Wǒ zǒu dào le wǔlóu.	I walked up to the fifth floor.

Zhídào míngtiān.	Until tomorrow.
Děng yíhuìr jiàn.	See you later.
Zàijiàn.	Until we see each other again.

7. "toward"

| Wǎng nàge fāngxiàng. | In that direction. |
| Tā wǎng gōngyuán de fāngxiàng zǒu. | She was walking toward/in the direction of the park. |

8. "from"

| Cóng Sìchuān dào Guǎngzhōu. | From Sichuan to Guangzhou. |
| Zìcóng wǒ kànjiàn le tā. | Since I saw him./Since the time I saw him. |

9. "on"

| Zài zhuōzi shàng.[35] | On the table. |
| Tā yǒu yìtiáo shǒupà zài tā de tóu shàng. | She had a handkerchief on her head. |

10. "for," "through"

Yíge zhōngtóu liùshí yīnglǐ.	Sixty miles an hour.
Wǒ huà le yí kuài qián mǎi le zhège.	I bought it for a dollar. (*lit.*, I spent one dollar to buy this one.)
Wǒ gěi le tā yí kuài qián yào zhège.	I gave him a dollar for this.
Wǒmen héngchuān Zhōngguó.	We passed through China.

Huǒchē chuānguò Xī'ān.	The train passes through Xian.
Tā chuānguò ménkǒu jìnlái.	He came in through the door.
Wǒ tì nǐ qù.	I'll go for/in place of you. (*lit.,* I'll replace you to go.)
Tā qù zhǎo yīshēng.	He went for the doctor. (*lit.,* He went to find the doctor.)
Wǒ liǎng nián zhīnèi huì bìmiǎn qù lǚxíng.	I'll be avoiding travel for two years.

11. Study these other expressions:

Wèishénme?	Why?/What was the reason?
Mùqián.	For the time being.
Zài zǎoshang.	In the morning./During the morning.
Míngtiān zǎoshang.	Tomorrow morning.
Míngtiān xiàwǔ.	Tomorrow afternoon.
Zài xiàwǔ.	During the afternoon./ In the afternoon.
Zài wǎnshang.	At night.
Tā yánzhe dàjiē zǒu.	He walked along the street.
Pìrú.	For example.
Jiéguǒ.	Consequently./As a result.
Dàtǐshàng.	In general.
Wánquán.	Completely.
Yīnwèi zhège yuányīn.	For that reason. (*lit.,* For this reason.)
Yīnwèi...	By reason of .../ On account of ...

Zuìhòu.	Finally./At last.
Zài zhèr fùjìn.	Around here.
Wǒ bù tóngyì qù.	I'm not in favor of going.
Wǒ zhīchí qù zuò.	I'm in favor of doing it.
Tiān na!	For goodness' sake!/ For heaven's sake!

12. "for," "in order to"

Wèile qù nàr.	In order to go there.
Tā dào Shànghǎi qù le.	He left for Shanghai.
Qù Guǎngzhōu de gōngchē.	The bus for Guangzhou.
Zhè fēng xìn shì gěi nǐ de.	The letter is for you. (*lit.*, This letter is for you.)
Míngtiān de kè.	The lesson for tomorrow.
Duì tā lái shuō hěn róngyì.	That's very easy for him.
Zhè shì wújiàzhí de.	It's worthless./It's good for nothing.

B.   WORD STUDY

gōngjī	attack
màoxiǎn	adventure/risk
shūshì	comfortable
yǒngqì	courage
bù yīlài fùmǔ/dúlì	independence
yǔyán	language
kǒuxìn	oral message
yìjiàn	opinion
jìjìng	silence

QUIZ 27

Match the Chinese words in the left column with their English translations in the right column.

1. *Zài zhōngwǔ.*	a.	On foot.
2. *Yìdiǎnr yìdiǎnr.*	b.	One by one.
3. *Zhuǎn yòu.*	c.	I come from Beijing.
4. *Yòng Zhōngguó Fāngfǎ.*	d.	It's made of wood.
5. *Gēn.*	e.	By day.
6. *Zǒulù.*	f.	Again.
7. *Wǒ cóng Běijīng lái.*	g.	On the table.
8. *Zhè shì yòng mùtóu zuò de.*	h.	To the right.
9. *Yīnwèi.*	i.	In that direction.
10. *Zài.*	j.	Little by little.
11. *Zài nàge fāngxiàng.*	k.	Until tomorrow.
12. *Báitiān.*	l.	At noon.
13. *Zhuǎn zuǒ.*	m.	Since I saw him.
14. *Yíge yíge.*	n.	In the Chinese manner.
15. *Zuì yuǎn dào Shànghǎi.*	o.	With.
16. *Liǎngtiān zhīhòu wǒ jiù zǒu le.*	p.	Instead of.
17. *Zài zhuōzi shàng.*	q.	To the left.
18. *Zhídào míngtiān wéi zhǐ.*	r.	On account of.
19. *Ér búshì.*	s.	As far as Shanghai.
20. *Zìcóng wǒ jiàn dào tā.*	t.	I'm leaving in two days.

ANSWERS

1—l; 2—j; 3—h; 4—n; 5—o; 6—a; 7—c; 8—d; 9—r; 10—f;
11—i; 12—e; 13—q; 14—b; 15—s; 16—t; 17—g; 18—k;
19—p; 20—m.

QUIZ 28

Match the Chinese words in the left column with their
English translations in the right column.

1. *Pìrú.*

a. I gave him ten dollars for this.

2. *Huǒchē chuānguò Běijīng.*

b. Sixty miles an hour.

3. *Wǒmen héngchuān Zhōngguó.*

c. Completely.

4. *Mùqián.*

d. For that reason.

5. *Wǒ huāle yí kuài qián mǎile zhège.*

e. Around here.

6. *Yīnwèi zhège yuányīn.*

f. For goodness' sake!

7. *Yíge zhōngtóu liùshí yīnglǐ.*

g. At last.

8. *Wánquán.*

h. For example.

9. *Wǒ gěi le tā shí kuài qián yào le zhège.*

i. I'm not in favor of going.

10. *Tiān na!*

j. For the time being.

11. *Zuìhòu.*

k. I bought it for a dollar.

12. *Tā chuānguò ménkǒu jìnlái.*

l. The train passes through Beijing.

13. *Zài zhèr fùjìn.*

m. I'll go for you.

14. *Wǒ tì nǐ qù.*

n. He came in through the door.

15. *Wǒ bù tóngyì qù.*

o. We passed through China.

ANSWERS

1—h; 2—l; 3—o; 4—j; 5—k; 6—d; 7—b; 8—c; 9—a;
10—f; 11—g; 12—n; 13—e; 14—m; 15—i.

QUIZ 29

Match the Chinese words in the left column with their
English translations in the right column.

1. *Zhè fēng xìn shì gěi   a. A bookcase.
   nǐ de.*
2. *Zhè shì wújiàzhí de.*   b. The lesson for
                                  tomorrow.
3. *Míngtiān de kè.*   c. In order to go there.
4. *Kuàiyào xiàyǔ le.*   d. He left for Shanghai.
5. *Wǒ zhīchí zuò.*   e. I'm studying to be a
                                  doctor.
6. *Yíge shūguì.*   f. He's about to leave.
7. *Wèile qù nàr.*   g. The letter is for you.
8. *Tā dào Shànghǎi qù.*   h. I'm in favor of doing
   le.   it.
9. *Tā kuàiyào zǒu le.*   i. It's worthless.
10. *Wǒ zài xuéxí zuò   j. It's about to rain.
    yīshēng.*

ANSWERS

1—g; 2—i; 3—b; 4—j; 5—h; 6—a; 7—c; 8—d; 9—f;
10—e.

LESSON 31

A. ON THE ROAD

Duìbuqǐ.	Pardon me./Excuse me.
Zhège shìzhèn jiào shénme míngzi?	What is the name of this town?
Wǒmen lí Hángzhōu yǒu duō yuǎn?	How far are we from Hangzhou?
Cóng zhèlǐ dào Huángshān yǒu duōshǎo gōnglǐ?	How many kilometers from here to Yellow Mountain?
Lí zhèlǐ yǒu shí gōnglǐ.	It's ten kilometers from here.
Lí zhèlǐ yǒu èrshí gōnglǐ.	It's twenty kilometers from here.
Cóng zhèlǐ zěnme qù Lìjiāng?	How do I get to Lijiang from here?
Yán zhe zhè tiáo lù zǒu.	Follow this road.
Nǐ kěyǐ gàosù wǒ zěnme qù zhège dìzhǐ ma?	Can you tell me how I can get to this address?
Nǐ zěnme qù zhège dìfang?	How do you get to this place?
Hěn yuǎn ma?	Is it very far?
Nǎ tiáo lù dào Shànghǎi zuì jìn?	What's the shortest way to get to Shanghai?
Wǒ yào zǒu nǎ yì tiáo lù?	Which road must I take?

B. WALKING AROUND

Nǐ yǒu zhège chéngshì de dìtú ma?	Do you have a map of the city?
Zhè tiáo jiē zài nǎr?	Where is this street?

Nǐ kěyǐ dài wǒ qù Shànghǎi Jiē ma?	Can you take me to Shanghai Street?
Jīnhuā Jiē shì zài zhèr fùjìn ma?	Is Jinhua Street near here?
Nǎr yǒu gōngyòng diànhuà?	Where is there a public phone?
Wǒ kěyǐ zài nǎr dǎ diànhuà?	Where can I make a phone call?
Chēzhàn lí zhèr yǒu duōshǎo tiáo jiē?	How many blocks away is the station? (*lit.*, How many streets away from here is the station?)
Chēzhàn lí zhèr yǒu duō yuǎn?	How far is the station? (*lit.*, How far away from here is the station?)
Zhè tiáo jiē jiào shénme míngzi?	What is the name of this street?
Nǐ kěyǐ gàosù wǒ zhè tiáo jiē zài nǎr ma?	Can you tell me where this street is?
Jīn Jiē zài nǎr?	Where is Gold Street?
Lí zhèr yuǎn ma?	Is it far from here?
Lí zhèr jìn ma?	Is it near here?
Yòubiānr dìsān tiáo jiē jiùshì le.	It's the third block to the right.
Wǎng zhèbiānr zǒu.	Go this way.
Wǎng qián zǒu.	Go straight ahead.
Zài lùkǒu wǎng zuǒ guǎi.	Go to the corner and turn left.
Zài dìyī ge lùkǒu wǎng zuǒ guǎi.	Take the first intersection to the left.
Chēkù zài nǎr?	Where is the garage?
Gōng'ānjú zài nǎr?	Where is the police station (*lit.*, public security bureau)?
Bówùguǎn zài nǎr?	Where is the museum?

C. BUS, TRAIN, SUBWAY, TAXI

Gōngchēzhàn zài nǎr?	Where is the bus stop?
Chēfèi shì duōshǎo qián?	How much is the fare?
Wǒ zài nǎyíge zhàn xiàchē?	At what stop do I get off?
Wǒ zài nǎr xiàchē?	Where do I get off?
Huǒchēzhàn zài nǎr?	Where is the train station?
Qù Běijīng de huǒchē cóng nǎyíge zhàn kāichū?	From which station does the train to Beijing leave?
Cóng Pānzhīhuā lái de huǒchē zài nǎr dào zhàn?	At which station does the train from Panzhihua arrive?
Zīxùn guìtái zài nǎr?	Where is the information booth (*lit.,* information counter)?
Nǐ kěyǐ gěi wǒ yífèn huǒchē shíkèbiǎo ma?	Will you please let me have a train schedule? (*lit.,* Could you give me a train schedule?)
Nǎyítàng huǒchē qù Dàlǐ?	Which is the train for Dali?
Zhè shì cóng Xiàmén lái de huǒchē ma?	Is this the train from Xiamen?
Qù Dàlián de huǒchē zài nǎr shàngchē?	Where do you get the train for Dalian?
Zài èr hào yuètái.	On track two. (*lit.,* On platform two.)
Wǎng Běijīng de huǒchē shénme shíhou kāi?	When does the train for Beijing leave?
Huǒchē gāng kāi le.	The train just left.
Huǒchē mǎshàng yào zǒu le.	The train is leaving right away.

Xiàyìbān huǒchē shénme shíhou kāi?	When does the next train leave?
Zài nǎr mǎi chēpiào?	Where are the tickets sold? (*lit.*, Where to buy tickets?)
Gěi wǒ yìzhāng qù Běijīng de dānchéng chēpiào.	Give me a one-way ticket to Beijing.
Tóuděngchēxiāng háishì èrděngchēxiāng?	First or second class?
Tóuděng.	First class.
Duōshǎo qián?	How much does it cost?
Yào zuò duō jiǔ?	How long does it take to get there?
Zhèr yǒu rén zuò ma?	Is this seat taken?
Wǒ kěyǐ bǎ[36] xíngli fàng zài zhèr ma?	May I put this suitcase here?
Wǒmen zài zhèr huì[37] tíng duō jiǔ?	How long do we stop here? (*lit.*, How long would we stop here?)
Wǒ zài zhèr zhuǎn huǒchē ma?	Do I change trains here?
Zhè liǎng huǒchē huì tíng Běijīng ma?	Does this train stop in Beijing?
Wǒ zài nǎr kěyǐ mǎi dào chēpiào?	Where can I buy a ticket?
Yǒu méiyǒu dìtiě dìtú?	Is there a subway map?
Zhège shì shénme zhàn?	What stop is this?
Wǒ zài shénme zhàn xiàchē?	At what stop do I get off?

---

[36] *Bǎ* is a preposition. When it is used, the verb follows the object of a sentence.
[37] *Huì* means "would" or "will."

Chūzūchē! Yǒu kòng ma? Taxi! Are you free?

Zài wǒ qù zhège dìzhǐ. Take me to this address.

Wǒ qiàn nǐ duōshǎo? How much do I owe you?

QUIZ 30

Match the Chinese words in the left column with their English translations in the right column.

1. *Shénme fāngfǎ zuì kuài dào…?* a. How far is the station?

2. *Wǒ zài nǎr kěyǐ dǎ diànhuà?* b. How do you get to this place?

3. *Zhè tiáo jiē zài nǎr?* c. Can you take me to… Street?

4. *Zài wǒ qù zhège dìzhǐ.* d. Where is the bus stop?

5. *Chēzhàn yǒu duō yuǎn?* e. What stop do I get off?

6. *Wǒ kěyǐ yòng nǐ de diànhuà ma?* f. Where can I phone?

7. *Nǐ kěyǐ dài wǒ qù… Jiē ma?* g. Where is this street?

8. *Wǒ zài shénme zhàn xiàchē?* h. What's the shortest way to get to…?

9. *Nǐ zěnme qù zhège dìzhǐ?* i. Take me to this address.

10. *Gōngchēzhàn zài nǎr?* j. May I use your telephone?

ANSWERS

1—h; 2—f; 3—g; 4—i; 5—a; 6—j; 7—c; 8—e; 9—b; 10—d.

SUPPLEMENTAL VOCABULARY 10: NATURE

nature	*dàzìrán*
tree	*shù*
flower	*huā*
forest	*sēnlín*
mountain	*shān*
field	*tiándì*
river	*hé*
lake	*hú*
ocean	*hǎiyáng*
sea	*hǎi*
beach	*hǎitān*
desert	*shāmò*
rock	*yánshí*
sand	*shā*
sky	*tiān*
sun	*tàiyáng*
moon	*yuèliang*
star	*xīng*
water	*shuǐ*
land	*lùdì*
plant	*zhíwù*
hill	*xiǎoshān*
pond	*chítáng*

LESSON 32

A. WRITING AND MAILING LETTERS

Wǒ xiǎng xiě yìfēng xìn.   I'd like to write a letter.

Nǐ yǒu qiānbǐ ma?   Do you have a pencil?

Nǐ yǒu bǐ ma?   Do you have a pen?
Nǐ yǒu yìxiē zhǐ ma?   Do you have some paper?
Nǐ yǒu xìnfēng ma?   Do you have an envelope?
Wǒ kěyǐ zài nǎr mǎi   Where can I buy a stamp?
  yóupiào?
Yóujú zài nǎr?   Where is the post office?
Wǒ xiǎng jì zhè fēng   I'd like to mail this letter.
  xìn.
Yào duōshǎo yóufèi?   What is the postage (for this
                                   letter)?
Zuìjìn de yóutǒng zài   Where is the nearest mailbox?
  nǎr?
Zài lùkǒu.   On the corner.

B.   TELEPHONES, FAXES, AND E-MAIL

Wǒ xiǎng fā yíge   I'd like to send a fax.
  chuánzhēn.
Diànhuàjú zài nǎr?   Where is the telephone office?
Zài shì zhōngxīn.   It's downtown.
Fā yìzhāng chuánzhēn How much is a fax to the
  dào Měiguó yào   United States?
  duōshǎo qián?
Wǒ yào fā yíge   I need to send an e-mail.
  diànyóu.
Wǒ kěyǐ shàngwǎng   Can I get on the Internet?
  ma?
Nǐ yǒu wǎngzhàn ma?   Do you have a Web site?
Diànnǎo zài nǎr?   Where is the computer?
Wǒ yào kàn wǒ de   I need to read my e-mail.
  diànyóu.
Zài lǚguǎn kěyǐ   Does the hotel have Internet
  shàngwǎng ma?   access? (lit., Can I go online
                                   in the hotel?)

| Wǒ yào fā jì fēng diànyóu. | I have to send several e-mails. |
| Wǒ yīnggāi yòng yíge hǎo de sōusuǒ yǐngqíng zuò xúnzhǎo. | I should do a search with a good search engine. |

C. TELEPHONING

Zhèr yǒu diànhuà ma?	Is there a phone here?
Wǒ kéyǐ zài nǎr dǎ diànhuà?	Where can I make a phone call?
Diànhuà zài nǎr?	Where is the telephone?
Diànhuàjiān zài nǎr?	Where is the phone booth?
Zài lǚguǎn de dàtīng.	In the hotel lobby.
Wǒ kě bùkéyǐ yòng nǐ de diànhuà?	May I use your phone?
Dāngrán kéyǐ! Yòng ba!	Of course, go ahead! (*lit.*, Use it!)
Búyào wàngjì bǎ nǐ de yídòng diànhuà fàng zài dàizi lǐ.	Don't forget to pack your cell phone in your bag.
Wǒ bù zhīdào kě bùkéyǐ zài wǒ qù de guójiā lǐ shǐyòng.	I don't know if it will work in all the countries I'm going to visit.
Búshì měi yíbù yídòng diànhuà dōu kéyǐ zài rènhé dìfang shǐyòng de.	Not all cellular phones work in all places.
Hěn duō gōngsī zài qítā guójiā yě tígòng fúwù.	Many phone companies also provide services in other countries.
Wǒ yào bó chángtúdiànhuà.	Give me long distance. (*lit.*, I need to call long distance.)

Dǎ diànhuà qù Shànghǎi yào duōshǎo qián?	How much is a phone call to Shanghai?
Wǒ yào bō èr-èr-bā-qī-wǔ—bā-èr.	I want 228-7582.
Búyào guàshàng.	Hold on a minute. (*lit.*, Don't hang up.)
Diànhuà zhànxiàn.	The line is busy.
Nǐ gěi wǒ de hàomǎ shì búduì de.	You gave me the wrong number.
Méiyǒu rén jiē.	There is no answer.
Huáng xiānsheng zài ma?	May I speak to Mr. Huang? (*lit.*, Is Mr. Huang here?)
Wǒ jiùshì.	Speaking. (*lit.*, I am.)
Zhèshì Chén Dànián.	This is Danian Chen speaking.
Shì Huáng xiānsheng ma?	Is this Mr. Huang?
Shì.	Yes./Speaking.
Nǎr zhǎo?	Who is this?

SUPPLEMENTAL VOCABULARY 11:
COMPUTERS AND THE INTERNET

computer and Internet	*diànnǎo jí hùliánwǎng*
computer	*diànnǎo*
keyboard	*jiànpán*
monitor/screen	*yíngguāngpíng/píngmù*
printer	*dǎyìnjī*
mouse	*huáshǔ*
modem	*tiáozhìjiětiáoqì*
memory	*cúnchǔqì*
CD-ROM	*guāngpán*
CD-ROM drive	*wéidú guāngdiéjī*
file	*wénjiàn*

document	*dàng'àn/wénjiàn*
cable	*diànxiàn*
DSL	*shùmǎ yònghù huílù*
Internet	*hùliánwǎng*
Web site	*wǎngzhàn*
webpage	*wǎngyè*
e-mail	*diànyóu*
chat room	*liáotiānshì*
Web log/blog	*bókè/wǎngshàngrìzhì*
instant message	*jíshí xùnxī*
attachment	*fùjiàn*
to send an e-mail	*fā diànyóu*
to send a file	*fā wénjiàn*
to forward	*zhuǎnjì*
to reply	*huífù*
to delete	*shānchú*
to save a document	*cúnchǔ dàng'àn*
to open a file	*dǎkāi wénjiàn*
to close a file	*guānbì wénjiàn*
to attach a file	*fùshàng wénjiàn*

LESSON 33

A.   WHAT'S YOUR NAME?

Nǐ jiào shénme (míngzi)?[38]	What's your name? (*lit.*, What first name are you called?)
Wǒ jiào Dànián.	My name is Danian.
Tā jiào shénme míngzi?	What's his name?
Tā jiào Xiǎoqiáng.	His name is Xiaoqiang.
Tā jiào shénme míngzi?	What's her name?

Tā jiào Měilì.	Her name is Meili.
Tāmen jiào shénme míngzi?	What are their names?
Tā jiào Dōngpíng. Tā jiào Měifāng.	His name is Dongping and hers is Meifang.
Tā jiào shénme míngzi?	What's his first name?
Tā jiào Xiǎoqiáng.	His first name is Xiaoqiang.
Tā xìng shénme?	What's his last name?
Tā xìng Huáng.	His last name is Huang.

B.   WHERE ARE YOU FROM?

Nǐ shì cóng shénme dìfang lái de?	Where are you from?
Wǒ shì cóng Běijīng lái de.	I'm from Beijing.
Nǐ zài nǎli chūshēng?	Where were you born?
Wǒ shì cóng Niǔyuē lái de.	I'm from New York.
Tā shì cóng shénme dìfang lái de?	Where is he from?
Tā shì cóng Guǎngzhōu lái de.	He's from Guangzhou.
Wǒ zài Měiguó chūshēng.	I was born in America.
Wǒ xiànzài zhù zài Tiānjīn.	I'm now living in Tianjin.

C.   HOW OLD ARE YOU?

Nǐ duō dà/nǐ jǐ suì?	How old are you?
Wǒ èrshí sì suì.	I'm twenty-four years old.
Dào jiǔyuè wǒ èrshí sì suì.	I'll be twenty-four in September. (*lit.,* By

	September I'll be twenty-four years old.)
Wǒ zài yī-jiǔ-liù-liù nián bāyuè shíjiǔ hào chūshēng.	I was born August 19, 1966.
Nǐ shénme shíhou shēngrì?	When is your birthday?
Wǒ yīyuè èrshí-sān hào shēngrì.	My birthday is on January 23.
Tā duō dà?	How old is he?
Tā sānshí suì.	He's thirty years old.
Nǐ yǒu jǐge xiōngdì?	How many brothers do you have?
Wǒ yǒu yíge gēge hé yíge dìdi.	I have one elder brother and one younger brother.
Gēge èrshí èr suì.	The older one is twenty-two.
Tā zài dàxué dúshū.	He studies at the University.
Dìdi shí qī suì.	The younger one is seventeen.
Tā zài gāozhōng niàn gāosān.	He's in his last year of high school. (*lit.*, He is studying grade three in high school.)
Nǐ yǒu duōshǎo ge jiěmèi?	How many sisters do you have?
Wǒ yǒu yíge mèimei.	I have one younger sister.
Tā jiǔ suì.	She's nine.

D. PROFESSIONS

Nǐ zuò shénme?	What do you do?
Wǒ shì lǜshī.	I'm a lawyer.
Nǐ zài nǎr shàngbān?	Where do you work?
Nǐ shì shénme zhíyè?	What's your profession?
Nǐ tàitai zuò shénme?	What does your wife do?
Nǐ xiānsheng zuò shénme?	What does your husband do?

Nǐ māma zuò shénme?	What does your mother do?
Nǐ bàba zuò shénme?	What does your father do?
Tā shì lǜshī.	He's a lawyer.
Tā shì jiànzhùshī.	He's an architect.
Tā shì lǎoshī.	He's/she's a teacher.
Tā shì dàxué jiàoshòu.	He's a university professor.
Tā shì yīshēng.	He's a doctor.
Tā shì shāngrén.	He's/she's a businessman/ businesswoman.
Tā shì nóngfū.	He's a farmer.
Tā zài zhèngfǔ lǐ bànshì.	He's in the government service.
Tā zài qìchē gōngchǎng shàngbān.	He works in an automobile factory.
Tā cóng zǎo dào wǎn gōngzuò.	She works from morning till night.

E.   FAMILY MATTERS

Nǐ zài zhèr yǒu méiyǒu qīnqì?	Do you have any relatives here?
Nǐ de jiārén quánbù dōu zhù zài zhèr ma?	Does all your family live here?
Chúle wàizǔfùmǔ.	Except my grandparents (on the maternal side).
Tāmen zhù zài jiànshuǐ fùjìn de nóngchǎng.	They live on a farm near Jianshui.
Nǐ gēn Huáng xiānsheng yǒu qīnshǔ guānxì ma?	Are you related to Mr. Huáng?

Tā shì wǒ de jiùfù.	He is my uncle on my maternal side.
Tā shì wǒ de shūfù.	He's my uncle on my paternal side.
Tā shì wǒ de biǎogē.	He's my cousin. (*lit.*, father's sister's or mother's sibling's son who is older than you)
Nǐ gēn Huáng tàitai yǒu qīnshǔ guānxì ma?	Are you related to Mrs. Huáng?
Tā shì wǒ de yímǔ.	She's my aunt. (*lit.*, mother's elder sister)
Tā shì wǒ de tángmèi.	She's my (younger) cousin. (*lit.*, father's sister's or mother's sibling's daughter who is younger than you)

F.   WORD STUDY

yǒuqù	interesting, funny
kuàijì	accounting, accountant
xiángqíng	detail
gùyuán	employee
pànduàn	judgment
jīròu	muscle
gōngyuán	park
cānguǎn	restaurant
méiguì	rose

SUPPLEMENTAL VOCABULARY 12: FAMILY AND RELATIONSHIPS

family and relationships	*jiātíng jí guānxì*
mother	*māma*
father	*bàba*

son	*érzi*
daughter	*nǚ'ér*
elder sister	*jiějie*
younger sister	*mèimei*
baby	*yīng'ér*
elder brother	*gēge*
younger brother	*dìdi*
husband	*xiānsheng/zhàngfu*
wife	*tàitai/qīzi*
aunt	*gūmǔ* (father's elder sister)/*gūgu* (father's younger sister)/*gūmā* (father's married sister)/*yímǔ* (mother's elder sister)/*āyí* (mother's younger sister)/*yímā* (mother's married sister)/*bómǔ* (father's elder brother's wife)/*shěnshen* (father's younger brother's wife)/*jiùmu* (mother's brother's wife)
uncle	*bófù* (father's elder brother)/*shūshu* (father's younger brother)/*jiùfù* (mother's brother)/*gūfu* (father's elder sister's husband)/*yífu* (mother's younger sister's husband)
grandmother	*nǎinai* (father's mother)/*wàipó* (mother's mother)
grandfather	*yéye* (father's father)/*wàigōng* (mother's father)

cousin	*biáojiě* (father's sister's daughter who is older than you)/*biáomèi* (father's sister's daughter who is younger than you)/*biáogē* (father's sister's son who is older than you)/*biáodì* (father's sister's daughter who is younger than you)/*tángjiě* (father's brother's daughter who is older than you)/*tángmèi* (father's brother's daughter who is younger than you)/*tanggè* (father's brother's son who is older than you)/*tángdì* (father's brother's son who is younger than you)
mother-in-law	*yuèmǔ* (wife's mother)/*pópo* (husband's mother)
father-in-law	*yuèfù*/*yuèzhàng* (wife's father)/*gōnggong* (husband's father)
stepmother	*jìmǔ*
stepfather	*jìfù*
stepson	*jìzǐ*
stepdaughter	*jìnǚ*
boyfriend	*nánpéngyou*
girlfriend	*nǚpéngyou*
fiancé(e)	*wèihūnfū* (male)/ *wèihūnqī* (female)
friend	*péngyou*

relative	*qīnqì*
to love	*ài*
to know (a person)	*rènshi*
to meet	*jiàn*
to marry	*gēn … jiéhūn* (to marry to …)/*jià* (a woman to marry a man)/*qǔ* (a man to marry a woman)
to divorce (someone)	*gēn … líhūn*
to get a divorce	*bàn líhūn*
to inherit	*jìchéng*

SUPPLEMENTAL VOCABULARY 13: ON THE JOB

jobs	*gōngzuò*
policeman/policewoman	*gōng'ān/jǐngchá*
lawyer	*lùshī*
doctor	*yīshēng*
engineer	*gōngchéngshī*
businessman/ businesswoman	*shāngren/shíyèjiā*
salesman/saleswoman	*tuīxiāoyuán/shòuhuòyuán*
teacher	*jiàoshī/lǎoshī*
professor	*jiàoshòu*
banker	*yínhángjiā*
architect	*jiànzhùshī*
veterinarian	*shòuyī*
dentist	*yáyī*
carpenter	*mùjiàng*
construction worker	*jiànzhùgōngrén*
taxi driver	*chūzùchēsījī*
artist	*yìshùjiā*
writer	*zuòjiā*
plumber	*guǎnzigōng*

electrician	*diàngōng*
journalist	*jìzhě*
actor/actress	*yǎnyuán*
musician	*yīnyuèjiā*
farmer	*nóngfū/nóngmín*
secretary/assistant	*mìshū/zhùlǐ*
unemployed	*shīyè/dàiyè*
retired	*tuìxiū*
full-time	*quánzhí*
part-time	*bànzhí*
steady job	*wěndìng de gōngzuò*
summer job	*shǔqīgōng*

LESSON 34

A. SHOPPING *(MǍI DŌNGXI)*

1. Zhège duōshǎo qián?
How much is this?

2. Liùshí kuài.
Sixty kuai.

3. Yǒu diǎnr guì. Yǒu piányi yìdiǎnr de ma?
That's rather expensive. Don't you have anything cheaper?

4. Tóng yíyàng de ma?
Of the same sort?

5. Tóng yíyàng de huòzhě shì lèisì de.
The same sort or something similar.

6. Zhèr yǒu yí ge.
There's this. (*lit.*, There is one.)

7. Nǐ méiyǒu qítā de kěyǐ gěi wǒ kànkan ma?
Haven't you any other kind you could show me?

8. Piányi yìdiǎnr de?
Less expensive?

9. Rúguǒ yǒu de huà...
If possible... (*lit.* If there is a possibility...)

10. Huòzhě nín huì xǐhuān zhège.
Perhaps you would like this.

11. Nà yào kànkan jiàqian.
That depends on the price.

12. Zhège sìshí wǔ kuài.
This one is forty-five kuai.

13. Wǒ xǐhuan zhège duō yìdiǎnr.
I like it better than the other one. (*lit.*, I like this one a little more.)

14. Zhège bǐjiào piányi.
It's cheaper.

15. Zhège zěnmeyàng? Piányi yìxiē háishì guì yìxiē?
How about this? Is it cheaper or more expensive?

16. Bǐjiào guì.
It's more expensive.

17. Nǐ háiyǒu qítā cúnhuò ma?
Haven't you anything else in stock?

18. Yǒuxiē xīnhuò hěn kuài jiù dào.
I'm hoping to receive some new styles soon. (*lit.*, There is some new merchandise coming very soon.)

19. Duō jiǔ?
How soon?

20. Guò jǐ tiān. Nín kěyǐ zhège zhōumò guòlái ma?
In a few days. Can you drop by toward the end of the week? (*lit.*, Can you come over this weekend?)

21. Wǒ huì... Zhège duōshǎo qián?
I'll do that... What's the price of this?

22. Yìshuāng sān kuài.
Three kuai a pair.

23. Gěi wǒ yìshuāng.
Let me have a pair.

24. Nín yào zìjǐ ná ma?
Will you take them with you? (*lit.*, Will you take them yourself?)

25. Wǒ xiǎng yào nǐmen sòng qù.
I'd rather have you send them.

26. Dìzhǐ háishì yíyàng ma?
Is the address still the same?

27. Yíyàng.
The same.

28. Zàijiàn.
Good-bye.

NOTE:

1. *Duōshǎo qián?* is a common way of asking about the price (*duōshǎo* means "how much/how many" and *qián* means "money"). Alternatively, one can say *Zhège yào duōshǎo qián?* (*lit.*, How much money does it need?)

2. One can also use *liùshí kuài qián* for "sixty dollars."

9. The expression *rúguǒ... de huà* means "if" and it can be used to form conditional sentences. You can use this expression in Chinese to suggest the probable consequences of an action, as in the following example: *Rúguǒ nǐ qù de huà, tā huì hěn gāoxìng.* (If you go, she will be very happy.)

16. *Bǐjiào* means "comparatively" and can be placed in front of an adjective to make it comparative. Thus *bǐjiào guì* means "more expensive"; *bǐjiào piányi* means "cheaper"; and *bǐjiào piàoliang* means "more beautiful."

17. *Háiyǒu* means "to have in addition to."

18. *Xīnhuò* means "new products."

19. "How soon?" is expressed with *duō jiǔ*, which literally means "how long?"

20. *Zhōumò* means "weekend."

QUIZ 31

1. *Yǒu diǎnr* _____ (expensive).
   a. *hǎo*
   b. *gāo*
   c. *guì*

2. *Yǒu* _____ (cheap) *yīdiǎnr de ma?*
   a. *yíyàng*
   b. *duō*
   c. *piányi*

3. *Tóng* _____ (same).
   a. *lèisì*
   b. *yíyàng*
   c. *kuài*

4. *Piányi* _____ (less) *de.*
   a. *guì*
   b. *yīdiǎnr*
   c. *jǐ tiān*

5. *Wǒ xǐhuān zhège* _____ (more) *yīdiǎnr.*
   a. *bǐjiào*
   b. *duō*
   c. *yíxiē*

6. *Nǐ* _____ (have) *qítā cúnhuò ma?*
   a. *yǒu*
   b. *méiyǒu*
   c. *qù*

7. *Yǒuxiē xīnhuò hěn kuài jiù* _____ (come).
   a. *chī*
   b. *qù*
   c. *dào*

8. *Duō* _____ (soon)?
   a. *guì*
   b. *kuài*
   c. *jiǔ*

9. _____ (Address) *háishì yíyàng ma?*
    a. *Dìzhǐ*
    b. *Cúnhuò*
    c. *Yī shuāng*

ANSWERS
1—c; 2—c; 3—b; 4—b; 5—b; 6—a; 7—c; 8—c; 9—a.

B.   GENERAL SHOPPING EXPRESSIONS

Wǒ yào mǎi...	I'd like to buy...
Zhège duōshǎo qián?	How much is it?
Hěn guì!	It's very expensive!
Nǐ yǒu piányi yīdiǎnr de ma?	Do you have something cheaper?
Wǒ xǐhuan... (de)	I prefer something...
Wǒ chuān... mǎ.	My size is... (*lit.*, I wear size...)[39]
Wǒ yào zhège.	I'll take it. (*lit.*, I want this.)

SUPPLEMENTAL VOCABULARY 14: CLOTHING

clothing	*yīfu*
shirt	*chènshān*
pants	*kùzi*
jeans	*niúzǎikù*
T-shirt	*tìxūshān*
shoe(s)	*xiézi*
sock(s)	*wàzi*
belt	*yāodài*
sneakers/tennis shoes	*qiúxié/jiāodǐbùxié*

---

[39] There are three main sizes in China: *dàmǎ* (large size), *zhōngmǎ* (medium size), and *xiǎomǎ* (small size). If the size is expressed by a specific number, the word *hào* is added after the number, e.g., *wǔhào* "size 5" (*lit.*, number 5).

dress	*lianyiqun/lǐfú*
skirt	*qúnzi*
blouse	*zhàoshān*
suit	*tàozhuāng*
hat	*màozi*
glove(s)	*shǒutào*
scarf	*wéijìn*
jacket	*duán shàngyī/jiākè*
coat	*wàitào*
earring(s)	*ěrhuán*
bracelet	*shǒuzhuó*
necklace	*xiàngliàn*
eyeglasses	*yǎnjìng*
sunglasses	*tàiyáng yǎnjìng*
watch	*shǒubiǎo*
ring	*jièzhǐ/zhǐhuán*
underpants	*chènkù*
undershirt	*hànshān*
bathing trunks	*yóuyǒngkù*
bathing suit	*yóuyǒngyī*
pajamas	*shuìyī*
cotton	*miánbù*
leather	*pígě*
silk	*sī*
corduroy	*dēngxīnróng*
nylon	*nílóng*
lacy	*huābiān*
size	*hào/chǐmǎ*
to wear/to put on	*chuān*

LESSON 35

A. BREAKFAST IN A RESTAURANT
(CĀNGUN CHĪ ZĂOCĀN)

1. **Nǐ yídìng hěn è le.**
You must be hungry.

2. **Shì a.**[40]
I certainly am.

3. **Wǒ fēicháng è.**
I'm terribly hungry.

4. **Fúwùyuán! Fúwùyuán!**
Waiter! Waiter!

5. **Shì.**
Yes, folks.

6. **Wǒmen yào sān ge zǎocān.**
We'd like breakfast for three.

7. **Nǐmen yǒu shénme hē de?**
What can you serve us?
(*lit.*, What drink do you have?)

8. **Kāfēi jiā niúnǎi, níngméngchá huòzhě nǎichá,
qiǎokèlì...**
Coffee with milk, tea with lemon or with milk, hot
chocolate...

---

[40] *A* is an exclamation word, which is placed at the end of a sentence to indicate
the affirmative meaning.

9. Zhèxiē yǐnliào pèi shénme chī de a?
What do you serve with it?

10. Miànbāo juǎn, bǐnggān...
Rolls, biscuits...

11. Yǒu huángyóu ma?
Is there any butter?

12. Yǒu de, nǚshì.
Yes, Madam.

13. Gěi wǒ yì bēi kāfēi hé yìxiē miànbāo juǎn.
Bring me a cup of coffee and some rolls.

14. Nǐ ne, Xiǎoqiáng? Nǐ yào chī shénme?
And you, Xiǎoqiáng? What are you going to eat?

15. Wǒ bù chī tài duō.
I don't eat very much.
(*lit.*, I don't eat too much.)

16. Nǐ pà pàng ma?
Your figure, I suppose?
(*lit.*, Are you afriad of getting fat?)

17. Bú shì—zhǐshì xíguàn le.
Not exactly—habit more than anything else. (*lit.*, No, it's only a habit.)

18. Nǚshì, nín yào shénme?
What will you have, Madam?
(*lit.*, Madam, what do you like?)

19. **Níngméngchá, bǐnggān hé yíge chǎodàn.**
Tea and lemon, biscuits, and an egg.
(*lit.,* Lemon tea, biscuits, and a scrambled egg.)

Later...

20. **Fúwùyuán, máfan nǐ gěi wǒ yí kuài cānjīn.**
Waiter, would you please bring me a napkin?

21. **Háiyào yí ge chā, xièxie.**
And a fork for me, please.

22. **Máfan nǐ gěi wǒmen duō yīdiǎnr táng.**
Please bring us a little more sugar.

23. **Ránhòu jiézhàng... Zhèli....**
And then let's have the check... Here you are.

24. **Xiānsheng, xièxie.**
Thank you, sir.

NOTE:
   3. *Fēicháng* means "very."
   4. The word *fúwùyuán* can be used for both "waiter"
      and "waitress" in Chinese.
   7. If you are asking about food, not drink, you can say
      Nǐmen yǒu shénme chī de.
   11. There is no word to express the concept of "any" in
      "Is there any...?" in Chinese. One simply says *Yǒu...
      ma?* which literally means "Is/are there?"
   21. *Hái* can mean "in addition."
   22. *Jiézhàng* literally means "to settle the bill."

QUIZ 32

1. _____ (We want) *sān ge zǎocān.*
    a. *Wǒmen yào*
    b. *Gěi wǒmen*
    c. *Xíguàn*

2. _____ (Is there) *huángyóu ma?*
    a. *Xièxie*
    b. *Yǒu*
    c. *Yíyàng*

3. *Gěi wǒ* _____ (same) *de.*
    a. *fēicháng*
    b. *yíyàng*
    c. *yìdiǎnr*

4. *Nǐ yào* _____ (eat) *shénme?*
    a. *gěi*
    b. *hē*
    c. *chī*

5. *Wǒ bù chī tài* _____ (much).
    a. *shǎo*
    b. *xiǎo*
    c. *duō*

6. *Máfan nǐ* _____ (bring me) *yí kuài cānjīn?*
    a. *zhèli*
    b. *gěi wǒ*
    c. *jiézhàng*

. _____ (terwards) *jiézhàng.*
    n
    ing
    ǒu

ANSWERS
1—a; 2—b; 3—b; 4—c; 5—c; 6—b; 7—c.

B.   TO EAT: *CHĪ*, TO DRINK: *HĒ*, TO TAKE: *NÁ*

1. To eat: *chī*

wǒ chī	*wǒmen chī*
nǐ chī	*nǐmen chī*
tā chī	*tāmen chī*
Wǒ bú chī ròu.	I don't eat meat.
Tā shénme dōngxi doū chī.	He eats anything.
Tāmen jìnqíng de chī.	They eat heartily.

2. To drink: *hē*

wǒ hē	*wǒmen hē*
nǐ hē	*nǐmen hē*
tā hē	*tāmen hē*
Nǐmen yào hē diǎnr shénme?	Do you want to drink something? (*lit.*, What do you want to drink a little bit?)
Tā hē de xiàng yì tiáo yú.	He drinks like a fish.

3. To take: *ná*

wǒ ná	*wǒmen ná*
nǐ ná	*nǐmen ná*
tā ná	*tāmen ná*
Wǒ ná zǒu le yì zhāng zhǐ.	I took away a piece of paper.
Nǐ ná zhe liǎng běn shū.	You are taking two books. (*lit.*, You are holding two books.)
Nǐmen ná qián dào Shànghǎi.	You take money to Shanghai.

C.   A SAMPLE MENU

CÀIDĀN	MENU
Xiǎolóngbāo	Steamed bun
Suān là tāng	Hot and sour soup
Gōng Bǎo jī dīng	Gong Bao diced chicken
Shànghǎi chǎomiàn	Shanghaiese fried noodle
Gūlūròu	Sweet-sour pork
Gānshāo míngxiā	Dry stewed prawns
Jiāoyán páigǔ	Fried pork loin with spiced salt
Gānbiǎn sìjìdòu	Dry-cooked string beans
Zhīma tāngyuán	Sesame dumplings

LESSON 36

A.   APARTMENT HUNTING *(ZHĀO FÁNGZI)*

1. **Wǒ shì lái kàn fángzi de.**
I've come to see the apartment.

2. **Nǎ yí tào?**
Which one?

3. **Chūzū nà tào.**
The one that is for rent.

4. **Yǒu liǎng tào.**
There are two.

5. **Nǐ kěyǐ shuōyishuō shì shénme yàngzi de ma?**
Can you describe them? (*lit.*, Can you talk a little bit what's like?)

6. **Zài wǔlóu nà tào méiyǒu jiājù.**
The one on the fifth floor is unfurnished.

7. **Lìngwài nà tào ne?**
And the other one?

8. **Zài èr lóu nà tào yǒu jiājù.**
The one on the second floor is furnished.

9. **Yǒu duōshǎo ge fángjiān?**
How many rooms do they have?

10. **Zài wǔ lóu nà tào yǒu sì ge wòshì, yí ge chúfáng hé yí ge yùshì.**
The one on the fifth floor has four bedrooms, a kitchen, and a bath.

11. **Shì duì zhe dà jiē ma?**
Does it face the street?

12. **Bù, duì zhe tíngyuàn.**
No, it faces a courtyard.

13. **Nà èr lóu nà tào ne?**
And the one on the second floor?

14. **Èr lóu nà tào yǒu yí ge wòshì, yí ge kètīng hé yí ge fàntīng.**
The one on the second floor has a bedroom, a living room, and a dining room.

15. **Yěshì duì zhe tíngyuàn ma?**
Does it also face out a courtyard?

16. **Bù, duì zhe dàjiē.**
No, it faces the street.

17. **Zūjīn duōshǎo?**
How much is the rent?

18. **Dà de nà tào yí ge yuè bā bǎi kuài, bù bāokuò shuǐfèi hé méiqì.**
The larger one is eight hundred kuai a month, plus water and gas.

19. **Yǒu jiājù nà tào ne?**
And the furnished one?

20. **Nà tào yí ge yuè yī qiān kuài, bāokuò shuǐdiàn hé méiqì.**
That one costs one thousand kuai a month, everything included.

21. **Shì shénme yàng de jiājù? Xīn de hái shì jiù de?**
What kind of furniture does it have? Is the furniture in good condition?

22. **Shì xiàndài jiājù, bǎoyǎng de hěn hǎo.**
It's modern furniture and it's in excellent condition.

23. **Shénme dōngxi yě yǒu, chúfáng yòngjù yě wánbèi.**
You'll find everything you need, even a complete set of kitchen utensils.

24. **Yào qiān zùyuè ma?**
Does one have to sign a lease?

25. **Nǐ yào gēn dàilǐ jiǎng.**
You'll have to see the renting agent for that.

26. **Yǒu shénme tiáojiàn?**
What are the terms?

27. **Xiān fù yí ge yuè de fángzū, hái yào fù yí ge yuè de yājīn.**
One month's rent in advance and another month's rent as a deposit.

28. **Jiùshì zhème duō?**
Is that all? (*lit.*, Is that much?)

29. **Dāngrán háiyào tūijiànrén.**
Of course, you'll have to give references.

30. **Duì le, yǒu meíyǒu diàntī?**
By the way, is there an elevator?

31. **Méiyǒu.**
No.

32. **Zhēn kěxī!**
What a shame!

33. **Chúle zhèxiē, fángzi tǐng xiàndàihuà.**
Aside from that, the house is very modern.

34. **Shénme yìsi?**
What do you mean?

35. Yǒu zhōngyāng nuǎnqì hé kōngtiáo, háiyǒu hòu lóutī.

There's central heating and air conditioning and a back stairway.

36. A, wǒ wàng le... yǒu méiyǒu rèshuǐ?

Oh, I forgot... Is there any hot water?

37. Dāngrán yǒu! Yùshì zuìjìn cái zhuāngxiū hǎo.

Of course! And the bathrooms were recently remodeled.

38. Kěyǐ kànyikàn fángzi ma?

Can one see the apartments?

39. Zhǐnéng zài shàngwǔ kàn.

Only in the morning.

40. Hǎo, wǒ míngtiān zǎoshang lái kànyikàn. Xièxie nǐ.

Very well, I'll come tomorrow morning. Thanks a lot.

41. Búkèqì.

You're welcome.

NOTE:

  6. *Méiyǒu jiājù* means "without furniture."

 11. *Dà jiē* literally means "big street." It can also mean "the main street."

 17. Alternatively, one can say *zūjīn duōshǎo qián?*

 20. *Bāokuò shuǐdiàn hé méiqì* means "to include water and gas." Generally, when the rent is said to include everything in China, it includes all utilities bills, not just water and gas, but electricity as well.

21. The expression *Xīn de hái shì jiù de* means "Is it new or old?"

22. *Bǎoyǎng de hěn hǎo* means "maintained very well."

23. *Chúfáng yòngjù yě wánbèi* means "kitchen's ustensils are complete."

24. *Zùyuè* "lease."

25. *Gēn dàilǐ jiǎng* literally means "with agent talk." In other words, "talk to the agent."

27. *Xiān fù* literally means "before pay," which translates as "to pay first." *Yājīn* means "deposit."

30. The expression *Duì le!* means "Right!" and indicates that the speaker suddenly remembered something that he or she wished to add.

37. The expression *Zuìjìn cái zhuāngxiū hǎo* means "It hasn't been renovated until recently." *Cái* means "not until."

QUIZ 33

1. *Wǒ shì* _____ (come) *kàn fángzi de*.
   a. *qù*
   b. *lái*
   c. *chī*

2. _____ (To rent) *nà tào*.
   a. *Chū*
   b. *Chūqián*
   c. *Chūzū*

3. _____ (There are) *liǎng tào*.
   a. *Yǒu*
   b. *Méiyǒu*
   c. *Zhè*

4. _____ (Without) *jiājù*.
   - a. *Bù*
   - b. *Yǒu*
   - c. *Méiyǒu*

5. *Yǒu* _____ (how) *ge fángjiān?*
   - a. *duō shǎo qián*
   - b. *duōshǎo*
   - c. *duō jiǔ*

6. *Shì duì zhe* _____ (street) *de ma?*
   - a. *chúfáng*
   - b. *dà fáng*
   - c. *dà jiē*

7. _____ (Also) *duì zhe tíngyuàn*.
   - a. *Yěshì*
   - b. *Búshì*
   - c. *Kěshì*

8. *Yí ge* _____ (month) *liángbǎi kuài*.
   - a. *yuè*
   - b. *xīngqī*
   - c. *nian*

9. *Nǐ* _____ (need to find) *fángzi*.
   - a. *huì zhǎo*
   - b. *bù zhǎo*
   - c. *yào zhǎo*

10. *Fángzi* _____ (very) *xiàndàihuà*.
    - a. *bù*
    - b. *tǐng*
    - c. *shì*

ANSWERS
1—b; 2—c; 3—a; 4—c; 5—b; 6—c; 7—a; 8—a; 9—c;
10—b.

B.   TALKING NEEDS, ETC.

Wǒ dùzi è.	I'm hungry.
Wǒ hěn kǒukě.	I'm thirsty.
Wǒ hěn kùn.	I'm sleepy.
Wǒ hěn lěng.	I'm cold.
Wǒ hěn rè.	I'm hot.
Wǒ shì duì de.	I'm right.
Wǒ tóutòng.	I have a headache.
Wǒ yátòng.	I have a toothache.
Tā bú duì.	He's not right.
Tāmen cuò le.	They're wrong.
Wǒ èrshí suì.	I'm twenty.

C.   TO HAVE: *YǑU*

1. I have

Wǒ yǒu zhège.	I have this./I've got this.
Wǒ shénme yě méiyǒu.	I don't have anything.
Nǐ yǒu ma?	Do you have it?
Wǒ méiyǒu.	I don't have it.
Wǒ yǒu shíjiān.	I have time.
Wǒ shénme qián yě méiyǒu.	I haven't any money.
Wǒ shénme shíjiān yě méiyǒu.	I haven't any time.
Tā shénme péngyou yě méiyǒu.	He hasn't any friends.
Nǐ zài Běijīng yǒ shénme péngyou ma?	Do you have (any) friends in Beijing?

Wǒ zài Běijīng méiyǒu shénme péngyou.	I don't have any friends in Beijing.
Nǐ yǒu xiāngyān ma?	Do you have a cigarette?
Wǒ méiyǒu.	I don't have any cigarettes. (*lit.,* No, I don't.)
Nǐ yǒu huǒ ma?	Do you have a light?
Wǒ méiyǒu huǒchái.	I don't have matches.
Nǐ zhěnme le?	What's the matter with you?
Wǒ méiyǒu shénme shì.	Nothing's the matter with me.
Nǐ yǒu duōshǎo qián?	How much money do you have?
Wǒ gēnběn shénme qián yě méiyǒu.	I haven't any money at all.
Wǒ yào...	I need...
Wǒ yào nàge.	I need that.

2. *Yào* means "to have to":

Wǒ yào qù.	I have to go./I must go.
Wǒ yào zǒu le.	I have to leave.
Wǒ yào xiě yì fēng xìn.	I have to write a letter.
Wǒ yǒu hěnduō shìqíng yào zuò.	I have a lot to do.

3. Do I have it?

Wǒ yǒu ma?	Do I have it?
Nǐ yǒu ma?	Do you have it?
Tā yǒu ma?	Does he have it?
Tā yǒu ma?	Does she have it?
Wǒmen yǒu ma?	Do we have it?
Nǐmen yǒu ma?	Do you have it?
Tāmen yǒu ma?	Do they have it?

4. Don't I have it?

Wǒ méiyǒu ma?	Don't I have it?
Nǐ méiyǒu ma?	Don't you have it?
Tā méiyǒu ma?	Doesn't he have it?
Tā méiyǒu ma?	Doesn't she have it?
Wǒmen méiyǒu ma?	Don't we have it?
Nǐmen méiyǒu ma?	Don't you have it?
Tāmen méiyǒu ma?	Don't they have it?

QUIZ 34

Match the Chinese words in the left column with their English translations in the right column.

1. *Wǒ shénme qián yě méiyǒu.*   a. I have a headache.

2. *Wǒ shénme dōngxi yě méiyǒu.*   b. Don't you have it?

3. *Tā bú duì.*   c. I don't have it.

4. *Wǒ hěn kùn.*   d. I'm cold.

5. *Tā yǒu ma?*   e. I'm hot.

6. *Wǒ méiyǒu.*   f. I don't have any money.

7. *Wǒ dùzi è.*   g. Does he have it?

8. *Wǒ hěn lěng.*   h. He's not right.

9. *Wǒ èrshí suì.*   i. I'm thirsty.

10. *Nǐ méiyěu ma?*   j. I have a lot to do.

11. *Wǒ yào zǒu le.*   k. I don't have anything.

12. *Wǒ hěn rè.*   l. I'm sleepy.

13. *Wǒ hěn kóukě.*   m. I'm hungry.

14. *Wǒ tóutòng.*   n. I have to leave.

15. *Wǒ yǒu hěnduō shìqíng yào zuò.*   o. I'm twenty years old.

ANSWERS
1—f; 2—k; 3—h; 4—l; 5—g; 6—c; 7—m; 8—d; 9—o;
10—b; 11—n; 12—e; 13—i; 14—a; 15—j.

SUPPLEMENTAL VOCABULARY 15: IN THE KITCHEN

in the kitchen	*zài chúfáng lǐ*
refrigerator	*bīngxiāng*
(kitchen) sink	*xǐcáo*
counter	*guìtái*
stove	*huǒlú*
oven	*kǎolú/kǎoxiāng*
microwave	*wēibōlú*
cupboard	*guìchú*
drawer	*chōutì*
plate	*pánzi*
cup	*bēi*
bowl	*wǎn*
glass	*bōlíbēi*
spoon	*chí*
knife	*dāo*
can	*guàntou/jīnshǔguàn*
box	*xiāng/hé*
bottle	*píng*
carton	*zhǐbǎnxiāng*
coffee maker	*(zhǔ) kāfēi jī*
tea kettle	*hú*
blender	*jiǎobànjī/zhàzhījī*
iron	*yùndǒu*
ironing board	*yùndǒu bǎn*
broom	*sàozhou*
dishwasher	*xǐwǎnjī*
washing machine	*xǐyījī*
dryer	*hōnggānjī*

to cook	*zhǔ/shāo (lit., to burn)*
to do the dishes	*xǐ pánzi (lit., to wash dishes)*
to do the laundry	*xǐ yīfu (lit., to wash clothing)*
dishwashing detergent	*qīngjiéjì*
laundry detergent	*xīyīyè*
bleach	*piǎobáijì*
clean/dirty	*gānjìng/zāng*

SUPPLEMENTAL VOCABULARY 16: IN THE BATHROOM

in the bathroom	*zài yùshì lǐ*
toilet	*cèsuǒ*
sink (wash basin)	*xǐliǎnpén*
bath tub	*yùgāng/yùpén*
shower	*línyù*
mirror	*jìngzi*
medicine cabinet	*yào guì*
towel	*máojīn*
toilet paper	*cèzhǐ*
shampoo	*xǐfàjì*
soap	*féizào*
bath gel	*xǐzǎoyè*
shaving cream	*guā hú gāo*
razor	*tìdāo*
to wash oneself	*xǐzǎo (lit., to take a bath)*
to take a shower/bath	*xǐzǎo*
to shave	*guā húzi*
cologne	*gǔlóngshuǐ*
perfume	*xiāngshuǐ*
deodorant	*chúchòujì*
bandage	*bēngdài*
powder	*fěn*

QUIZ 35

Match the Chinese words in the left column with their
English translations in the right column.

1. *xǐ pánzi*   a. cup
2. *bēi*   b. mirror
3. *cèsuǒ*   c. to have a shower
4. *jìngzi*   d. toilet
5. *xǐzǎo*   e. to do the dishes

ANSWERS
1—e; 2—a; 3—d; 4—b; 5—c.

LESSON 37

A.   COULD YOU GIVE ME SOME INFORMATION?

1. Duìbuqǐ.
Pardon me.

2. Yǒu shénme yào bāngmáng ma?
What can I do for you?

3. Nǐ kěyǐ gěi wǒ yìxiē zīliào ma?
Could you give me some information?

4. Hǎo. Méi wèntí.
Gladly. (*lit.*, Yes, no problem.)

5. **Wǒ bù shúxī zhège chéngzhèn, bù zhīdào zěnme zǒu.**
I don't know this town and I can't find my way around.

6. **À, zhège hěn jiǎndān.**
Well, it's quite simple.

7. **Nǐ zhīdào, zài zhèr wǒ shì yí ge mòshēngrén.**
You see, I'm a stranger here.

8. **Zhèyàng de huà, wǒ gěi nǐ jièshào yíxià zhège chéngzhèn.**
In that case, I'll show you the town.
(*lit.*, In this case, I'll introduce this town a little to you.)

9. **Fēicháng gǎnxiè nǐ.**
Thank you very much.

10. **Nǐ kànjiàn jiējiǎo nà zuò dàlóu ma?**
Do you see that large building on the corner?

11. **Yǒu yí miàn qízi nà zuò?**
The one with the flag?

12. **Duì. Méiyǒu cuò. Nà zuò shì yóuzhèngjú, duìmiàn shì...**
That's right. That's the post office. Opposite it, on the other side of the street...

13. **Nǎr?**
Where?

14. **Zài nàbiānr. Nǐ kànjiàn nà zuò yǒu yí ge zhōng de dàlóu ma?**
Over there. Do you see that other building with the clock?

15. **À, duì, wǒ xiànzài kàndào le.**
Oh, yes, now I see.

16. **Nà jiùshì shìzhèngfǔ.**
That's the city hall.

17. **Xiànzài wǒ míngbai le... duì le, zhè tiáo jiē jiào shénme míngzi?**
Now I see... By the way, what's the name of this street?

18. **Zhèngjiē.**
Main Street.

19. **Jǐngchájú zài nǎr?**
Where is the police station?

20. **Zài jiēwěi. Yīzhí wǎng qián zǒu.**
At the end of the street. Go straight ahead.

21. **Rúguǒ wǒ méi kànjiàn ne?**
What if I miss it? (*lit.*, What if I didn't see?)

22. **Nǐ bú huì kàn bú jiàn de. Nà shì yí dòng dà lóu, wàimiàn wéi zhe tiěsīwǎng... nǐ kànjiàn nà jiā shāngdiàn ma?**
You can't miss it. It's a big building surrounded by an iron fence...You see that store?

23. **Nǎ yì jiā? Zài yòubiānr nà jiā ma?**
Which store? The one on the right?

24. **Duì, chuāngkǒu yǒu yí ge dà hóng shízì nà jiā.**
Right, the one with a large red cross in the window.

25. **Shí yì jiā yàofáng ma?**
Is it a pharmacy?

26. **Shì, nà shì yì jiā yàofáng. Yīshēng zhù zài pángbiānr. Tā de míngzi jiù zài ménshang.**
Yes, it's a pharmacy. The doctor lives right next door. His name's on the door.

27. **Tā de zhěnsuǒ yě zài nàr ma?**
Does he have his office there as well?

28. **Shì, dànshì tā měitiān zǎoshang dōu zài yīyuàn lǐ.**
Yes, but he spends every morning at the hospital.

29. **Yīyuàn zài nǎr?**
Where's the hospital?

30. **Guò liǎng ge lùkǒu jiùshì yīyuàn, jiù zài gōnglù de qiánbiānr.**
The hospital is two blocks from here, just before you come to the main highway.

31. **Wǒ zěnme huí lǚguǎn?**
How can I get back to my hotel?

32. **Cóng zhèlǐ zǒu. Nǐ kàn nàr, zài... pángbiānr.**
Go this way. You see it there, next to the...

33. **...diànyǐng. Duì bú duì?**
...movies. That's right, isn't it? (*lit.,* Correct or not?)

34. Duì.
Yes. (*lit.*, Correct.)

35. Xiànzài wǒ míngbai le.
Now I understand.

36. Nǐ wèishénme bù mǎi yì běn lǚyóu zhǐnán?
Why don't you buy yourself a guidebook?

37. Zhège zhǔyi búcuò. Wǒ kěyǐ qù nǎr mǎi?
That's a good idea. Where can I buy one?

38. Zài chēzhàn huòzhě rènhé shūbàotānr.
In the station or at any newspaper stand.

39. Chēzhàn lǐ zhèr yuǎn ma?
Is the station far from here?

40. Chēzhàn zài Dōngfānglù de jìntóu.
The station is at the end of Dongfang Road.

41. Zhèr fùjìn nǎr yǒu shūbàotānr?
Where's there a newspaper stand near here?

42. Zài zhège lùkǒu yǒu yí ge.
There's one on this corner.

43. Fēicháng gǎnxiè nǐ.
Thank you very much.

44. Búkèqi. Wǒ hěn lèyì bāngmáng.
Don't mention it. I'm very glad to have been of help to you. (*lit.*, I'm very willing to help.)

45. **Wǒ hěn xìngyùn pèng dào nǐ. Nǐ zhēn de hěn shúxī zhège chéngzhèn.**
I was certainly lucky to meet you. You really know this town very well.

46. **Yīdiǎnr yě bù qíguài. Wǒ jiùshì shìzhǎng!**
It's not surprising. I'm the mayor!

NOTE:

7. *Zhīdào* means "to know."
10. *Jiējiǎo* means "street corner."
16. *Shìzhèngfǔ* means "city government."
19. In China, the police are called *gōng'ān*, which literally means "public security."
20. *Jiēwěi* means "the end of the street."
24. *Chuāngkǒu* means "window."
30. *Lùkǒu* literally means "the mouth of the road." *Sān ge lùkǒu* means "three blocks" or literally "the mouths of three roads."

QUIZ 36

1. *Zhège hěn* _____ (simple).
    a. *bāngmáng*
    b. *jiǎndān*
    c. *fēicháng*

2. *Wǒ gěi nǐ jièshào zhège* _____ (town) *yí xià*.
    a. *yīyuàn*
    b. *chéngzhèn*
    c. *chēzhàn*

3. *Nǐ kàn de jiàn* _____ (corner) *nà zuò dàlóu*.
    a. *lùkǒu*
    b. *jiēwěi*
    c. *pángbiānr*

4. *Nà jiùshì* _____ (post office).
   a. *jiē*
   b. *yóuzhèngjú*
   c. *yīyuàn*

5. *Nǐ kànjiàn nà jiā* _____ (store) *ma?*
   a. *derecha*
   b. *shāngdiàn*
   c. *casa*

6. _____ (Doctor) *zhù zài pángbiānr.*
   a. *Yīshēng*
   b. *Yàofáng*
   c. *Míngzi*

7. *Tā de míngzi jiù zài* _____ (door) *shang.*
   a. *chē*
   b. *mén*
   c. *lóu*

8. *Tā de* _____ (clinic) *yě zà nàr.*
   a. *yàofáng*
   b. *shāngdiàn*
   c. *zhěnsuǒ*

9. *Jiù zài gāosù gōnglù de* _____ (before).
   a. *pángbiānr*
   b. *qiánbiānr*
   c. *hòubiānr*

10. *Wǒ kěyǐ qù nǎr* _____ (buy)?
    a. *mǎi*
    b. *chī*
    c. *kàn*

ANSWERS

1—b; 2—b; 3—a; 4—b; 5—b; 6—a; 7—b; 8—c; 9—b;
10—a.

B. SIGHT-SEEING

Yǒu nǎ xiē míngshèng gǔjì?	Which are the historic sights? (*lit.,* What historic sights are there?)
Jìniànpǐndiàn zài nǎr?	Where is a souvenir shop?
Wǒ xiǎng qù shāngyèqū.	I want to go to the business district.
Wǒ xiǎng qù zhèngfǔ dàlóu.	I want to go to the government palace.
Jǐngsè hěn mírén.	The view is breathtaking.
Zhège dìfang yóukè xīxī hěn duō.	This place is very touristy.

SUPPLEMENTAL VOCABULARY 17: AROUND TOWN

around town	*chéngzhèn yóulǎn*
town	*chéngzhèn*
city	*chéngshì*
village	*cūnzhuāng*
car	*chē*
bus	*gōngchē*
train	*huǒchē*
taxi	*chūzūchē*

subway/metro	*dìtiě*
traffic	*jiāotōng*
building	*dàlóu/dàxià*
apartment building	*gōngyù dàlóu*
library	*túshūguǎn*
restaurant	*fàndiǎn/fànguǎn*
store	*shāngdiàn*
street	*jiē*
park	*gōngyuán*
train station	*huǒchēzhàn*
airport	*fēijīchǎng*
airplane	*fēijī*
intersection	*shízì lùkǒu*
lamppost	*lùdēngzhù*
streetlight	*lùdēng*
bank	*yínháng*
church	*jiàotáng*
temple	*miàoyǔ/sìyuàn*
mosque	*qīngzhēnsì*
sidewalk	*rénxíngdào*
bakery	*miànbāodiàn*
butcher shop	*ròudiàn*
café/coffee shop	*kāfēidiàn*
drugstore/pharmacy	*yàofáng*
supermarket	*chāojí shìchǎng*
market	*shìchǎng*
shoe store	*xiédiàn*
clothing store	*fúzhuāngdiàn*
electronics store	*diànzǐ qìjiàn shāngdiàn*
bookstore	*shūdiàn*
department store	*báihuò shāngdiàn*
mayor	*shìzhǎng*
city hall/municipal building	*shìzhèngfǔ/ shìzhèng dàlóu*

to buy	*mǎi*
to go shopping	*qù mǎi dōngxi*
near/far	*jìn/yuǎn*
urban	*chéngshì*
suburban	*jiāoqū/shìjiāo*
rural	*nóngcūn*

LESSON 38

A. THE MEDIA AND COMMUNICATIONS (*CHUÁNMÉI HÉ TŌNGXÙN*)

1. Zhōu Lì: Wǒ bù xiǎng nǐ qù mǎi jīntiān de bàozhǐ.

Li Zhou: I didn't want you to buy the newspaper today.

2. Lǐ Péng: Wèishénme bù mǎi? Fāshēng le shénme shì?

Peng Li: Why not? (*lit.*, Why not to buy?) What happened?

3 Z: Bàozhǐ de biāotí dōushì lìng rén zhènjīng de xīnwén. Tóubǎn shàng de dōushì zāinàn, qiǎngjié, móushā, qiángjiān, dǎzhàng hé hànzāi de xīnwén—méiyǒu bié de dōngxi.

Z: The newspaper headlines bring shocking news. The front page has news about disasters, robberies, murders, rapes, wars, and droughts—nothing else.

4. L: Rúguǒ méiyǒu zhèxiē xīnwén, dāngrán zuì hǎo, dànshì zhèxiē dōushì shìshí.

L: It would be better if there weren't any such news, but they are real events.

5. **Z: Rúguǒ wǒmen cóng guòqù xuéxí!**
Z: If only we learned from the past.

6. **L: Yěxǔ nǐ bú yìnggāi kàn tóubǎn huòzhě
shèlùn, zhèyàng jiù kěyǐ bìmiǎn kàn dào lìng rén
zhènjīng de xīnwén.**
L: Maybe you shouldn't read (*lit.*, look at) the first page or
the editorials to avoid the shocking news.

7. **Z: Wǒ duì cáijīng, yùndòng, shūpíng de
bǎnmiàn hé fēnlèi guǎnggào dōu méi xìngqù.**
Z: The financial pages, sports, book reviews, and classified sections don't interest me much.

8. **L: Nǐ kěyǐ kàn tiánzì yóuxì, mànhuà huòzhě
màntán lán, lìng zìjǐ kuàilè.**
L: You could entertain yourself with the crossword puzzle
and the comic strips or the gossip column.

9. **Z: Zuì hǎo bú yào mǎi bàozhǐ, ...bú yào kàn.**
Z: It's better not to buy the paper...not to read it.

10. **L: Zhège bùdān zhǐshì xīnwén jiè de guòcuò.
Kējì, bǐrú xiàng hùliánwǎng, ràng wǒmen yòng
gèng kuài de fāngshì zhīdào quánshìjiè búxìng de
shìqíng. Dānshì zǒnghuì yǒu yìxiē yǒuqù de, wǒ
kěndìng yě huì yǒu hǎo de xīnwén!**
L: It's not only the fault of the press. Technology, like the
Internet, for example, allows us to learn about all of the
world's misfortunes with greater speed. But there's
always something interesting, and I'm sure that there will
be good news, too!

NOTE:

1. *Jīntiān de bàozhǐ* means "today's newspaper."

3. *Lìng rén zhènjīng de* is an adjectival clause used to translate the English adjective "shocking." Literally, it means "to make people shocked." *Méiyǒu bié de dōngxi* means "not to have other things."

4. *Shìshí* means "the fact." The expression *rúguǒ... dāngrán zuì hǎo, dànshì...* is used in conditional sentences. For example, *Rúguǒ nǐ qù, dāngrán zuì hǎo, dànshì nǐ bú qù* means "It would be best if you had gone, but you didn't."

6. *Kàn bàozhǐ/shū*, not *dú bàozhǐ/shū* is used to express the English "to read a newspaper/book." Literally, *kàn bàozhǐ/shū* means "to look at a newspaper/book," while *dú shū*, means "to study."

7. *Wǒ duì... méi xìngqù* is used to express that a person has no interest in someone or something. For example, *Wǒ duì nǐ méi xìngqù* means "I'm not interested in you."

B. AT THE AIRPORT *(ZÀI JĪCHǍNG)*

1. **Líng: Xiānsheng, máfán nǐ, zhè shì wǒ de jīpiào, hùzhào hé qiānzhèng.**
Ling: Pardon me, sir, here are our tickets, passports and visas.

2. **Zhíyuán: Xiǎojie, duìbuqǐ. Zhège hùzhào bú shì nǐ de, shì yíge xiǎo nǚháir de.**
Staff: Excuse me, madam. This passport isn't yours. It belongs to a young girl.

3. **Líng: Bú shì wǒ de? Zāogāo! Duìbuqǐ, wǒ yídìng nòng cuò le. Wǒmen de nǚér méiyǒu gēn wǒmen yìqǐ lǚxíng. Děng yíxià, zhè běn cái duì.**

L: It isn't mine? Damn! I'm sorry. I have indeed made a mistake. Our daughter isn't traveling with us. One moment. ...Well, this is the one.

4. **Zhíyuán: Hángbān yánchí le. Bādiǎnbàn zài èrshísān hào mén dēngjī. Nǐ yào tuōyùn nǐ de xíngli ma?**
S: The flight is delayed. It will leave from gate 23 at 8:30. (*lit.,* Boarding at gate 23 at 8:30) Do you want to check (your) luggage?

5. **Líng: Wǒ bù xūyào, dànshì tā yào.**
L: Mine I don't, but his I do.

6. **Zhíyuán: Zhè shì shōujù. Wǎng yòu zǒu. Tōngguò bǎoān, ránhòu nǐ yào xiàng hǎiguān shēnbào.**
S: Here is the receipt. Go to the right. Pass through security and then you will have to make a customs declaration.

7. **Líng: Wǒmen xiǎng yào kào zhe chuānghu de wèizhi.**
L: We'd like to have window seats.

8. **Zhíyuán: Zài chūjìngmén de yòubiānr yǒu yíge gōngzuò rényuán huì ānpái wèizhi gěi nǐ. Zhù nǐ lǚtú yúkuài!**
S: Right at the departure gate there'll be an agent who will assign you the seats. Have a good trip!

NOTE:
  3. Literally, *Wǒ nòng cuò le* means "I did it incorrectly."
  4. *Tuōyùn* means "to entrust (a company) to deliver something."

5. *Bù xūyào* means "I don't need."
6. *Xiàng hǎiguān shēnbào* means "to declare something to customs."
8. The rather formal expression *Zhù nǐ lǚtú yúkuài* translates as "I wish you a pleasant trip." The same sentiment can be expressed in a less formal way by using *Zhù nǐ yílù shùnfēng*.

QUIZ 37

A. CHUÁNMÉI HÉ TŌNGXÙN

1. *Zài bàozhǐ shang kànjiàn shénmen xīnwén?*
   a. *dúshū*
   b. *dǎzhàng*
   c. *xiànzài*

2. *Wǒmen cóng nǎr xuéxí?*
   a. *wèilai*
   b. *xiànzài*
   c. *guòqù*

3. *Wǒmen cóng nǎr kàn dào xīnwén?*
   a. *jīchǎng*
   b. *bàozhǐ*
   c. *diànhuà*

4. *Tóubǎn dōushì lìng rén zhènjīng de* _____ (news).
   a. *bàozhǐ*
   b. *biāotí*
   c. *xīnwén*

5. *Bàozhǐ yǒu hěnduō* _____ (sections/pages).
   a. *tiáo*
   b. *bǎn*
   c. *gè*

B.   ZÀI JĪCHǍNG

1. *Nà shì shéi de hùzhào?*
   a. *tā nǚér de*
   b. *tā zìjǐ de*
   c. *tā xiānsheng de*

2. *Hángbān* _____ (delay) *le.*
   a. *yánchí*
   b. *dào*
   c. *kāi*

3. *Tā yào qù* _____ (customs) *shēnbào.*
   a. *jīcháng*
   b. *háiguān*
   c. *bǎoān*

4. *Zhù nǐ* _____ (travel) *yúkuài.*
   a. *lái*
   b. *gōngzuò*
   c. *lǚtú*

ANSWERS
A.
1—b; 2—c; 3—b; 4—c; 5—b;
B.
1—a; 2—a; 3—b; 4—c.

C. THE MOST COMMON VERBS

1. To do, to make: *zuò*

Wǒ zìjǐ zuò.	I made (did) it myself./I'll do it myself.
Biérén gàosù tāmen zuò shénme, tāmen jiù zuò shénme.	They'll always do what they're told. (*lit.,* Whatever the others tell them to do, they'll do it.)
Wǒ huì zuò dào zuìhǎo.	I'll do my best to go.
Jǐnkuài zuò.	Do it as soon as possible.

2. To go: *qù*

Wǒ míngnián qù Zhōngguó.	I'm going to China next year.
Tā bù gēn nǐ qù.	He's going to go without you. (*lit.,* He doesn't go with you.)
Wǒ zuótiān qù le jiàn tā.	I went to see him yesterday.
Wǒ míngtiān huì qù kàn tāmen.	I'll go to visit them tomorrow.
Kuài diǎnr qù.	Go quickly.
Nǐ zuótiān yǒu méiyǒu qù kàn diànyǐng?	Did you go to the movies yesterday?
Zǒu ba!	Let's go!
Wǒmen zuótiān wǎnshang qù le diànyǐngyuàn.	We went to the theater last night.

3. To come: *lái*

Nǐ gēn wǒ yìqǐ lái, shì búshì?	You're coming with me, aren't you?

Tā jīngcháng lái wǒ jiā.	He always comes to my house.
Tā shénme shíhou lái?	When will she come?
Tāmen chángcháng lái shìqū.	They come to the city often.
Tāmen míngtiān lái jiàn wǒmen.	They're coming to see us tomorrow.
Tāmen jīntiān xiàwǔ huì lái jiàn wǒmen.	They'll come to see us this afternoon.
Míngtiān dàgài zhège shíjiān lái.	Come about this time tomorrow.

4. To walk, to go: *zǒu(lù)*

Wǒ yìlù zǒu lái le.	I walked all the way. (*lit.,* I walked and came all the way.)
Wǒmen huì yìqǐ zǒu.	We'll walk together.
Zǒu kuài diǎnr.	Walk faster.

5. To give: *gěi*

Nǐ kěyǐ míngtiān gěi wǒ ma?	Can you give it to me tomorrow?
Wǒ zuótiān gěi le tā.	I gave it to him yesterday.
Wǒ huì gěi wǒ kěyǐ gěi de.	I'll give what I can.

6. To have: *yǒu*

Wǒ méiyǒu shénme shíjiān.	I haven't any time.
Nǐ yào jǐnkuài ná dào.	You have to get it as soon as possible.

Wǒmen yǒu kèrén zài jiā lǐ.	We have guests at home.
Tā yào jīntiān yìzǎo chūqù.	He had to go out early today.
Nǐ huì yǒu shíjiān ma?	Will you have time?
Wǒ jīntiān wǎnshang yào qù yīnyuèhuì.	I have to go to a concert tonight.

7. To say/to speak: *shuō*

Tā shuō tā zǒu le.	He said he was leaving.
Tā shuō tā míngtiān huì lái.	She says she'll come tomorrow.
Tāmen cónglái bù shuō shénme.	They never say anything.
Tā jīngcháng xiǎng shuō shénme jiù shuō.	He always says what he thinks.
Nǐ xǐhuān shuō shénme jiù shuō.	Say whatever you like.
Nǐ jué de tā huì shuō shénme?	What do you think he'll say?

8. To put: *fàng*

Wǒ bǎ zhège fàng zài zhuōzi shang.	I put it on the table.
Nǐ huì bǎ zhège fàng zài nǎr?	Where are you going to put it?
Bǎ suǒyǒu dōngxi fàng zài tā zìjǐ de dìfang.	Put everything in its place.
Bǎ zhuōzi fàng zài kàojìn chuānghu de dìfang.	Put the table near the window.
Wǒ hěn fàngxīn.	I feel very relieved.
Tā zuótiān fàngjià.	He had a holiday yesterday.

9. To put (on)/to wear: *chuān*

Wǒ bù xiǎoxīn chuān le nǐ de màozi.	I put your hat on by mistake.
Chuān shàng nǐ de xīn tàozhuāng.	Put on your new suit.

10. To want: *xiǎng/yào/xiǎngyào*

Wǒ xiǎng qù.	I want to go.
Rúguǒ wǒmen bú qù, tā Bú huì qù.	He won't want to go if we don't go with him.

11. To bring: *dàilái*

Wǒ wàng le dàilái.	I forgot to bring it.
Dài yìxiē qián lái.	Bring some money with you.
Tā gěi tā dàilái le yí fèn lǐwù.	He brought her a present.

12. To leave: *líkāi*

Wǒ xīngqīsān líkāi.	I'm leaving on Wednesday.
Tā cóng zhèbiānr líkāi le.	He went out this way.

13. To see: *kàn/jiàn*

Méiyǒu yǎnjìng tā kàn bú jiàn.	He can't see well without his glasses.
Wǒ zuótiān jiàn dào tā.	I saw him yesterday.
Xiànzài nǐ kàn dào wǒ shuō de shì de.	Now you'll see that what I say is true.

14. To know: *zhīdào/rènshi/shúxī*

Wǒ zhīdào zhè shì zhēn de	I know it's true.
Tā rénshi nǐ.	He knows you.
Wǒmen bú tài shúxī zhège chéngshì.	We don't know this city very well.

15. Can: *kěyǐ*

Wǒ kěyǐ zài nǎr fā chuánzhēn?	Where can I send a fax?
Nǐ jīntiān wǎnshang kěyǐ lái ma?	Can you come tonight?

SUPPLEMENTAL VOCABULARY 18: ENTERTAINMENT

entertainment	*yúlè*
movie/film	*diànyǐng*
to go to the movies	*qù kàn diànyǐng*
to see a movie	*kàn diànyǐng*
movie theater	*diànyǐngyuàn*
theater	*jùyuàn*
to see a play	*kàn xìjù*
opera	*gējù*
concert	*yīnyuèhuì*
club	*jùlèbù*
circus	*mǎxì*
ticket	*piào*
museum	*bówùguǎn*
gallery	*huàláng/měishùguǎn*
painting	*huà*
sculpture	*diāokè/diāosù*
television program	*diànshì jiémù*

to watch television	*kàn diànshì*
comedy	*xǐjù*
documentary	*jìlùpiàn*
drama	*xìjù*
book	*shū*
magazine	*zázhì*
to read a book	*kàn shū*
to read a magazine	*kàn zázhì*
to listen to music	*tīng yīnyuè*
song	*gēqǔ*
band	*yuèduì*
the news	*xīnwén*
talk show	*qīngtán jiémù/fǎngtán jiémù*
to flip channels	*xuǎntái*
to change channels	*zhuǎntái*
to have fun	*wán de gāoxìng*
to be bored	*mèn*
funny	*yǒuqù/hǎowán*
interesting	*yǒu yìsi*
exciting	*lìng rén xīngfèn*
scary	*kěpà*
party	*shèjiāo jùhuì*
dancing party	*wǔhuì*
restaurant	*fànguǎn/fàndiàn*
to go to a party	*qù wǔhuì*
to have a party	*gǎo wǔhuì*
to dance	*tiàowǔ*

QUIZ 38

1. *Tā cóng nàbiānr_____* (to leave) *le.*
   a. *wàng*
   b. *líkāi*
   c. *dàilái*

2. *Wǒ hěn* _____ (relieved).
    a. *fàngxīn*
    b. *chuánzhēn*
    c. *gěi*

3. *Nǐ zuòtiān* _____ (to give) *le tā.*
    a. *qù*
    b. *kàn kàn*
    c. *gěi*

4. *Nǐ*_____ (think) *tā huì shuō shénme?*
    a. *yǒu yìsi*
    b. *júe de*
    c. *kàn*

5. _____ (Walk) *kuài diǎnr.*
    a. *Kāi*
    b. *Fàng*
    c. *Zǒu*

ANSWERS
1—b; 2—a; 3—c; 4—b; 5—c.

LESSON 39

A.   WHAT'S IN A NAME?

Tā jiào shénme míngzi?
What's his name?

Tā jiào Huáng Hǎi.
His name is Huang Hai.

Gēn tā yìqǐ de nàge nǚshì jiào shénme míngzi?
What's the name of the young lady with him?

Tā jiào Lǐ Huì.
Her name is Li Hui.

Tā bàba jiào shénme míngzi?
What's her father's name?

Tā bàba jiào Lǐ Chéng.
Her father's name is Li Cheng.

Wǒ bù míngbai wèishénme tā xìng Huì, tā bàba xìng Chéng, Tāmen liǎng ge dōu jiào Lǐ.
I can't understand why her last name is Hui and her father's last name is Cheng. Their first names are both Li, aren't they?

Nǐ cuò le. Tā bú xìng Huì, tā bàba yě bú xìng Chéng. Huì hé Chéng shì míngzi, Lǐ shì xìng.
You're wrong. Her last name isn't Hui and her father's isn't Cheng. Li is their last name.

Duìbuqǐ. Wǒ bù míngbai.
Excuse me but I don't understand.

Wǒ jiěshì gěi nǐ tīng ba. Zhōngguó rén de xìng zài míngzi de qiánbiānr.
I'll explain it to you. In Chinese, the last name comes before the first name.

Zhēn de?
Really?

Bǐrúshuō, wǒ jiào Zhāng Wéi. Zhāng shì wǒ de xìng, Wéi shì wǒ de míngzi.
For instance, I'm called Zhang Wei. Zhang is my last name and Wei is my first name.

Xiànzài wǒ míngbai le. Qiánbiānr nàge shì xìng.
Now I see. The word in front is the last name.

Duì le. Nǐ kěyǐ jiào Lǐ xiǎojie.
That's right. You can call her Miss Li.

Tā māma jiào shénme míngzi?
What's her mother's name?

Tā māma jiào Hé Fāng.
Her mother's name is He Fang.

Wèishénme tā xìng Hé?
Why is her last name He?

Yīnwèi Hé shì tā yuánlái de xìng. Zài Zhōngguó, nǚxìng jiéhūn zhīhòu, tōngcháng bú huì gǎi xìng.
Because He is her maiden name. In China, women usually don't change their last name after marriage.

Nà wǒ zěnme jiào tā?
Then how should I address her?

Nǐ kěyǐ jiào tā Hé nǚshì, huòzhě Lǐ tàitai.
You can use her maiden name and call her Ms. He, or you can use her married name and call her Mrs. Li.

B. NOTES ON PERSONAL NAMES IN CHINESE

The last name always precedes the first name in China. When making a new acquaintance, one usually asks for a person's last name by using the expression *Qǐng wèn nǐ guì xìng?* which literally means "What's your honorable last name?" Expressions *xiānsheng* (Mr.), *tàitai* (Mrs.), and *xiǎojie* (Miss) are used in combination with the last names to address strangers and new acquaintances.

First names are used only with friends, relatives, or peers. They can consist of one or more syllables, e.g., *Xīng* and *Dōng Fāng*.

Sometimes, the expression *xiǎo* is placed before a person's last name to indicate a certain degree of intimacy, e.g., *Xiǎo Huáng. Xiǎo* is more commonly used when addressing people younger than or equal in age to oneself.

LESSON 40

A. FUN IN CHINESE

MÉI GUĀNXI (IT DOESN'T MATTER)

—Xiǎojie, wǒ xiǎng kàn yīshēng. — Miss, I want to see the doctor.

—Yīshēng xiànzài hěn máng. Nǐ xià ge xīngqī zài lái ba. — The doctor is very busy now. Come again next week.

—Xià ge xīngqī? Wǒ yǐjīng sǐ le. — Next week? I will have died by then.

—Méi guānxi. Nǐ zài lái ba. — It does not matter. Just come back.

NOTE:

kàn yīshēng "to see a doctor"
máng "to be busy"
zài lái "to come again"
yǐjīng "already"
sǐ le "died"
méi guānxi "it doesn't matter (*lit.*, no relation)"

NǍLI, NǍLI! (WHERE, WHERE!)

Peter hěn àimù piàoliang de nǚ gēshǒu Huáng Zhēn. Yǒu yì tiān, yǒu rén gěi tā jièshào Huáng Zhēn. Tā fēicháng xīngfèn. Tā shuō:

Peter really likes the beautiful singer Huang Zeng. One day, he was introduced to Huang Zeng at a party. He was very excited and said:

—*Huáng xiǎojie, nǐ shì wǒ jiàn guò de zuì piàoliang de nǚháizǐ!*

—Miss Huang, you're the most beautiful girl I've ever seen!

Huáng Zhēn qiānxū de huídá:

Huang Zeng replied humbly:

—*Nǎli, nǎli!*

—Thank you for the compliment!

Peter bù míngbai. Tā wèn zìjǐ: "Wèishénme tā shuō 'nǎli, nǎli'?"

Peter was puzzled. He asked himself, "Why did she say 'Where, where'?"

NOTE:

piàoliang "beautiful"
xīngfèn "to be excited"
qiānxū "humbly"
huídá "to reply"

nǎli, nǎli! Literally, "where, where," idiomatically, a humble expression used to thank for a compliment.

QǏNG WĚN... (PLEASE KISS...)

Nancy xué le yìnián Zhōngwén. Tā juédìng zìjǐ yíge rén qù Zhōngguó jǐ ge yuè.	Nancy has studied Chinese for a year and decides to go to China for a couple of months by herself.
Zhèshì tā dìyícì qù wàiguó. Tā mílù le, zhǎo bú dào lǚguǎn. Yúshì tā wèn yíge lùguò de lǎorén:	This is her first time visiting a foreign country. She gets lost and can't find her hotel, so she approaches (*lit.*, asks) a man who is passing.
—*Qǐng wèn...*	—Please kiss...
Nà nánrén chījīng de kàn zhe tā, ránhòu dàxiào.	The man looks at her in surprise and laughs.
Nancy zài shì yícì:	Nancy tries to ask again:
—*Qǐng wèn...*	— Please kiss...
Nà nánrén shuō: "Xiǎojie, wǒ shòu chǒng ruò jīng! Wǒ yào xiān jiǎnchá wǒ de xuěyā."	The man says, "Madam, your offer is very flattering, but I need to check my blood pressure."

NOTE:
Qǐngwèn is "may I ask" and *qǐngwěn* means "please kiss." There is a significant difference in tone between *wèn*, "to ask" and *wěn*, "to kiss," which can be easily confused by students of Chinese.
juédìng "to decide"
zìjǐ yíge rén "by oneself/alone"
dìyícì "for the first time"

wàiguó "foreign country"
mílù "got lost"
zhǎo bú dào "can't find"
yúshì "then, so"
lùguò "passing by"
lǎorén "old man"
chījīng "in surprise"
ránhòu "then"
dàxiào "to laugh"
xiān "first"
jiǎnchá "to check"
xuěyā "blood pressure"
shòu chǒng ruò jīng "to be overwhelmed by flattery and honor"

ZHÈLI MÉIYǑU HUÁNGJĪN (NO GOLD HERE)

Cóngqián yǒu yíge rén, tā jiào Zhāng Sān. Yǒu yì tiān, tā zhǎo dào hěn duō huángjīn. Tā pà biérén tōuzǒu tāde huángjīn. Yúshì tā zài hòuyuàn wā le yíge dà dòng, bǎ huángjīn mái qǐlái.

Once upon a time there was a man. His name was Zhang San. One day, he found a lot of gold. He was afraid that other people would steal his treasure. So, he dug a big hole in the backyard and buried the gold in it.

Tā yòu pà biérén zhǎo dào huángjīn. Yúshì tā xiǎng dào yíge fāngfǎ. Tā zài dìshang fàng le yíge mùpái, shàngbiānr xiě zhe:

Then, he became afraid that someone would find the gold, so he thought of a solution. He put a wooden sign on the ground saying:

—Zhèli méiyǒu huángjīn.

—No gold here.

Tā kàn le hěn gāoxìng, He looked at it happily,
  ránhòu tā qù shuìjiào. then went home to sleep.
Zhāng Sān zǒu le zhīhòu, Immediately after he left,
  tā de línjù Lǐ Sì his neighbor Li Si came over
  mǎshang zǒu guòlái, and stole all the gold. He
  tōuzǒu le suǒyǒu de was afraid that Zhang San
  huángjīn. Tā pà Zhāng would know he was the
  Sān zhīdào shì tā tōuzǒu thief. So he also put a
  le huángjīn. Yúshì tā yě wooden sign on the ground.
  dìshang fàng le yíge It read:
  mùpái, shàngbiānr
  xiě zhe:
—*Nǐ de línjù Lǐ Sì* —Your neighbor Li Si
  méiyǒu tōuzǒu nǐ de didn't steal your gold.
  huángjīn

NOTE:
huángjīn "gold"
cóngqián "once upon a time"
zhǎo dào "found"
pà "to be afraid"
biérén "other people"
tōuzǒu "stole"
hòuyuàn "backyard"
wā "to dig"
dà dòng "big hole"
bǎ huángjīn mái qǐlái "buried the gold"
xiǎng dào "think of (something)"
fāngfǎ "solution, method"
dìshang "on the ground"
fàng "to put"
mùpái "wooden sign"
xiě "to write"
ránhòu "then"

shuìjiào "to sleep"
zhīhòu "after"
línjù "neighbor"
zǒu guòlái "to come over"
suǒyǒu "all"
méiyǒu tōuzǒu "didn't steal"

B. IMPORTANT SIGNS IN CHINESE CHARACTERS

男	Men
女	Women
卫生间or 厕所 or 洗手间	Lavatory
有人	Closed (*lit.*, there is person)
无人	Open (*lit.*, there is no person)
不准抽烟	No Smoking
不准进入	No Admittance
敲	Knock
铃	Ring
私人	Private
查询	Inquire Within
停! or 止步!	Stop!
去!	Go!
小心!	Look out!
危险!	Danger!
慢走	Go slowly!
绕道	Detour
警告	Caution
保持右走	Keep to the Right
桥	Bridge
不准停车	No Parking
衣帽间	Check Room
兑换	Money Exchanged
资料	Information

等候室	Waiting Room
不要伸出窗外	Don't Lean Out (of the Window)
飞机场	Airport
铁路	Railroad
快车	Express
慢车	Local (*lit.,* slow car)
站	Stop (bus, train, etc.)
不可张贴	Post No Bills
修理中	Under Repair
入口	Entrance
出口	Exit
配家具房子	Furnished Rooms
房子	Apartments
油漆未干	Wet Paint
十字路口	Crossroads
肉店	Butcher
饼店	Bakery
牛奶	Dairy
裁缝店	Tailor Shop
鞋店	Shoe Store
理发店	Barber Shop
菜市场 or 市场	Grocer
药房 or 药店	Pharmacy/Drugstore
糖果店	Confectioner/Candy Store
文具店	Stationery Store
信箱	Mail Box
酒吧	Bar/Tavern
公安局	Police Station
酒	Wines
油站	Gas Station
书店	Bookstore
市政府	City Hall
点心 or 小吃	Refreshments
冷(水)	Cold (Water)
热(水)	Hot (Water)

QUIZ 39

Match the Chinese words in th left column with their English translation in the right column.

1. 入口   a. No Smoking
2. 绕道   b. Express
3. 不可伸出窗外   c. No parking
4. 有人   d. Open
5. 无人   e. Exit
6. 不准抽烟   f. Information
7. 快车   g. Detour
8. 不准停车   h. Entrance
9. 出口   i. Closed
10. 资料   j. Don't Lean Out (of the Window)

ANSWERS

1—h; 2—g; 3—j; 4—d; 5—i; 6—a; 7—b; 8—c; 9—e; 10—f.

FINAL QUIZ

1. _____ (May I ask) *huòchēzhàn zài nǎr?*
   a. *Yǒu méiyǒu*
   b. *Qǐng wèn*
   c. *Wèishénme*

2. *Nǐ*_____ (can) *gàosu wǒ nǎr yǒu fàndiàn ma?*
   a. *kěyǐ*
   b. *bù néng*
   c. *shì*

3. *Nǎr* _____ (there is) *hǎo fànguǎn?*
   a. *shì*
   b. *yǒu*
   c. *qù*

4. _____ (Give) *wǒ yìxiē miànbāo.*
   a. *Xué*
   b. *Jué*
   c. *Gěi*

5. _____ (I need) *qián.*
   a. *Wǒ yào*
   b. *Wǒ méiyǒu*
   c. *Wǒ bù*

6. _____ (I would like) *yì bēi kāfēi.*
   a. *Wǒ xǐhuān*
   b. *Wǒ yǎo qù*
   c. *Wǒ xiǎng yào*

7. *Wǒ gěi nǐ*_____ (introduce) *wǒ de péngyou.*
   a. *jièshào*
   b. *rènshi*
   c. *shúxī*

8. *Wǒ de shū* _____ (in) *nǎr?*
   a. *zài*
   b. *shì*
   c. *méi*

9. *Wǒ kěyǐ* _____ (send) *chuánzhēn ma?*
   a. *fā*
   b. *zǒu*
   c. *zuò*

10. *Nĭ* _____ (know how to speak) *Zhōngwén ma?*
    a. *huì qù*
    b. *shuō*
    c. *huì shuō*

11. _____ (Go) *nàli.*
    a. *Qù*
    b. *Shuō*
    c. *Nǎr*

12. *Wŏ huì zuò dào* _____ (the best).
    a. *zuìhǎo*
    b. *hǎo*
    c. *bú yóngyi*

13. *Nĭ* _____ (call) *shénme míngzi?*
    a. *shuō*
    b. *jiào*
    c. *mǎi*

14. *Yí ge* _____ (week) *yŏu duōshǎo tiān?*
    a. *xīngqī*
    b. *nián*
    c. *yuè*

15. *Xiànzài* _____ (what time)?
    a. *jǐdiǎn*
    b. *shíjiān*
    c. *fēn*

16. *Wŏ* _____ (don't have) *xiāngyān.*
    a. *yě yŏu*
    b. *méiyŏu*
    c. *yŏu*

17. *Nǐ* _____ (want) *yìxiē shuǐguǒ ma?*
    a. *xiǎng*
    b. *yǒu*
    c. *yào*

18. _____ (Allow) *wǒ gěi nǐ jièshào wǒ de péngyou.*
    a. *Shì*
    b. *Ràng*
    c. *Lìng*

19. *Nǐ kěyǐ* ____ (describe) *shì shénme yàngzi de ma?*
    a. *kànkan*
    b. *shuōshuo*
    c. *qǐngqǐng*

20. *Dǎ diànhuà dào Shànghǎi yào* _____ (how much)?
    a. *duōshǎo qián*
    b. *duō jiǔ*
    c. *duō dà*

21. *Wǒmen yào sān ge* _____ (breakfast).
    a. *zǎocān*
    b. *wǔfàn*
    c. *jiǔ*

22. *Xiànzài* _____ (1:45).
    a. *yī diǎn sìshí*
    b. *yī diǎn sān kè*
    c. *chà yī kè sān diǎn*

23. *Wǒ* _____ (tomorrow morning) *qù.*
    a. *míngtiān xiàwǔ*
    b. *míngtiān zǎoshang*
    c. *míngtiān wǎngshang*

24. *Wǒ* _____ (can I) *bāng nǐ ma?*
    a. *cóng*
    b. *huì*
    c. *kěyǐ*

25. *Méi* _____ (relation).
    a. *wèntí*
    b. *guānxi*
    c. *shíjiān*

ANSWERS

1—b; 2—a; 3—b; 4—c; 5—a; 6—c; 7—a; 8—a; 9—a; 10—c; 11—a; 12—a; 13—b; 14—a; 15—a; 16—b; 17—c; 18—b; 19—b; 20—a; 21—a; 22—b; 23—b; 24—c; 25—b.

SUMMARY OF CHINESE GRAMMAR

1. PRONUNCIATION AND THE *PĪNYĪN* SYSTEM

a. 23 initial sounds

b	like *b* in *bear*
p	like *p* in *poor*
m	like *m* in *more*
f	like *f* in *fake*
d	like *d* in *dare*
t	like *t* in *take*
n	like *n* in *now*
l	like *l* in *learn*
z	like *ds* in *yards*
c	like *ts* in *its*
s	like *s* in *sibling*
zh	like *dge* in *judge*
ch	like *ch* in *church*
sh	like *sh* in *hush*
r	like *r* in *rubbish*
j	like *g* in *gene*
q	like *ch* in *cheese*
x	like *sh* in *shoe*
g	like *g* in *get*
k	like *c* in *cow*
h	like *h* in *help*
w	like *w* in *wet*
y	like *y* in *yellow*

Note that the comparison of Chinese sounds to English sounds is only approximate.

b. 36 final sounds

a	like *a* in *ma*
ai	like *y* in *my*
ao	like *ou* in *pout*
an	like *an* in *élan*
ang	like *ong* in *throng*
o	like *o* in *or*
ou	like *oa* in *float*
ong	like *ong* in *long*
e	like *er* in *nerve*
ei	like *ay* in *day*
en	like *un* in *under*
eng	like *ung* in *mung*
i (after *z,* *c, s, zh,* *ch, sh*)	like *r* in *thunder*
i	like *ee* in *see*
ia	like *yah*
iao	like *eow* in *meow*
ian	like *yan*
iang	like *yang*
ie	like *ye* in *yes*
iu	like *yo* in *yo-yo*
iong	like *young*
in	like *in* in *sin*
ing	like *ing* in *sing*
u	like *u* in *flu*
ua	like *ua* in *suave*
uai	like *wi* in *wide*
uan	like *wan*
uang	like *wong* with a strong *u* at the beginning
uo	like *wo* in *won't*
ui	like *weigh*

un	like *won* but with a shorter *o* sound
ü	like *eu* in *rheumatic*
üan	like *ü* plus the *en* like in *pen*
üe	like *ü* plus the *e* like in *debt*
ün	like *ü* plus *n*
er	like *are*

c. Tones

There are four tones in Chinese. They are marked above the vowel of each syllable. In the case of diphthongs, the tone is marked over a single vowel in the following order of priority: *a, o, e, i, u.* When *i* and *u* combine to form a diphthong, the tone marker is placed over the second vowel.

Take the vowel *a* as an example:

First tone:	*ā*
Second tone:	*á*
Third tone:	*ǎ*
Fourth tone:	*à*

Here are a few examples of diphthongs:

ai
First tone:	*āi*
Second tone:	*ái*
Third tone:	*ǎi*
Fourth tone:	*ài*

ui
First tone:	*uī*
Second tone:	*uí*
Third tone:	*uǐ*
Fourth tone:	*uì*

iu

First tone:	*iū*
Second tone:	*iú*
Third tone:	*iǔ*
Fourth tone:	*iù*

d. Neutral tone

Some syllables are "toneless" or pronounced with a neutral tone. There are no tone markers above the vowels of such syllables. Examples of toneless syllables are particles *ma* and *ne*, which are always written and pronounced with a neutral tone.

For example:

Nǐ hǎo ma?
How are you?

Wǒ hěn hǎo. Nǐ ne?
I am fine. How about you?

e. Tone changes

Double third tones

When two syllables with third tones are next to each other, the first syllable with a third tone is usually pronounced as a half third tone, which sounds like a second tone. The *Pīnyīn* tone mark remains the same.

For example:

Nǐ hǎo ma?
How are you?

Yī "one" and *bù* "not"

Yī undergoes three different types of tone changes.

When *yī* is used alone, at the end of a word or as an ordinal number, it is pronounced with a first tone.

> For example:
> *yī, èr, sān*   *xīngqīyī*
> one, two, three   Monday
>
> *dìyī*   *yī-qī-qī-liù nián*
> the first   year 1776

If it precedes a syllable with the fourth tone, *yī* is pronounced *yí*. For example:

> *yíhùir*   *yíwàn*
> a while   ten thousand

If it precedes a syllable with the first, second or third tone, *yī* is pronounced *yì*.

> For example:
> *yìqiān*   *yìzhí*
> one thousand   all along

If it comes between two duplicate syllables, *yī* is pronounced with the neutral tone.

> For example:
> *shì yi shì*   *zuò yi zuò*
> try a little bit   do a little bit

Bù has two types of tone changes.

When *bù* is used alone, at the end of a word, or when it precedes a first, second or third tone syllable, it remains unchanged and is pronounced *bù*.

For example:
Bù! Wǒ bù chī.
No! I don't eat it.

Wǒ bù zhīdào.
I *don't* know.

When it precedes a syllable with the fourth tone, it is written and pronounced *bú*.

For example:
Wǒ bú huì qù.
I *won't* go.

When it is found between two duplicate syllables, it is written and pronounced *bu*.

For example:
Hǎo bu hǎo?
Okay?
(*lit.,* Good or not good?)

f. Use of apostrophe

When a syllable starting with *a, o* or *e* immediately follows another syllable, an apostrophe is added to keep the two syllables separate and prevent any confusion of meaning.

For example:
píng'ān (píng + ān, not *pín +gān)*
safe
pèi'ǒu (pèi + ǒu, not *pè + iǒu)*
spouse
Cháng'é (cháng + é, not *chán + gé)*
Lunar Fairy

2. PARTS OF SPEECH

a. Nouns

Nouns in Chinese denote people and objects, as well as abstract concepts, such as time, direction and location.

> For example:
> *Wǒ shì xuésheng.*
> I am a *student.*

> *Xiànzài shì sāndiǎn.*
> *Now* it's *three o'clock.*

> *Wǒ zhù zài Shànghǎiguǎngchǎng.*
> I live in *Shanghai Square.*

> *Tàyáng zài dōngfāng shēngqǐ.*
> *The sun* rises in *the east.*

A noun can modify another noun or can be modified by an adjective.

> For example:
> *Zhè shì Zhōngguó píjiǔ.*
> This is Chinese *beer.*

> *Tā shì hǎo háizi.*
> He/she is a good *boy/girl.*
> (*lit.,* He/she is a good *child.*)

Chinese does not make use of articles with nouns, unlike English ("a/an" and "the"). To say "She is a̲ teacher" in Chinese, simply say *tā shì lǎoshī* (*lit.,* She is teacher). However, there are different words in Chinese to translate the English "a/an" and "the" when that is absolutely necessary. Neither of them are exactly equivalent to the uses of English articles.

Use a numerical qualifier, followed by the measure word, to suggest the meaning of "a/an."

> *Gěi wǒ yī běn shū.*
> Give me one/a book.

Use the demonstrative pronoun *nà* "that" to suggest the meaning of "the."

> *Nà ge nánháizi qù yóuyǒng le.*
> That the boy went swimming.

b. Verbs

In Chinese, verbs are used to describe actions, behaviors and emotions. They can be placed immediately after the subject or, in a manner quite different from English, they can come at the end of a sentence.

> For example:
> *Wǒ zǒu.*
> I *walk.*

> *Tā xué Zhōngwén.*
> He *learns* Chinese.

> *Tā xǐhuan dòngwù.*
> She *likes* animals.

> *Wǒ kěnéng gēn péngyou yìqǐ qù.*
> I will probably *go* with my friends.

The negative form of a verb is obtained by placing the word *bù* "not" directly in front of it.

> For example:
> *Tā bù xǐhuan kàn diànshì.*
> He *does not like* watching television.

> *Nǐ bú yìnggāi qù.*
> You *should not* go.

There are no verb conjugations in Chinese. A verb does not change its form depending on the subject. Verbs have the same forms when used with singular or plural pronouns. Furthermore, verbs do not change their form to express the different tenses. Different tenses are expressed in Chinese by adding specific helping words to the verb.

c. Adjectives

Adjectives modify nouns and describe characteristics of people and things. An adjective is placed before the noun it modifies.

> For example:
> *yí ge hěn gāo de nánháizi*
> a very *tall* boy
>
> *piàoliang de dōngxi*
> *pretty* things

An adjective can be modified by an adverb such as *hěn* (very).

> For example:
> *Zhège píngguǒ hěn tián.*
> This apple is *very sweet.*

In Chinese equational sentences, adjectives are not linked to nouns with the verb "to be," as in English.

> For example:
> *Tā piàoliang.*
> She *is* pretty. (*lit.,* she pretty)

An adjective is made negative by placing the word *bú* before it.

For example:
Tā bú gāo.
He is *not* tall. (*lit.,* he not tall)

d. Numerals

Cardinal numbers are used to indicate quantity and numbering.

yī	*èr*
one	two
sān	*bǎi*
three	a hundred
etc.	

Ordinal numbers are used to indicate order and sequencing.

dìyī	*dìèr*
the first	the second
etc.	

e. Measure words

A measure word is a word used obligatorily between a number word and a noun.

For example:
sì ge rén
four people

liǎng běn shū
two books

f. Pronouns

Pronouns take the place of nouns and fall into three categories in Chinese: personal pronouns, demonstrative pronouns and interrogative pronouns or question words.

Often, pronouns are implied, rather than being actually stated in Chinese. The English word "it," for example, is not translated in Chinese expressions of time, e.g. *liǎng diǎn* "It is two o'clock" (*lit.* two o'clock).

g. Adverbs

As in English, adverbs in Chinese are used to modify verbs and adjectives, as well as other adverbs. Their purpose is to clarify the words they modify by answering to the questions how, when, where, or why. In general, they are placed in front of the verbs they modify.

The word *hěn* (very) is probably the most used adverb in the Chinese language. Like *zuì* (the most) and *tài* (too), it is placed immediately before the adjective it modifies. A typical example of its usage is:

> *Nǐ shuō de hěn hǎo*
> You speak very well.

Adverbs used to modify verbs include *mǎshàng* (immediately) and *yìqǐ* (together).

h. Prepositions

Prepositions relate a noun or a pronoun to another word, usually in regard to position, direction, space, or time. They usually precede a noun in Chinese. A commonly used locative preposition *zài* is used in the following sentence:

> *Wǒ zài jiā lǐ.*
> I am at home. (*lit.,* I at home inside)

i. Conjunctions

Chinese uses different conjunctions to link words, phrases and sentences.

For example:
píngguǒ hé xiāngjiāo
apple *and* banana

píngguǒ huòzhě xiāngjiāo
apple *or* banana

Wǒ yīnwèi bìng le, suǒyǐ wǒ bùnéng qù.
Since I am sick, (*lit.* therefore, so) I cannot go.

Wǒ xiǎng qù, kěshì wǒ tài máng.
I want to go, *but* I am too busy.

j. Verb suffixes

The Chinese language uses verb suffixes to indicate the time of an action. There are three verb suffixes: *le, zhe* and *guò*. *Le* is used to indicate a completed action; *zhe* is used to indicate an ongoing activity or state of being; and *guò* is used to indicate a continuous action.

k. Particles

Particles are short invariable words that are very commonly used in the Chinese language.

De is used frequently and when placed after a pronoun, it makes the pronoun possessive.

For example:
Zhè shì wǒ de shū.
This is my book.

Zhè jiā fàndiàn de cài hěn hǎo.
This restaurant's food is very good.

The particle *de* can also be used to form adverbial expressions. In this case, *de* is placed immediately after a verb and followed by an adjective.

> For example:
> *Tā zuò de hěn hǎo.*
> He does it very well.

Note that three different Chinese characters correspond to the *Pinyin* word *de*— 的, 得 and 地. These are three different words with different functions, but the same pronunciation.

Particles *ma* and *ne* are known as "ending particles" because they are placed at the end of sentences to create questions.

> For example:
> *Nǐ hǎo ma?*
> How are you?
>
> *Nǐ ne?*
> How about you?

The particle *ba* is placed at the end of sentences to form polite regrets.

> For example:
> *Qǐng jìnlái ba!*
> Please come in!

l. Exclamation

Exclamatory words, such as *na*, *le*, and *ya*, are used to help express strong feelings, such as surprise, joy, or shock. They are used in combination with other words and are always placed at the end of sentences.

For example:
Tiān na!
My God!
(*lit.,* Heaven!)

Zāo le!
Darn it!

Zhēn zāogāo ya!
It's really bad!
(*lit.,* Really bad!)

m. Sound words

Sound words are used to express speakers' emotions, such as sorrow, happiness, or anger. They typically stand alone and are placed before an accompanying sentence.

For example:
Ai! Nà jiā lǚguǎn zài nǎr?
Gosh! Where is that hotel?

Hāhā! Wǒ hěn gāoxìng!
Ha ha! I am very happy!

3. NOUNS

There is no distinction in form between singular and plural nouns in Chinese. A number or a measure word can be placed in front of a noun to designate it as either singular or plural.

For example:
yí ge píngguǒ
one *apple*

liǎng ge píngguǒ
two *apples*

The ending *men* can be used to create plural nouns, but only if they refer to human beings. Adding *men* will also make the noun definite, i.e., refer to a specific group of people.

> For example:
> *Háizimen ài chī tángguǒ.*
> The children like eating candy.

> *Lǎoshīmen jìnlái le.*
> The teachers came in.

When *men* is added to the noun *rén*, the resulting noun is indefinite and generic.

> For example:
> *Rénmen ài tā.*
> People like him/her.

If a number or measure word precedes a noun, *men* cannot be used.

> For example:
> *liǎng ge háizi* (correct)
> two children

> *liǎng ge háizimen* (incorrect)
> two children

4. PERSONAL PRONOUNS AND POSSESSIVE PRONOUNS

<u>Personal Pronouns</u>

Singular personal pronouns in Chinese are:

1st person	I/me	*wǒ*
2nd person	you/you	*nín* (fml.)
	you/you	*nǐ* (infml.)
3rd person	he, she, it/	*tā*
	him, her, it	

There is no difference among the personal pronouns for "he," "she," and "it" in pronunciation. *Tā* is used for all. However, the Chinese characters for *tā* "he," *tā* "she," and *tā* "it" are different.

Chinese does not distinguish between subject and object pronouns. For example, the word *wǒ* means both "I" and "me."

> For example:
> *Wǒ xǐhuan tā, tā yě xǐhuan wǒ.*
> I like him and he likes me, too.

Plural personal pronouns in Chinese are:

1st person	we/us	*wǒmen*
2nd person	you/you	*nǐmen*
3rd person	they/them	*tāmen*

Note that there is no special formal form for the 2nd person plural pronoun *nǐmen*. Instead, phrases *nín liǎng wèi* (you two/both of you) or *nín jǐ wèi* (several of you) can be used.

For example:
Nín liǎng wèi qǐng zùo.
You two (*pl. fml.*), please sit down.

Nín jǐ wèi yào dào nǎli?
Where do you (*pl. fml.*) need to go?

Tā (it) is usually used to refer to an animal or an object.

Tā shì chǒngwù.
It is a pet.

Wǒ zuì ài tā.
I like it the most.

In colloquial language, *tāmen* is not normally used to replace plural nouns for animals or objects. Instead, plural demonstrative pronouns are used.

However, if a noun referring to an animal is the object of a sentence immediately following another sentence in which the animal was identified as a species, *tāmen* can be used. This use of *tāmen* occurs rarely in Chinese.

For example:
Wǒ yǒu sān zhī māo. Wǒ hěn xǐhuan tāmen.
I have three cats. I like them a lot.

When *tā* (it) refers to an object, it is usually omitted from the sentence when it can be understood from the context.

For example:
Nà běn shū hěn hǎokàn. Nǐ kàn guò méiyǒu?
This book is very interesting. Have you read (it) yet?

Unlike in English, one never uses *tā* (it) as the subject of a sentence when talking about weather.

>For example:
>*Xiàyǔ.*
>It is raining.
>
>*Hǎo tiān.*
>It is sunny.

Possessive pronouns

Possessive pronouns consist of personal pronouns followed by the particle *de*.

	Singular	
1st person	my/mine	*wǒ de*
2nd person	your/yours	*nín de* (fml.)
	your/yours	*nǐ de*
3rd person	his, her, its/ his, hers, its	*tā de*

	Plural	
1st person	our/ours	*wǒmen de*
2nd person	your/yours	*nǐmen de*
3rd person	their/theirs	*tāmen de*

5. DEMONSTRATIVE PRONOUNS: *ZHÈ* AND *NÀ*
===

Chinese had two demonstrative pronouns: *zhè* "this" and *nà* "that." A measure word must be placed between a demonstrative pronoun and a noun that it modifies.

>For example:
>*zhè běn shū*   this book
>*nà běn shū*   that book

In the plural, *xiē* is used:

zhè xiē shū	these books
nà xiē shū	those books

In colloquial language, *zhè* and *nà* are pronounced as *zhèi* and *nèi* when combined with a measure word:

zhèi běn shū	this book
nèi běn shū	that book

The noun that follows *zhè* or *nà* can be left out if its meaning is clear from the context.

For example:

Zhè běn shū shì nǐ de.
This book is yours.

Zhè běn shì nǐ de.
This (one) is yours.

6. INDEFINITE PRONOUNS

There are several types of indefinite pronouns in Chinese. Indefinite pronouns such as "anyone," "nobody," "anything," or "anytime" consist of question words (who, what, when, where, why, etc.) and *yě*.

anyone	*shéi + yě*
anything	*shénme dōngxi + yě*
anytime	*shénme shíhòu + yě*
anywhere	*nǎr + yě*
nobody	*shénme rén + yě*

For example:
Wǒ shéi yě bú jiàn.
I don't see *anyone.*

Tā shénme dōngxi yě chī.
He eats *anything*.

Nǐ nǎr yě bú zhù.
You don't live *anywhere*.

Nǐ xǐhuan shénme shíhou lái yě kěyǐ.
Come over *anytime* you like.

Shénme rén yě kěyǐ qù.
Anyone can go.

When indefinite pronouns function as subjects, they can also be formed using *rènhé* "any" and *yě* as follows:

anyone	*rènhé rén + yě*
anything	*rènhé dōngxi + yě*
anytime	*rènhé shíhou + yě*
anywhere	*rènhé dìfang + yě*
nobody	*méiyǒu rén*

For example:
Rènhé rén yě kěyǐ qù.
Anyone can go.

Rènhé dōngxi yě huì biàn.
Anything can change.

Rènhé shíhou yě kěyǐ.
Anytime is fine.

Rènhé dìfang yě kěyǐ.
Anywhere is fine.
(*lit.*, Anywhere can be.)

Méiyǒu rén lái.
Nobody came.

The indefinite pronouns "someone" and "somebody" are
expressed with *yǒu rén,* while the indefinite pronoun
"something" is expressed with *diǎn dōngxi.*

Yǒu rén zài zhèr.
Someone is here.
(*lit.,* There is person here.)

Yǒu rén zhǎo nǐ.
Somebody is looking for you.

Wǒ yǒu diǎn dōngxi gěi nǐ.
I have *something* to give you.

The indefinite pronouns "wherever," "whoever," and
"whatever" are formed with *wúlùn* "no matter," question
words (who, what, where, etc.), and *yě.*

wherever	*wúlùn...nǎr...yě*
whoever	*wúlùn...shéi...yě*
whatever	*wúlùn...shénme...yě*

For example:
Wúlùn nǐ qù nǎr, wǒ yě qù.
Wherever you go, I will go.

Wúlùn shì shéi, wǒ yě bú huì jiàn.
Whoever it is, I will not see him/her.

Wúlùn wǒ chī shénme, tā yě chī.
Whatever I eat, he/she eats.

7. NUMBERS

<u>Cardinal numbers 1 to 10</u>

one	*yī*	six	*liù*
two	*èr*	seven	*qī*
three	*sān*	eight	*bā*
four	*sì*	nine	*jiǔ*
five	*wǔ*	ten	*shí*

<u>Cardinal numbers 11 to 100</u>

eleven	*shí yī* (10 + 1)	sixteen	*shí liù* (10 + 6)
twelve	*shí èr* (10 + 2)	seventeen	*shí qī* (10 + 7)
thirteen	*shí sān* (10 + 3)	eighteen	*shí bā* (10 + 8)
fourteen	*shí sì* (10 + 4)	nineteen	*shí jiǔ* (10 + 9)
fifteen	*shí wǔ* (10 + 5)	twenty	*èrshí* (2 x 10)

thirty	*èrshí* (3 x 10)	seventy	*qīshí* (7 x 10)
forty	*sìshí* (4 x 10)	eighty	*bāshí* (8 x 10)
fifty	*wǔshí* (5 x 10)	ninety	*jiǔshí* (9 x 10)
sixty	*liùshí* (6 x 10)	one hundred	*yībǎi* (10 x 10)

twenty-three	*èrshí sān* (20 + 3)
fifty-six	*wǔshí liù* (50 + 6)
forty-nine	*sìshí jiǔ* (40 + 9)
ninety-nine	*jiǔshí jiǔ* (90 + 9)

<u>Cardinal numbers from 200 to 100,000,000</u>

two hundred	*èrbǎi/liǎngbǎi*
one thousand	*yīqiān*
ten thousand	*yīwàn**
one million	*yībǎiwàn*
ten million	*yīqiānwàn*
one hundred million	*yīyì*
one billion	*shíyì*

* Note that "ten thousand" is not *shíqiān* as would be expected.

Líng is used to express the zero in numbers.

104	*yībǎi líng sì*
1,032	*yīqiān líng sānshí èr*
1,004	*yīqiān líng sì*
10,004	*yīwàn líng sì*
1,050	*yīqiān líng wǔshí*

The word *yī* is added before *shí* in numbers ending in the numerals 10 through 19.

111	*yībǎi yīshí yī*
312	*sānbǎi yīshí èr*
210	*èrbǎi yīshí*
519	*wǔbǎi yīshí jiǔ*

More examples:

2,010	*èrqiān líng yīshí*
8,100,243	*bābǎi yīshíwàn líng èrbǎi sìshí sān*
987,654,321	*jiǔyì bāqiān qībǎi liùshíwǔwàn sìqiān sānbǎi èrshí*

The number two is expressed in two different ways in Chinese. *Èr* is used for counting and numeric expressions, such as *shí èr* twelve or *èrbǎi* two hundred. *Liǎng* is used in combination with nouns.

Ordinal numbers

Dì is added to a cardinal number in order to form an ordinal number.

For example:

one	*yī*	the first	*dì yī*
nine	*jiǔ*	the ninth	*dì jiǔ*

8. MEASURE WORDS

When a noun is modified by a number word or a demonstrative pronoun, a measure word is needed between the number word or the demonstrative pronoun and the noun. Different nouns require the use of different measure words.

For example, the measure word *běn* needs to be added between *yī* and *shū* to form the complete expression *yī běn shū* "one book/a book."

The measure word changes according to the category to which the given noun belongs. There are different measure words for nouns denoting round objects, flat objects, items of clothing, people, etc.

Measure words are classified in to the following categories:

a. Nature of the object

Measure word	Category	Examples
zhī	animals[41]	*yī zhī jī* (one/a chicken)
		yī zhī māo (one/a cat)
		yī zhī niǎo (one/a bird)
zhī	utensils	*yī zhī bēi* (one/a cup/glass)
		yī zhī wǎn (one/a bowl)
		yī zhī guō (one/a pot)
tái	machinery	*yī tái jīqì* (one/a machine)
		yī tái diànnǎo (one/a computer)
		yī tái diànshì (one/a television)

[41] Special measure words are used for the following three animals: *yī tiáo gǒu* (one/a dog), *yī tóu niú* (one/a cow), and *yī pǐ mǎ* (one/a horse).

jiàn	clothing (top)	*yī jiàn chènyī* (one/a shirt)
		yī jiàn fēngyī (one/a wind break)
tiáo	clothing (bottom)	*yī tiáo kùzi* (one/a pair of pants)
		yī tiáo qúnzi (one/a skirt)
bǎ	something with handle	*yī bǎ cháhú* (one/a teapot)
		yī bǎ yǔsǎn (one/an umbrella)
		yī bǎ shànzi (one/a Chinese fan)
		yī bǎ yǐzi (one/a chair)
zuò	large and imposing objects	*yī zuò sān* (one/a mountain)
		yī zuò dàlóu (one/a building)
liàng	vehicles	*yī liàng qìchē* (one/a car)
jiā	families or enterprises	*yī jiā fànguǎn* (one/a restaurant)
		liǎng jiā rénjia (two families)
ge[42]	people	*yī ge rén* (one/a person)
		liǎng ge láoshī (two teachers)

b. Shape of the object

Measure word	Category	Examples
zhāng	flat surface	*yī zhāng zhǐ* (one/a piece of paper)
		yī zhāng bàozhǐ (one/a newspaper)

---

[42] The polite form is *wèi*. For example: *yī wèi láoshī* (one/a teacher).

		yī zhāng zhàopiàn (one/a photo)
		yī zhāng chuáng (one/a bed)
zhī	pointed and thin or like a branch	*yī zhī bǐ* (one/a pen)
		yī zhī qiāng (one/a gun)
		yī zhī jūnduì (one/a troop)
lì	granular	*yī lì mǐ* (one/a grain of rice)
		yī lì zhǒngzi (one/a seed)
kē	small and round	*yī kē yǎnlèi* (one/a tear round drop)
		yī kē hóngdòu (one/a red bean)
tiáo	long and thin	*yī tiáo lù* (one/a road)
		yī tiáo tóufa (one/a hair)
		yī tiáo xiàn (one/a string)
pán	something round and flat or shaped like a plate	*yī pán wéiqí* (one/a game of Chinese checkers)
		yī pán cídài (one/a tape)

c. Words for containers that function as measure words

Measure word	Category	Examples
bēi	cup	*yī bēi shu* (one/a cup of water)
dài	bag	*yī dài píngguǒ* (one/a bag of apples)
pán	plate	*yī pán cài* (one/a dish)
xiāng	box	*yī xiāng lājī* (one/a box of garbage)

d. Measure words denoting quantity

Measure word	Category	Examples
duì[43]	pair[44]	*yī duì xiézi* (one/a pair of shoes)
		yī duì kuànzi (one/a pair of chopsticks)
shuāng	pair	*yī shuāng wàzi* (one/a pair of socks)
		yī shuāng yǎnjing (one/a pair of eyes)
fù	pair	*yī fù yǎnjìng* (one/a pair of glasses)
qún	group	*yī qún yāzi* (one/a group of ducks)
		yī qún rén (one/a group of people)
dá	dozen	*yī dá jīdá* (one/a dozen eggs)
chuàn	cluster	*yī chuan pútáo* (one/a cluster of grapes)

e. Measure words *xiē, jǐ,* and *yīdiǎnr*

Xiē can combine with a demonstrative pronoun or the number word *yī* to signify an undetermined quantity of something. *Yī* is the equivalent of "some," "several," or "a few" in English. "*Jǐ* + measure word" used to denote a smaller amount than *xiē*, while *Yī diǎnr* means "a little."

For example:

[43] The measure word *zhī* is used with *duì* and *shuāng* when it is necessary to single out one object from the pair, e.g., *yī zhīwàzi* (one/a sock).

[44] "A pair of trousers" is *yī tiáo kùzi* and "a pair of scissors" is *yī bǎ jiǎodāo* in Chinese.

nà xiē rén	those people
yī xiē shū	some books
jǐ ge rén	people
yī diǎnr yán	a little salt

Xiē can be used with countable and uncountable nouns. *Yī diǎnr* is only used with uncountable nouns and *jǐ* is only used with countable nouns.

f. Amounts or portions of things

Measure word	Category	Examples
kuài	piece	*yī kuài dàngāo* (one/a piece of cake)
dī	drop	*yī dī shuǐ* (one/a drop of water)
cè	volume	*yī cè shū* (one/a volume of a set of books)

j. Units of measurement

cùn	inch	*chǐ*	foot
yīnglǐ	mile	*gōngchǐ/mǐ*	meter
gōnglǐ	kilometer	*gōngjīn*	kilogram
jīn	catty[45]	*bàng*	pound

The table below shows the different units of measure used in Mainland China, Taiwan and Hong Kong.

[45] 1 catty = 600 gr.

Units of measure	Mainland China	Taiwan	Hong Kong
Length	*mǐ* (meter)/ *gōnglǐ* (kilometer)	*mǐ* (meter)/ *gōnglǐ* (kilometer)	*chǐ* (foot)/*gōnglǐ* (kilometer)
Weight	*gōngjīn* (kilogram)	*gōngjīn* (kilogram)	*bàng* (pound)/ *gōngjīn* (kilogram)/ *jīn* (catty)

k. The measure word *gè*

Gè is the most extensively used measure word. It is used especially with those nouns that don't have particular measure words assigned.

> For example:
> *yī ge píngguǒ*   one/an apple
> *yī ge zhàoxiàngjī*   one/a camera

In addition, it is also used for abstract things, such as dreams and ideas.

> For example:
> *yī ge xīngqī*   one/a week
> *yī ge mèng*   one/a dream
> *yī ge zhǔyi*   one/an idea

As a general rule, each noun combines with one specific measure word. A few nouns can combine with more than one measure word.

> For example:
> *yī tái diànnǎo* or *yī bù diànnǎo* (one/a computer)
> *yī ge diànyǐng* or *yī bù diànyǐng* (one/a film)

9. "VERB-OBJECT" VERBS

Special two-syllable verbs exist in Chinese that consist of verbs and their objects. For example, the verb *chīfàn* consists of the word *chī* (to eat) and *fàn* (cooked rice). The object is usually not translated in English.

> For example:
> *Wǒ chīfàn.*
> I eat.
> (*lit.,* I eat cooked rice.)
>
> *Tā kàichē.*
> He drives.
> (*lit.,* He opens car.)

Not all two-syllable verbs in Chinese are "verb-object" verbs. Most verbs, such as *jiǎnchá* (to examine), do not fall into this category. This is an important distinction because "verb-object" verbs require special treatment under certain circumstances. When a "verb-object" verb is modified by a verb suffix, such as *le* or *guò*, the suffix is added between the verb and the object. In the case of other two-syllable verbs, the suffix is added after the verb.

> For example:
> *Wǒ chī le fàn.*
> I ate.
>
> *Wǒ jiǎnchá le.*
> I examined.

10. EXPRESSING A COMPLETED ACTION WITH *LE*

The suffix *le* is put after a verb to indicate that an action has been completed or that something is different from the way it was in the past, including a change in seasons.

Because *le* can also be used to refer to something that has not yet happened, its function is very different from the simple past tense in English.

> For example:
> *Tā qù le Shànghǎi.*
> He *went* to Shanghai.
>
> *Qiūtiān lái le.*
> *Now it's* autumn.
>
> *Fēijī kuài qǐfēi le.*
> The plane *is about* to take off.

11. EXPRESSING A PAST ACTION USING *GUÒ*

The suffix *guò* is placed after a verb to indicate that an action took place during a period of time from the past until now. It is usually translated as the present perfect tense in English.

> For example:
> *Wǒ qù guò Zhōngguó.*
> I have been to China.

Here is how to form a question using *guò*:
> *Nǐ qù guò Zhōngguó méiyǒu?*
> *Have you ever been* to China?

The positive and negative answers to this question are:
> *Wǒ qù guò.*
> Yes, I *have been.*
>
> *Wǒ hái méi qù guò.*
> No, I *haven't been yet.*
>
> *Wǒ méi (yǒu) qù guò.*
> No, I *have never been before.*

Note that the word "no", which is typically used at the start of a reply in English, is merely implied in Chinese.

12. USE OF *ZÀI* TO DENOTE AN ONGOING ACTION

The word *zài* is placed before a verb to indicate that an action is continuous and ongoing. It is equivalent to the present continuous tense in English.

> For example:
> *Wǒ zài kàn shū.*
> I *am reading*.
>
> *Tāmen zài gōngzuò.*
> They *are working*.

13. USE OF *ZHE* TO DENOTE AN ONGOING STATE OF BEING

Placing the word *zhe* after a verb also indicates continuous action, but refers to a state of being rather than a kinetic activity. Like *zài*, it is similar to the "ing" form in English.

> For example:
> *Tā zhàn zhe.*
> He *is standing*.
>
> *Nǐ ná zhe yì běn shū.*
> You *are holding* a book.

Note that the difference between *zài* and *zhe* is subtle. *Zài* refers to a continuous active motion, while *zhe* refers to a frozen action or state of events that continues in time.

> For example:
> *Tā zài zhuān yīfu.*
> She *is putting* on clothes.
>
> *Tā chuān zhe yí jiàn hóngsè de yīfu.*
> She *is wearing* a red piece of clothing.

14. USE OF *HUÌ* TO EXPRESS FUTURE ACTION

Huì has different meanings in Chinese depending on how it is used. One of its uses is to express action that takes place in the future. When placed immediately before a main verb in a sentence, it is equivalent to both "shall" or "will" in English.

> For example:
> *Wǒ míngtiān huì qū Shànghǎi.*
> I *shall* go to Shanghai tomorrow.
>
> *Tā děng yīhuìr huì gěi nǐ.*
> He *will* give it to you in a while.
> (*lit.*, He *will* give you in a while.)

15. TO HAVE: *YǑU*

Yǒu is used to indicate possession. The negative form of *yǒu* is *méiyǒu*.

> For example:
> *Wǒ yǒu liǎng běn shū.*
> I *have* two books.
>
> *Nǐ yǒu sān tiáo gǒu.*
> You *have* three dogs.
>
> *Tā méiyǒu qián.*
> He *does not have* money.

The question forms of *yǒu* are:
> *Nǐ yǒu qián ma?*
> Do you *have* money?
>
> *Nǐ yǒu méiyǒu qián?*
> *Don't* you *have* money?
> (*lit.*, Do you *have* money *or not?*)

The positive and negative answers to these questions are:

> *Yǒu.*
> Yes, I do.

> *Méiyǒu.*
> No, I don't.

Méiyǒu can also be used to formulate negative questions in the following manner:

> *Nǐ méiyǒu qián ma?*
> *Don't* you have money?

The positive and negative answers to this question are:

> *Bú shì. Wǒ yǒu.*
> Yes. I have (money).
> (*lit.,* No. I have money.)

> *Shì. Wǒ méiyǒu.*
> No. I don't (have money).
> (*lit.,* Yes. I don't have money.)

Note that, in the first example, "no" in Chinese is equivalent to "yes" in English because the reply in Chinese expresses disagreement with the question asked and implies a rejection of the idea that the person questioned may not have any money. Fully stated, the first reply reads as follows in Chinese: "No, that's not true. I do have money." In English, this translates as: "Yes, I have money." A similar situation occurs in the second example, where the answer "yes" in Chinese is equivalent to the answer "no" in English. In this case, the reply reads as follows in Chinese: "Yes, you are right. I don't have money." In English, this translates as: "No, I don't have money."

16. THERE IS/ARE: *YŎU* AND *SHÌ*

There are two ways to indicate existence in Chinese. One
is to use *yŏu* (there is/there are) in a sentence with the following word order: place word + location word + *yŏu* +
subject.

> For example:
> *Xuéxiào (lĭ) yŏu hěnduō xuésheng.*
> *There are* a lot of students in the school.
> (*lit.,* School inside there are lots of students.)
>
> *Gōngyuán lĭ yŏu yì tiáo gŏu.*
> *There is* a dog in the park.
> (*lit.,* Park inside there is a dog.)

The other way to indicate existence is to use *shì* in a sentence with the following word order: place word + location word + *shì* + place word. Note that the object here
must be singular.

> For example:
> *Gōngyuán de hòubiānr shì xuéxiào.*
> *There is* a school behind the park.
> (*lit.,* The back of the park is school.)

17. USE OF PREPOSITION *ZÀI* AND OTHER LOCA-
TION WORDS

The preposition *zài* is used to specify location.

> For example:
> *Wŏ zài xuéxiào (lĭ).*
> I am in school.
>
> *Tā zài Měiguó.*
> He is in the U.S.

A number of auxiliary words are also used in Chinese to
specify additional information about location. These words

are positioned following a place name or a place word in a sentence.

> For example:
> *Wǒ de shū zài zhuōzi de xiàbiānr.*
> My book is *under* the table.

Location words

in front of	*qiánbiānr*
behind	*hòubiānr*
above	*shàngbiānr*
under	*xiàbiānr*
on the left	*zuǒbiānr*
on the right	*yòubiānr*
beside	*pángbiānr*
between	*zhōngjiān*
inside/in	*lǐ(biānr)*
outside	*wàibiānr*

The positioning of *zhōngjiān* is different from that of other location words. It requires the following sentence structure: "A *hé* B *de zhōngjiān*," where A and B are separate place names or words.

18. MODAL VERBS

There are three types of modal verbs in Chinese. They are used as follows:

a. To indicate possibility

Among its many applications, the modal verb *huì* can be used to express whether something may happen or not. *Huì* is always placed immediately before the main verb for this purpose.

For example:
Jīntiān huì xiàxué.
It *may* snow today.

Tā bú huì lái.
He *may* not come.

Note that *huì* can also mean "to be able" or "know how to."

For example:
Wǒ huì shuō Yīngwén hé Zhōngwén.
I (*know how to*) speak English and Chinese.

Another word that expresses possibility in Chinese is the modal verb *kěyǐ* (can). *Kěyǐ* must precede the main verb in a sentence, but does not need to be placed immediately before it.

For example:
Tā kěyǐ chī shí wǎn fàn.
He *can* eat ten bowls of rice.

Wǒ kěyǐ gēn nǐ qù.
I *can* go with you.

When used in questions, *kěyǐ* is placed after the main verb and separated by a comma. It can stand alone as a one-word answer, meaning "yes."

Nǐ míngtiān qù, kěyǐ ma?
Can you go tomorrow?
(*lit.*, You go tomorrow, can you?)

Kěyǐ.
Yes, I can.

b. To express desire or willingness

Yào (to want) and *xiǎng* (to want/would like) are both used to express willingness. The first indicates a stronger sense of desire.

> For example:
> *Wǒ yào zhù zài xuéxiào fùjìn.*
> I *want* to live near the school.

> *Wǒ xiǎng hē yì bēi kāfēi.*
> I *would like* to drink a cup of coffee.

c. To express necessity

Yīnggāi (should) is placed before the main verb to show that an action is imperative. It can be separated from the main verb by an adverb that further qualifies the action.

> For example:
> *Nǐ yīnggāi mǎshàng zuò fēijī qù Běijīng.*
> You *should* take the plane to go to Beijing immediately.

Děi (to have to/must) is widely used in colloquial language to show a sense of necessity. It is placed in front of the main verb, although sometimes it is separated from that verb by an adverb or adverbial phrase.

> For example:
> *Nǐ děi zǎo yìdiǎnr huíqù.*
> You *have to* go back earlier.

The modal verbs listed above can all be negated with *bù* except for the verb *děi*. The negative form of *děi* does not exist. Instead, one can say:

> *Nǐ yīdìng bù kěyǐ chī.*
> You *mustn't* eat.

19. ADVERBIAL USE OF *DE*

In Chinese, the word *de* is placed between a verb and an adjective (verb + *de* + adjective) to form an adverbial expression that describes how an action is done. *De* is always placed immediately following the verb for this purpose.

> For example:
> *Tā chī de hěn kuài.*
> He eats very fast.
>
> *Nǐ shuō de hěn hǎo.*
> You speak very well.

If the verb has an object, then the verb has to be repeated and the object must be placed between the twin verbs.

> For example:
> *Wǒ shuō Zhōngwén shuō de hěn bù hǎo.*
> I don't speak Chinese very well.
> (*lit.,* I speak Chinese not very well.)

Note that, in Chinese characters, *de* (地) differs from the possessive *de* (的), although both have the same pronunciation.

20. MANY, SOME, ALL, EVERY

The words *hěn duō* and *bù shǎo* are used to signify "many/a lot of/quite a few," while *yīxiē* is used to signify "some" in Chinese. They both precede the noun they modify.

> For example:
> *Wǒ yǒu bù shǎo gǒu.*
> I have *quite a few* dogs.

Zhōngguó yǒu hěn duō rén.
There are *a lot of* people in China.

Tā yǒu yìxiē wèntí.
He has *some* questions.

Please note that no measure word is used between *hěn duō/bù shǎo* or *yìxiē* and the nouns they qualify.

Quánbù is "all" and *měi* is "every." It is not necessary to add a measure word between *quánbù* and a noun it modifies. However, you do need to add a measure word between *měi* and a noun.

For example:
Quánbù rén dōu sǐ le.
All of the people died.

Měi ge rén dōu sǐ le.
Everyone died.

Wǒ měi tiān shàngxué.
I go to school *every* day.

Note that in the last example, it is not necessary to add a measure word between *měi* and *tiān,* since *tiān* itself can function as a measure word. The same rule applies to the expression *měi nián* (every year). However, it is necessary to add a measure word when saying *měi ge xīngqī* (every week) and *měi ge yuè* (every month).

"All" and "every" can be expressed using duplicate measure words and *dōu.*

For example:
Gēgè rén dōu xǐhuan tā.
Everyone likes him. (*lit., All the people* like him.)

Běnběn shū dōu hěn guì.
Every/all book(s) is/are expensive.

21. FORMING SIMPLE QUESTIONS

There are two types of simple questions in Chinese. The first type of a simple question is formed by placing the particle *ma* at the end of a sentence. Note that the word order of a simple question with *ma* is the same as the word order of the answer to that question.

For example:
Nǐ qù ma?
Do you go?

Wǒ qù.
Yes, I do.

Zhāng xiānsheng zhù zài zhèr ma?
Does Mr. Zhang live here?

Tā zhù zài zhèr.
Yes, he does.

Tā pǎu de kuài ma?
Does he run fast?

Tā pǎu de kuài.
Yes, he does.

The second type of a simple question is formed by placing the word *bú* between the two elements of a reduplicated verb or adverb. The question particle *ma* is not needed.

> For example:
> *Nǐ qù bú qù?*
> Do you go or not?

> *Wǒ qù.*
> Yes, I do.

> *Tā pǎu de kuài bú kuài?*
> Does he run fast?

> *Tā pǎu de kuài.*
> Yes, he does.

22. QUESTIONS WITH THE PARTICLE *NE*

The particle *ma* is typically used at the end of a sentence to ask a simple question, while *ne* is usually used to succinctly ask the same question without repeating it.

> For example:
> *Nǐ xǐhuan hē chá ma?*
> Do you like drinking tea?

> *Wǒ xǐhuan. Nǐ ne?*
> Yes, I do. How about you?

23. QUESTION WORDS

shénme	what
shénme shíhou	when
nǎli/nǎr	where
nǎ/něi + measure word	which (*sg.*)
nǎ/něi + *xiē*	which (*pl*)
shéi/shuí	who/whom
duōshǎo qián	how much (money)

duōshǎo/jǐ + measure word	how many
duōshǎo	how much
zěnme(yàng)	how
wèishénme	why

Here are examples:

Nǐ jiào shénme míngzi?
What is your name?
(*lit.*, What name are you called?)

Nǐ shénme shíhou qù Zhōngguó?
When do you go to China?

Huǒchēzhàn zài nǎli/nǎr?
Where is the train station?

Nǎ/Něi běn shū shì nǐ de?
Which book is yours?

Nǎ/Něi xiē shū shì nǐ de?
Which books are yours?

Tā shì shéi/shuí?
Who is he/she?

Shéi/Shuí shì Huáng xiānsheng?
Who is Mr. Huang?

Zhè jiàn yīfu duōshǎo qián?
How much is this clothing?

Nǐ yǒu duōshǎo xuésheng?
How many students do you have?

Nǐ yǒu jǐ ge xuésheng?
How many students do you have?

Nǐ yǒu duōshǎo lìliàng?
How much strength/power do you have?

Tā zuìjìn zěnmeyàng?
How is he recently?

Nǐ wèishénme bú qù?
Why don't you go?

24. OR

Huòzhě and *háishì* both mean "or" in Chinese. *Huòzhě* is used in statements, while *háishì* is used in questions. Both *huòzhě* and *háishì* can be placed between nouns or noun phrases.

For example:
Wǒ huì qù Shànghǎi huòzhě Běijīng.
I'll go to Shanghai or Beijing.

Nǐ hē huòzhě wǒ hē dōu kěyǐ.
Either you or I can drink it.
(*lit.*, You drink or I drink, both are fine.)

Nǐ xǐhuan wǒ háishì tā?
Do you like me or him?

Nǐ jīntiān qù háishì míngtiān qù?
Do you go today or tomorrow?

25. YES-NO QUESTIONS

The way the answers "yes" and "no" are expressed in Chinese depends on how questions are asked. Generally

speaking, these answers require a repetition of the verb
used in the question.

For example:

Q1:   Nǐ shì Zhāng xiǎojie ma?
Are you Miss Zhang?

Wǒ shì.
Yes, I am.

Wǒ bú shì.
No, I am not.

Q2:   Nǐ huì shuō Yīngwén ma?
Do you know how to speak English?

Wǒ huì.
Yes, I do.

Wǒ bú huì.
No, I don't.

Q3:   Nǐ qù ma?
Do you go?

Wǒ qù.
Yes, I do.

Wǒ bú qù.
No, I don't.

Normally, the particle *bù* (not) is placed before the verb
in negative answers. This rule holds true for most but
not all verbs. The verb *yǒu* (to have) is an exception.

26. NEGATIVE PARTICLES *BÙ* AND *MÉIYŎU*

Bù and *méiyŏu* are used in negative statements.

Bù is usually used in negative statements in the present, future or continuous tense.

> For example:
> *Wŏ bù hē jiŭ.*
> I *don't* drink alcohol.
>
> *Wŏ bú huì jiŭ.*
> I *won't* go/leave.
>
> *Tā bú zài fàndiàn.*
> He *is not* in the hotel.
>
> *Huáng xiānsheng bú zài gōngzuò.*
> Mr. Huang *is not* working (at this moment).

Méiyŏu is used in negative statements denoting completed actions or actions that are translated using the present perfect tense in English. *Méiyŏu* is also the negative form of the verb *yŏu*.

> For example:
> *Wŏ méiyŏu hē jiŭ.*
> I didn't drink alcohol.
>
> *Wŏ méiyŏu hē guò jiŭ.*
> I have never drunk alcohol before.
>
> *Wŏ méiyŏu liăng wàn kuài.*
> I don't have twenty thousand dollars.

27. USAGE OF "TO BE": *SHÌ*

The use of the verb *shì* (to be) in Chinese is very different from its usage in English. The most striking difference is that, in Chinese, *shì* is never placed between a noun and an adjective in an equational sentence.

> For example:
> *Tā gāo.*
> He is tall. (*lit.,* he tall)

The uses of *shì* are as follows:

a. *Shì* is used between a subject noun and a predicate noun in an equational sentence.

> For example:
> *Měiguó de shǒudū shì Huáshèngdùn.*
> America's capital *is* Washington.

> *Jīngyú shì yī zhǒng dòngwù.*
> The whale *is* one kind of animal.

Shì can also be used to indicate existence or a state of being. (Refer to Item 16 above.)

b. *Shì* is used between two identical nouns and this pattern is repeated for two different nouns in the same sentence to indicate that the two nouns are not related and must not be mistaken for one another.

> For example:
> *Nín shì nín, wǒ shì wǒ, qǐng nín bù yào hùn zài yìqǐ.*
> You are you, I am I, please don't confuse the two.

c. *Shì* is used in compound sentences whose first half uses *shì* between two identical nouns, adjectives or verbs to mean "although."

For example:
Hǎo shì hǎo, jiù shì guì le yīdiǎnr.
Although it's good, it's a little bit expensive.
(*lit.,* Good to be good, but expensive more a little bit.)

Rén shì hǎo rén, jiùshì tài shòu.
Although he is a good person, he is too thin.

28. USE OF *SHÌ... DE*

The grammatical structure *shì... de* is used to place emphasis on specific elements in a sentence. Generally, the word that follows *shì* is the one that is emphasized.

In sentences that answer questions about where, when, how, or for what purpose an action takes place, the word *shì* comes immediately in front of the verb and *de* usually comes at the end of the sentence.

For example:
Tā shì cóng Běijīng lái de.
He *is from* Beijing. (emphasis on location)

Wǒ shì lái mǎi nǐ de chē de.
I've come to buy your car. (emphasis on purpose)

When emphasis is on the subject, *shì* is placed immediately in front of it.

For example:
Shì wǒ chī píngguǒ de.
I'm the one who ate the apple. (emphasis on "I")

When emphasis is on the object, *shì* comes before the verb and *de* is placed in front of the object rather than at the end of the sentence.

For example:
Wǒmen shì hē de chá.
We drank tea. (emphasis on "tea")

29. *HÉ* AS A CONJUNCTION WORD

Hé is equivalent to the word "and" in English, but its usage is much more limited. It can only be used to connect nouns or noun phrases.

For example:
Wǒ xǐhuan qū lǚxíng hé kànshū.
I like traveling *and* reading.

Wǒ hé tā yìqǐ zuò huǒchē.
He *and* I take the train together.

Note that in Chinese, *wǒ* (I) can precede other pronouns in a group, as in *wǒ hé tā* (I and he).

Hé can also be used as the equivalent of the English preposition "with".

For example:
Wǒ hé Huáng xiānsheng chǎojià.
I quarrel *with* Mr. Huang.

30. USE OF *DŌU*

The word *dōu* means "all" or "both" when it is placed before the main verb in a sentence containing more than one subject. When the subject refers to two individuals, *dōu* means "both." When the subject refers to more than two individuals, *dōu* means "all." It also means "all" when referring to uncountable and nationality nouns.

For example:
Huáng xiānsheng hé Huáng tàitai dōu bú zài.
Both Mr. Huang and Mrs. Huang are not here.

Bob, Bill hé Susie dōu shì xuésheng.
Bob, Bill, and Susie are *all* students.

Māo, gǒu hé zhū dōu shì dòngwù.
Cats, dogs, and pigs are *all* animals.

Wǒmen dōu shì Měiguórén.
We are *all* American.

31. EXPRESSIONS OF TIME AND PLACE

When combined with the preposition *zài*, words that express time or location usually precede the main verb in a sentence. When both time and location expressions are used in a sentence, the location expression usually precedes the time expression.

For example:
Wǒ zài túshūguǎn děng nǐ.
I'll wait for you *in the library*.

Wǒ zài Měiguó niànshū.
I study *in America*.

Tā měitiān qīdiǎn shàngbān.
He goes to work *at seven everyday*.

Wǒ xīngqīsān zài huǒchēzhàn děng nǐ.
I'll wait for you *at train station on Wednesday*.

32. COMPARISON

a. Comparative adjectives

The properties of two nouns can be compared using the grammatical structure "A *bǐ* B + adjective," which means "A has a property greater than B."

> For example:
> *Wǒ bǐ nǐ dà.*
> I am *older* than you.
> (*lit.*, I am bigger than you.)
>
> *Zhè běn shū bǐ nà běn shū guì.*
> This book is more expensive than that one.

To express the exact degree of difference between two properties, words specifying age or amount are placed immediately after the comparative adjective.

> *Wǒ bǐ nǐ dà sān suì.*
> I am three years *older* than you.

b. Comparative adverbs

Two adverbial expressions can be compared using the structure "A + verb + *de bǐ* + B + adjective," which means "A is doing something to a greater degree than B."

> For example:
> *Wǒ zǒu de bǐ nǐ kuài.*
> I run *faster* than you do.

c. Similarity

There are two ways to express similarity between the properties of two objects. One can use the expression *yǒu… nàme* (as… as) as follows.

> *Wǒ yǒu nǐ nàme gāo.*
> I am *as* tall *as* you.

Alternatively, one can use the grammatical structure "A + *hé* + B + *yíyàng* + adjective."

> For example:
> *Wǒ hé nǐ yíyàng gāo.*
> I am *as* tall *as* you.
> (*lit.,* I and you are the same height.)

d. Superlative

The superlative form of an adjective is formed by placing the word *zuì* immediately before it.

> For example:
> *Zhè jiā fàndiàn zuì hǎo.*
> This hotel is *the best*.

> *Tā de chē zuì kuài.*
> His car is *the fastest*.

33. TELLING TIME

The following sentence is used to ask about the time.
> *Xiànzài shì jǐdiǎn?*
> What time is it now?

The answer to this question takes the following form:
> *Xiànzài shì...*
> It's... now.

a. Hours

Each hour is expressed with a numeral + *diǎn*.
For example:

1:00	*yīdiǎn*	one o'clock
2:00	*liǎngdiǎn*	two o'clock
10:00	*shídiǎn*	ten o'clock

b. Minutes

Fēn means "minute" in Chinese. Minutes on the clock are expressed as follows:

1:10	*yīdiǎn shífēn*	ten past one
		(*lit.,* one o'clock ten minutes)
6:01	*liùdiǎn líng yìfēn*	one minute after six
		(*lit.,* six o'clock one minute)

Chinese has the following expressions for the half hour and the quarter hour.

3:15	*sāndiǎn yíkè*	a quarter past three
		(*lit.,* three o'clock a quarter)
9:30	*jiǔdiǎn bàn*	half past nine
		(*lit.,* nine o'clock half)
5:45	*wǔdiǎn sānkè*	a quarter to six
		(*lit.,* five o'clock three quarters)

One can also say:

5:45	*chà yíkè liùdiǎn*	a quarter to six
		(*lit.,* a quarter less than six)

The following expressions can be added to the time specified: *zǎoshang* (early morning), *shàngwǔ* (morning), *zhōngwǔ* (noon), *xiàwǔ* (afternoon), *wǎnshang* (night/evening), or *bànyè* (middle of the night). These words have to be put before the hour.

For example:

zǎoshang qīdiǎn	7:00 a.m.
	(*lit.,* morning seven o'clock)
shàngwǔ shídiǎn bàn	10:30 a.m.
	(*lit.,* morning ten o'clock)

bànyè liǎngdiǎn	2:00 a.m. (*lit.*, middle of the night two o'clock)
wǎnshang jiǔdiǎn	9:00 p.m. (*lit.*, night nine o'clock)

The time periods expressed by these words are as follows:

after midnight	*bànyè*
before 10 a.m.	*zǎoshang*
after 10 a.m.	*shàngwǔ*
12:00 p.m.	*zhōngwǔ*
before 6 p.m.	*xiàwǔ*
after 6 p.m.	*wǎnshang*

34. DATES

a. Year

2005	*èr-líng-líng-wǔ nián* (*lit.*, year 2005)
1872	*yī-bā-qī-èr nián* (*lit.*, year 1872)
1776	*yī-qī-qī-liù nián* (*lit.*, year 1776)

this year	*jīnnián*
last year	*qū'nián*
year before last	*qiánnián*
next year	*míngnián*
year after next	*hòunián*

b. Month

January	*yīyuè*
February	*èryuè*
March	*sānyuè*
April	*sìyuè*
May	*wǔyuè*
June	*liùyuè*
July	*qīyuè*

August	*bāyuè*
September	*jiǔyuè*
October	*shíyuè*
November	*shíyīyuè*
December	*shíèryuè*

this month	*zhège yuè*
last month	*shàng ge yuè*
month before last	*qián ge yuè*
next month	*xià ge yuè*
month after next	*xià xià ge yuè*

c. Week

Monday	*xīngqīyī/lǐbàiyī*
Tuesday	*xīngqièr/lǐbàièr*
Wednesday	*xīngqīsān/lǐbàisān*
Thursday	*xīngqīsì/lǐbàisì*
Friday	*xīngqīwǔ/lǐbàiwǔ*
Saturday	*xīngqīliù/lǐbàiliù*
Sunday	*xīngqītiān/lǐbàitiān*

this week	*zhège xīngqī*
last week	*shàng ge xīngqī*
week before last	*qián ge xīngqī*
next week	*xià ge xīngqī*
week after next	*xià xià ge xīngqī*

d. Day

1st day of the month	*yīhào/yīrì*
5th day of the month	*wǔhào/wǔrì*
31st day of the month	*sānshíyīhào/sānshíyīrì*

today	*jīntiān*
yesterday	*zuótiān*
day before yesterday	*qiántiān*
tomorrow	*míngtiān*
day after tomorrow	*hòutiān*

Note that both *hào* and *rì* mean "day of the month." *Hào* is more colloquial and *rì* is more formal.

The order of words in dates is: year, month, day, and weekday.

For example:

July 4, 1776	*yī-qī-qī-liù nián qīyuè sìhào* (*lit.,* 1776 year, July 4)
Friday, December 25, 2005	*èr-líng-líng-wǔ nián shíèryuè èrshíwǔhào xīngqīwǔ* (*lit.,* 2005 year, December 25, Friday)

35. MONEY EXPRESSIONS

The name of the currency used in China is *rénmínbi* (RMB). The basic unit is called *yuán* (dollar). One *yuán* contains ten *jiǎo* (ten cents). One *jiǎo* contains one hundred *fēn* (cents). Colloquially, *yuán* is pronounced as *kuài* and *jiǎo* is pronounced as *máo*.

To ask about the price, use the expression *Duōshǎo qián?* where *qián* means "money."

Zhè ge (yào) duōshǎo qián?
How much is this one?
(*lit.*, This one needs how much money?)

To answer the above question, say:
Zhè ge sānshí kuài qián.
This costs thirty dollars.

Zhè ge sānshí kuài wǔ máo.
This costs thirty dollars and five cents.

When the price is a round figure, *qián* can be eliminated
after *kuài* in the answer.

Zhè ge sānshí kuài.
This one costs thirty dollars.

In colloquial language, *máo* or *fēn* can also be dropped.

Zhè ge sānshí kuài wǔ.
This one costs thirty dollars and five cents.

36. COMMANDS AND REQUESTS

a. Commands

The imperative form of a verb is formed by placing the
particle *ba* at the end of a sentence in which it is con-
tained.

For example:
Shuì ba!
Go to sleep!

Zǒu ba!
(Let's) go!

To formulate a negative command, *bié* is placed before the verb. The particle *ba* is not needed.

> For example:
> *Bié shuì!*
> Don't sleep!
>
> *Bié zŏu!*
> Don't go!

b. Requests

The expression *Nĭ kĕyĭ…?* (Can you…?) is used to begin a request.

> For example:
> *Nĭ kĕyĭ guān mén ma?*
> *Can you* close the door?

One can also add the word *duìbuqĭ* (excuse me) when making a request.

> For example:
> *Duìbuqĭ, nĭ kĕyĭ bāng wŏ ma?*
> *Excuse me, can you* help me?

37. BASIC FACTS ABOUT CHINESE CHARACTERS

Chinese does not have an alphabet where each character corresponds to a sound in the language. Instead, characters denote individual words. For example, the character 花 is pronounced *huā* and means "flower." The shape and structure of some characters is associated with pictures derived from an ancient form of Chinese writing. For example, 人 is the character for "man" in Chinese. It reminds of a person standing with his two legs apart.

Chinese characters fall into many different meaning categories. Sometimes, it is possible to tell the category of a character from its root symbol, called "a radical," even if you are not familiar with it. For example, when the radical 艹 is written on top of a character, the character is associated with plants, as in 草 *cǎo* (grass). When the radical 冫 is written on the left side of a character, the character is associated with ice, as in 冰 *bīng* (ice). If the radical 氵 is written on the left side of a character, the character is associated with water, as in 河 *hé* (river).

There are over 10,000 Chinese characters. An educated Chinese person knows about 5,000 characters. Characters can either stand alone or combine with one another to form compound vocabulary words. The meaning of these compound words can be very different from the meanings of the individual characters they contain, which makes written Chinese a highly complex and difficult system to master. For example, the word 电脑 *diànnǎo* contains characters 电 *diàn* (electricity) and 脑 *nǎo* (brain) and means "computer." Another example is 地铁 *dìtiě*, where 地 *dì* means "earth" and 铁 *tiě* means "iron," but the compound word means "subway."

Chinese characters are written in strokes and according to a set pattern of rules that govern the direction and sequence of the strokes. Just as writers of English follow specific rules of penmanship and develop individualized handwriting, so the Chinese spend much time practicing their characters and personalize their style of writing until, for many, it becomes an art form, known as calligraphy. An average Chinese starts learning how to write characters as early as at the age of three and is encouraged to perfect his or her handwriting since good penmanship is regarded as a gauge of character throughout China.

Here is a list of one hundred most essential Chinese characters:

	Character	Pronunciation	Meaning
1.	一	yī	one
2.	二	èr	two
3.	三	sān	three
4.	四	sì	four
5.	五	wǔ	five
6.	六	liù	six
7.	七	qī	seven
8.	八	bā	eight
9.	九	jiǔ	nine
10.	十	shí	ten
11.	百	bǎi	hundred
12.	千	qiān	thousand
13.	万	wàn	ten thousand
14.	大	dà	big
15.	中	zhōng	middle
16.	小	xiǎo	small
17.	车	chē	car
18.	电	diàn	electricity
19.	云	yún	cloud
20.	雨	yǔ	rain
21.	火	huǒ	fire
22.	水	shuǐ	water
23.	山	shān	mountain
24.	上	shàng	on, above
25.	下	xià	under
26.	左	zuǒ	left
27.	右	yòu	right

28.	前	qián	in front of
29.	后	hòu	behind
30.	书	shū	book
31.	菜	cài	dish, vegetable
32.	鸡	jī	chicken
33.	鸭	yā	duck
34.	牛	niú	cow
35.	羊	yáng	sheep
36.	猪	zhū	pig
37.	鱼	yú	fish
38.	酒	jiǔ	wine
39.	笔	bǐ	pen
40.	字	zì	character
41.	是	shì	to be
42.	几	jǐ	several
43.	美	měi	beautiful
44.	国	guó	country
45.	高	gāo	tall, high
46.	低	dī	low
47.	不	bù	not
48.	没	méi	not to have
49.	有	yǒu	to have, there is/there are
50.	也	yě	also
51.	了	le	(verb suffix)
52.	东	dōng	east
53.	南	nán	south
54.	西	xī	west
55.	北	běi	north
56.	人	rén	people
57.	今	jīn	at present
58.	我	wǒ	I, me
59.	你	nǐ	you
60.	他	tā	he
61.	她	tā	she

62.	来	lái	come
63.	去	qù	go
64.	们	men	(plural particle)
65.	做	zuò	do
66.	元	yuán	dollar
67.	两	liǎng	two
68.	再	zài	again
69.	见	jiàn	see
70.	刀	dāo	knife
71.	分	fēn	separate, minute, cent
72.	到	dào	until, reach
73.	力	lì	strength
74.	加	jiā	plus
75.	又	yòu	also
76.	口	kǒu	mouth
77.	门	mén	door
78.	叫	jiào	call
79.	名	míng	first name
80.	和	hé	and
81.	茶	chá	tea
82.	在	zài	in, on, at
83.	坐	zuò	sit
84.	报	bào	report, newspaper
85.	外	wài	outside
86.	内	nèi	inside
87.	天	tiān	sky
88.	太	tài	too (excessive), very
89.	好	hǎo	good, well
90.	姓	xìng	last name
91.	学	xué	learn
92.	文	wén	written language
93.	家	jiā	home, family
94.	写	xiě	write
95.	对	duì	correct

96.	老	lǎo	old
97.	年	nián	year
98.	月	yuè	month, moon
99.	日	rì	day, sun
100.	从	cóng	from

LETTER, FAX, AND E-MAIL WRITING

FORMAL INVITATIONS

Wedding Invitation

Jǐn dìng yú èr líng líng wǔ nián shí èr yuè shí bā rì(xīngqītiān) wéi zhǎngzǐ Yóu Wéi yǔ Huáng Zhēn Zhēn xiǎojie zài Shànghǎi Dà Jiàotáng jǔxíng hūnlǐ. shì wǎn jiǎzuò Dōngfāng lù yībǎi hào Shànghǎi Fàndiàn èr lóu jìng bèi xǐzhuó gōnghòu guānglín

Lǐ Guāng
jìng yuē

Hūnlǐ shíjiān:	*Shàngwǔ shí diǎn = zhāngwǔ shíèr diǎn*
Hūnlǐ dìdiǎn:	*Nánjīng lù wǔ hào*

Xiàwǔ sìshí gōnghòu
Bāshí rùxí
Lǐ Zhái diànhuà: *1234-567*

The wedding ceremony of my eldest son You Wei and Miss Zhen Zhen Huang is scheduled to take place on Sunday, December 18, 2005, at the Shanghai Church. A wedding reception will be held on the same night on the second floor of the Shanghai Hotel, which is located at 100 Dongfang Road. We respectfully look forward to your honorable presence.

Guang Li
sincerely invites you to attend

Wedding ceremony time:	10 a.m.–12 noon
Wedding ceremony address:	5 Nanjing Road
Wedding reception:	4 p.m.
Wedding banquet:	8 p.m.
Li family's phone number:	1234-567

NOTE:
Generally, a printed reply card is not sent along with the wedding invitation. A guest usually replies by phone. When the guest arrives at the reception, he/she presents his/her gift—usually cash, placed in a red envelope along with a note—to the family that hosts the banquet.

Here is one way to write the note that acompanies the gift.

Jǐn jù fēiyí fèngshēn hèjìng

(Name of the guest)
jūgōng

Here is a small gift for you. (lit., An insignificant gift is presented to you.)

Humbly,
(Name of the guest)

NOTE:
The name and the closing of a letter in Chinese have to be written in two lines in the bottom righthand portion of the letter if the letter is written in a horizontal format. In China, letters can also be written in a vertical format, in which case the name and the closing are placed in the bottom lefthand corner in a manner parallel to English letter writing.

DINNER INVITATION

Jín dìng yú èr líng líng wǔ nián shí yuè èrshí hào (xīngqīsì) kāiyè, bìng yú wǎnshang liùshí yú Běijīng Fàndiàn guìbīntīng jìng bèi fēizhuó gōnghòu guānglín

*Běijīng diànnǎo gōngsī jīnglǐ
Hé Wén jìng yuē*

Dìdiǎn: Dà Yuán Jiē yìbǎi èrshí hào

A dinner party celebrating the founding of our company
is scheduled to be held in the VIP room of the Beijing
Hotel at 6 p.m. on Thursday, October 20, 2005.

I look forward to your honorable presence.

Wen He
sincerely invites you to attend

Address: 120 Da Yuan Street

Reply

Hé Wén jīnglǐ dà jiàn: jiēfèng
táijiǎn, xīn xī
guì gōngsī kāiyè shè yàn, kěxǐ kěhè. Kěxī dāngtiān wèi kè
chūxí, jìng qǐng yuánliàng.
Jìng fèng huālán yǐ zuò, liáo biǎo xièyì. Jí hòu
Jūn'ān

Chén Guó Ān
jìng qǐ

Honorable manager Wen He,

I received your invitation to attend the dinner to be held
on October 20, 2005 to celebrate the founding of your company. Congratulations on this auspicious occasion!
Unfortunately, I cannot attend on that day and beg for
your forgiveness.
As a token of my best wishes, I would like to present you
with a basket of flowers.

I wish you all the best!

Yours Respectfully,
Guo An Chen

INFORMAL LETTER

Xiǎo Líng,

   *Shōu dào nǐ de láixìn le, xièxie! Shíjiān guò de zhēn kuài.
Wǒ yǐjīng xué le Zhōngwén yì nián le. Zhège shǔjià wǒ
dǎsuan qù Zhōngguó lǚxìng liǎng ge yuè, érqiě dào
Shànghǎi kàn nǐ hé nǐ de jiārén. Wǒ xiǎng qù kànkan zài
zhàopiānr lǐ de fēngjǐng. Wǒ yě xiǎng chángchang gège
dìfang bùtóng de Zhōngguó shíwù. Nǐ kěyǐ gěi wǒ tuījiàn
yìxiē dìfang ma?*

   *Zhè shì wǒ dìyīcì qù Zhōngguó. Nǐ kěyǐ gàosu wǒ yīnggāi
dài shénme dōngxi qù Zhōngguó, yào zhùyì shénme
ma? Liùyuè hé qīyuè qù Zhōngguó lǚxíng hǎo bù hǎo? Nǐ*

yào bú yào wǒ zài Měiguó dài shénme dōngxi gěi nǐ? Qǐng gàosu wǒ. Qǐng dài wǒ wènhòu nǐ de jiārén.

Wǒ xīwàng hěn kuài shōu dào nǐ de huíxìn.

Zhù nǐ shēnghuó yúkuài!

Jennifer Crowley Shàng
Èr líng líng wǔ nián yīyuè sānshí hào

January 30, 2005

Dear Xiao Ling:

I am glad to have received your letter. Thank you very much! Time goes so fast. I have been studying Chinese for a year. This summer, I plan to go to China for two months and would like to visit you and your family in Beijing. I am eager to see the magnificant scenery that I have observed in photos. I would also like to try a variety of delicious Chinese foods from different regions throughout the country. Could you recommend some places I should visit during this trip?

This is my first trip to China. Could you tell me what I should take with me and what I should be aware of? Is it good to travel to China in June and July? Do you need anything from the U.S.? Please let me know if you want me to bring you something special. Kindly send my regards to your family.

I look forward to hearing from you soon.

I wish you all the best.

Your friend,
Jennifer Crowley

FORMS OF SALUTATION AND COMPLIMENTARY CLOSINGS

A. SALUTATIONS

FORMAL

xiānsheng	Sir:
nǚshì	Madam:
xiǎojie	Miss:
xiānsheng dà jiàn	Honorable Sir:
nǚshì dà jiàn	Honorable Madam:
xiǎojie dà jiàn	Honorable Miss:
xiānsheng tái jiàn	Dear Sir:
nǚshì tái jiàn	Dear Madam:
xiǎojie tái jiàn	Dear Miss:
jīnglǐ tái jiàn	Dear manager:
jiàoshòu dà jiàn	Honorable professor:

INFORMAL

In an informal letter, one simply uses the recipient's first name in the salutation.

B. COMPLIMENTARY CLOSINGS

FORMAL

The following expressions are equivalents of "Sincerely" and are placed after the name of the writer:

Jǐn qǐ
Jìng qǐ
Jìng shàng

In a business letter, the writer usually places his/her title before his/her full name, followed by one of the closings. As in the case of other forms of Chinese letter writing, the name and the closing in a business letter have to be written in two lines in the bottom right-hand corner of the page if the letter is written in a horizontal format. Here is an example:

ABC *gōngsī jīnglǐ*
Huáng Dà jǐn qǐ

Sincerely,
Da Huang
ABC company manager

INFORMAL

Yǒu	(Your) Friend,
Ài nǚ	(Your) Loving Daughter,
Ài ér	(Your) Loving Son,

In an informal letter, the word *shàng* needs to be placed after the writer's name in a closing. An informal closing should look like this:

Ài ér
Dà Wéi shàng

Your Loving Son,
Da Wei

ADDRESSING ENVELOPES

Jì Shànghǎi Nánjīng Lù yī líng líng wǔ hào
Shànghǎi Dàxià shì bā lóu
Zhōng Měi Gōng Sī
Yóubiān yī líng líng líng yī
Lǐ Dà Tóng jīnglǐ shōu

Běijīng Háidiàn Qū
Jiěfàng Lù bā hào
Guāngmíng Dàxià wǔ lóu wǔ shì
Yóubiān èr líng líng líng sān
Huáng Dōng fù

From: Huang Dong
Room 5 Guangmíng Building 5th Fl.
8 Jiefang Road
Beijīng Haidian Region
Postal code 20003

> To: Zhong Mei Gong Si
> Shanghai Building 18th Fl.
> 1005 Nanjing Road
> Shanghái 10001
> (Attn: Mr. Da Tong
> Li, manager)

NOTE:
Jì means "to send to" and identifies the address to which the letter is sent.
Shōu means "to receive" and indicates the recepient.
Fù means "to give" and functions here in a manner similar to the word "from" in English. It identifies the sender of the letter.
Yóubiān means "postal zip code."

The envelope format in Chinese is very different from that in English. In Chinese, the addresses, including the return address, begin with the country name, then give the city, town or village name, followed by the street name, the street address, the name of the building, the floor number, the room number and finally, the name of the sender or the recipient.

Importantly, unlike in English, the sender's address is placed at the bottom of the envelope and the recipient's is placed in the upper left-hand corner.

FAXES AND E-MAIL

The formats for faxes and e-mails are very similar.

Fax

Shōu jiàn rén:	*Chéng Lóng xiānsheng*
Chuánzhēn hàomǎ:	*1234-567*
Fā xìn rén:	*John Robson (chuánzhēn: 9876-5432)*
Zhǔtí:	*Héyuē*

Chén xiānsheng dà jiàn:

(body text)

John Robson shàng

Fùběn chéng: Táng Tǒng xiāngsheng

Attn:	Mr. Long Chen
Fax no.:	1234-567
From:	John Robson (Fax: 9876-5432)
Subject:	Contract

Dear Mr. Chen,

(body text)

Yours sincerely,

John Robson

c.c.: Mr. Tong Tang

E-mail

Shōu jiàn rén:	*Chéng Lóng xiānsheng*
Fā xìn rén:	*John Robson*
Zhǔtí:	*Héyuē*
Fùběn chéng:	*Táng Tǒng xiāngsheng*

Chén xiānsheng dà jiàn:

(body text)

John Robson shàng

To: Mr. Long Chen
From: John Robson (Fax: 9876-5432)
Subject: Contract
c.c.:   Mr. Tong Tang

Dear Mr. Chen,

(body text)

Yours sincerely,

John Robson